ULTIMATE
SPY

PIPE WITH CONCEALMENTS

SMERSH CREDENTIALS

SHOULDER HOLSTER

COIN WITH BLADE

SURREPTITIOUS ENTRY KIT

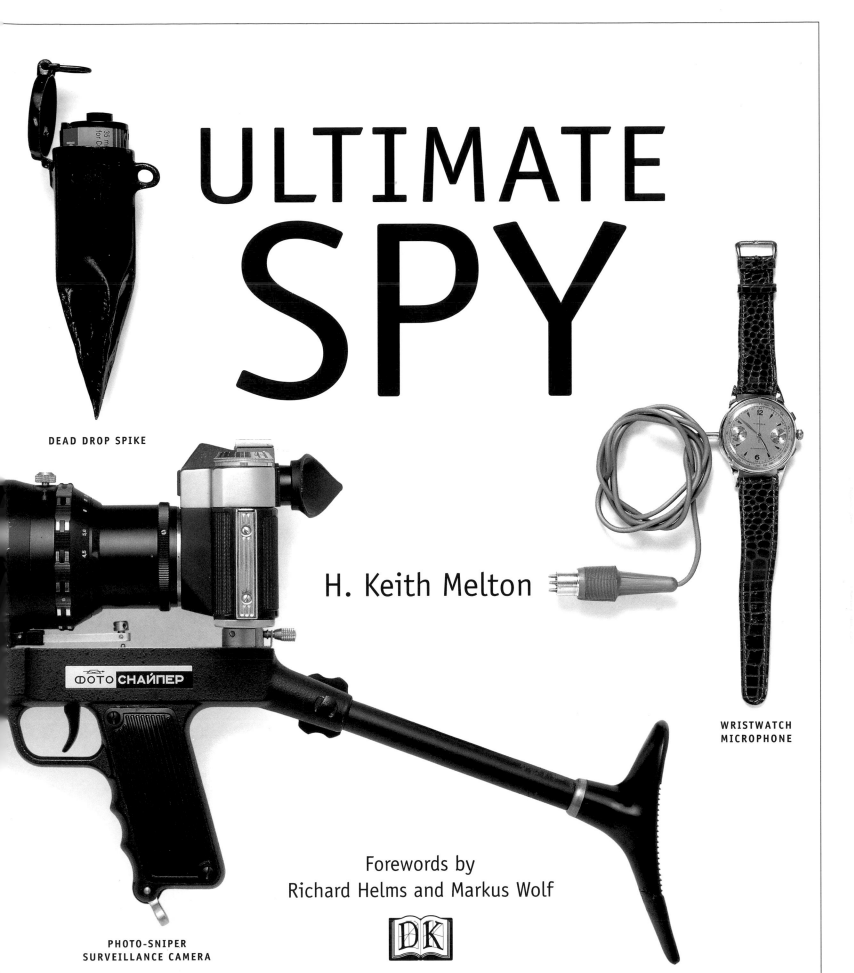

ULTIMATE SPY

DEAD DROP SPIKE

H. Keith Melton

WRISTWATCH MICROPHONE

ФОТО СНАЙПЕР

PHOTO-SNIPER
SURVEILLANCE CAMERA

Forewords by
Richard Helms and Markus Wolf

DK

LONDON, NEW YORK, MUNICH, MELBOURNE, AND DELHI

SECOND EDITION
Project Editor Jolyon Goddard
Project Art Editor Sara Freeman

DTP Designer Julian Dams
Editorial Assistance Janet Mohun, Teresa Pritlove

US Editor Margaret Parish

Editorial Manager Andrea Bagg
Senior Managing Editor Martyn Page
Managing Art Editor Louise Dick

Picture Research Anna Grapes
Production Louise Daly

FIRST EDITION
Project Editor Louise Tucker **Editor** Nicholas Turpin **Consultant Editors** Paul Cornish, Hayden B. Peake
Senior Editor Edward Bunting **Project Art Editor** Clare Shedden **Designer** Christina Betts
Managing Editor Martyn Page **Managing Art Editors** Philip Gilderdale, Bryn Walls
Senior Managing Editors Ruth Midgley, Josie Buchanan, Krystyna Mayer
Senior Managing Art Editor Lynne Brown
Production Alison Jones **Picture Research** Anna Lord

Second American Edition, 2002

03 04 05 10 9 8 7 6 5 4 3 2

Published in the United States by DK Publishing, Inc.
375 Hudson Street, New York, NY 10014

Copyright © 1996, 2002 Dorling Kindersley Limited, London
Text copyright © 1996, 2002 H. Keith Melton

Library of Congress Cataloging-in-Publication Data
Melton, H. Keith (Harold Keith), 1944-
    Ultimate spy/ by H. Keith Melton ; forewords by Richard Helms and Markus Wolf.--
Rev. ed.
        p. cm.
    Includes index.
    ISBN 0-7894-8972-4 (alk. paper)
    1. Espionage. 2. Intelligence service. I. Title.

JF1525.I6 M45 2002
327/12--dc21   2002019483

Reproduced by Colourscan, Singapore
Printed and bound in the Slovak Republic by TBB

See our complete product line at
www.dk.com

CONTENTS

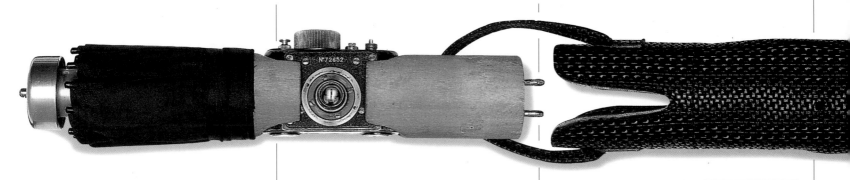

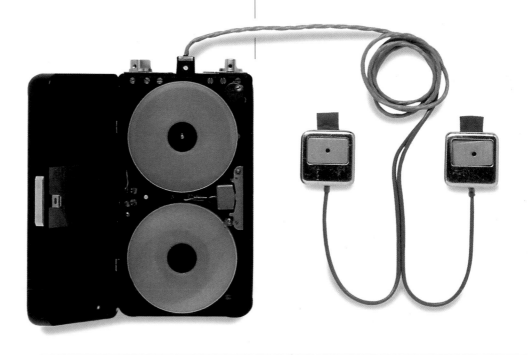

When I began my career in the Office of Strategic Services in the 1940s, books on espionage equipment and methods did not exist. By the end of World War II, available books contained black-and-white photographs and were classified. Not until 1991, with the publication of OSS *Special Weapons and Equipment: Spy Devices of WWII*, could the public learn about the secret devices that helped to win World War II. The book's author, Keith Melton, began collecting spy gear after his service in Vietnam. He is now recognized as the preeminent private collector and authority in the field.

In 1996, Mr Melton broadened his approach and tackled the history of espionage in the first edition of *Ultimate Spy*. The concise entries with their spectacular color illustrations made it a wonderful introduction to this fascinating world. Many of the espionage devices included had never before been seen in the West.

This expanded edition of *Ultimate Spy* includes entries on recent spy cases, the role of computers and the internet, and new items of equipment used by the Russian intelligence agencies and the East German HVA (Foreign Intelligence Service), which was headed by my former adversary Markus Wolf. Two of my favorite items are an HVA clothes-iron concealment, which is an ordinary-looking iron with a false bottom, and a miniature KGB camera hidden inside a conventional cigarette lighter.

Beyond the attraction of the spy devices, this extraordinary book offers readers insight into the problems faced by today's intelligence agents as they work against post-Cold War espionage and terrorist threats. *Ultimate Spy* is a brilliant contribution to the literature of intelligence. By demonstrating how the espionage threats of the past have been met, it justifies the optimism of our profession that we can rise to future challenges.

Richard Helms
Former Director of the CIA

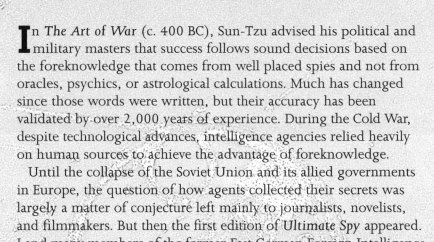

In *The Art of War* (c. 400 BC), Sun-Tzu advised his political and military masters that success follows sound decisions based on the foreknowledge that comes from well placed spies and not from oracles, psychics, or astrological calculations. Much has changed since those words were written, but their accuracy has been validated by over 2,000 years of experience. During the Cold War, despite technological advances, intelligence agencies relied heavily on human sources to achieve the advantage of foreknowledge.

Until the collapse of the Soviet Union and its allied governments in Europe, the question of how agents collected their secrets was largely a matter of conjecture left mainly to journalists, novelists, and filmmakers. But then the first edition of *Ultimate Spy* appeared. I and many members of the former East German Foreign Intelligence Service, the HVA, were surprised to discover a book that included elegant photographs of spy equipment, from Keith Melton's unique collection, and accurate descriptions of clandestine techniques that we had spent our careers keeping secret from Western intelligence agencies. This new edition shows many new items of equipment and brings us up to date with post-Cold War intelligence activities.

I am pleased to make this small contribution to a book that describes significant cases and illuminates the history of the equipment and methods used by spies. It is important for everyone to know how intelligence services and agents function and to understand that as the technology changes, the basic methods of espionage remain the same. Providing the foreknowledge to keep nations secure in this time of increased international terrorist threats is in large part the responsibility of intelligence and security services. This book helps make clear how they go about it.

Markus Wolf
Former Head of the East German Foreign
Intelligence Service, the HVA

WHO SPIES?

Infrared receiver
This small device was controlled remotely to trigger a hidden surveillance camera.

THE SPECIFIC ACT of gathering information from an enemy is rarely carried out by an intelligence officer in person. To accomplish this task, intelligence officers recruit agents who, perhaps by virtue of their position, have access to the information required. Officers who recruit and handle agents are known as case officers. Most work from an embassy under some form of official cover (see p. 194) and are protected legally by diplomatic immunity. Others may operate without diplomatic immunity, perhaps living under an assumed identity. When recruiting agents, case officers are guided by the factors most likely to motivate people to become spies. These can be summed up by the acronym MICE – money, ideology, compromise, and ego.

Aldrich Ames
Ames (b.1941) voluntarily became a KGB mole and revealed CIA secrets to the Soviets in exchange for $2.7 million. By his own account, he offered his services to pay off his debts and to finance his wife's spending habits.

M = MONEY

Financial problems, such as deep debt or greed for material possessions, are fertile ground for those who recruit agents. This has proved to be true in both capitalist and communist countries. Many Soviet intelligence officers were lured into spying for the West by the offer of a solution to money problems. The CIA (see p. 46) sometimes succeeded in targeting officers of the KGB (see p. 50) who were unable to pay back operational funds that they had used personally.

The major KGB successes that have come to light in recent years were also achieved by exploiting greed. The most significant American agents in the history of the KGB and SVR (see p. 62), Aldrich Ames (see p. 190), John Walker, Jr. (see p. 54), Harold James Nicholson, Earl Edwin Pitts, and Robert Phillip Hanssen (see p. 64), all offered their services in return for financial reward.

I = IDEOLOGY

A person may alternatively be led into becoming an agent because of a belief in the ultimate superiority of the social and political institutions of a foreign country. During the 1930s in particular, the Soviet

George Blake
Inspired by communism, Blake (b.1922) served the KGB as a mole within Britain's MI6.

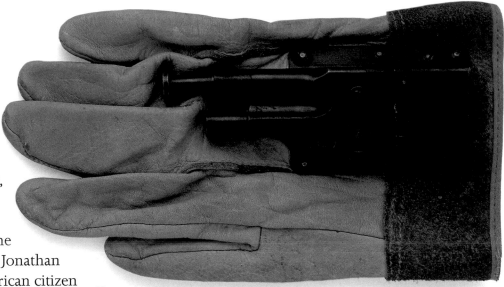

Union was able to recruit agents by exploiting the attraction that communism held for many in the West at that time. These included five idealistic students who were to become the Soviet Union's chief spies in Britain – Kim Philby, Anthony Blunt, Guy Burgess, Donald Maclean, and John Cairncross. Despite the decline of communism, ideology remains a factor in the recruitment of agents. Jonathan Pollard was an American citizen who worked at the US Naval Intelligence Support Center. He agreed to spy for Israel because of his ideological commitment to Zionism. Like many others, his motivation for spying was mixed – he was later to accept money from the Israelis.

John Vassall
While working as a clerk at the UK embassy in Moscow, Vassall (b.1924) was compromised and recruited by the KGB.

C = COMPROMISE

A first step in recruitment by compromise is to identify an element in a potential agent's lifestyle that he or she would not wish others to know about. Homosexuals, for instance, at least in the immediate postwar decades, often risked ruin if their private lives were revealed. This made it possible for the KGB to recruit John Vassall when he was an embassy clerk in Moscow (see p. 192). In 1955 the Soviets carried out an intricate operation in which they set him up in an embarrassing situation, took photographs, and used these to blackmail and entrap him. Seven years later in London, Vassall was convicted of passing secrets to the Soviets between 1956 and 1962.

The KGB kept special hotel rooms in Moscow that were used for photographing visiting Westerners in compromising circumstances – with prostitutes, for instance. With pictures in hand, the KGB could usually

Glove pistol
During World War II, the US Navy's Office of Naval Intelligence conceived this self-defense weapon for possible use by intelligence support and other administrative personnel who were stationed close to the front line.

blackmail its target individuals into becoming agents. Today, homosexuality and, of course, many heterosexual relationships, are no longer such effective means of coercion. On the other hand, financial and marital difficulties are still exploited with success.

E = EGO

Case officers are often trained to appeal to the egos of candidates vulnerable to intellectual flattery in order to entrap them. Typically, a case officer might commission a candidate to write articles for publication. Initially they may be on safe, unclassified subjects. If asked, later, to write on subjects of a more sensitive nature, the writer may already be ensnared by the praise, money, and possibly the sense of adventure gained through previous efforts.

Hugh Hambleton was lured to the KGB by flattery and a sense of adventure (see p. 192). Despite an awareness of the risks involved, some subjects continue in the belief that they can outwit intelligence professionals.

Hugh Hambleton
The KGB used flattery to recruit Hambleton (b.1922), an academic who later rose to the rank of professor.

WHAT DO SPIES DO?

THE PEOPLE WHO APPEAR IN THIS BOOK have all been active within the general field of intelligence, covert action, or special military operations. In a broad sense, these individuals can be brought together under the term "spies," but this is not a precise term. First, depending on one's point of view, the word may carry dishonorable overtones and be taken by some people as an insult. There are cases where this is appropriate. And yet there are other people working in this field – equally spies – on whose skills and strengths their country relies for its survival. Second, the fictional world of spying is one of action and excitement, but the reality is infinitely more discreet, professional, and subtle.

Wristwatch microphone
This fake watch contained a microphone that was connected to a tape recorder hidden beneath the user's clothing.

Maria Knuth
Knuth began her spy career in 1948 as a courier for Polish intelligence in West Berlin.

VARIETY OF ROLES

Those entering a career in special military operations must face the unglamorous aspects of military life, as in the other armed forces. The physical training is hard; so is the competition with others aiming to be selected for special duties. For those who are chosen, training will become much more diverse, since there are many different roles in today's special military forces, each requiring a course of specialized training.

There are many different roles, too, in the intelligence agencies. Similar roles, and similar structures, occur in each country. Typically, there is one agency for intelligence – the gathering of sensitive information – and one for counterintelligence – defense against enemy spies. An important distinction exists between officers, most of whom are career members of their agency, and agents, whose status varies with the country and the individual, and whether they are operating in war or in peacetime. A case officer is one who recruits and runs agents, and may try to encourage case officers of hostile nations to defect or act as moles. An agent is assigned tasks in intelligence or various other covert activities but is not an agency employee.

Some officers deal with administration and support, which generally accounts for about 25 percent of all agency staff. The other 75 percent are usually divided equally between analysis and operations, and what follows is a brief overview of some of their roles.

THE COURIER

Couriers are the links between the agents and their controllers. They sometimes also serve as cutouts – intermediaries who enable the system to work with no contact between sender and receiver. If neither of these two parties knows the other, they will be unable to betray one another. Some couriers work in embassies, collecting information from local agents. The Israeli agency Mossad makes use of couriers called *bodlim* to do this. Other couriers transport intelligence across international borders, sometimes in the guise of diplomatic couriers, as in the case of Alfred Frenzel (see p. 48).

Concealments
Intelligence agencies often use ingenious adaptations of everyday objects as hiding places for secret information or equipment.

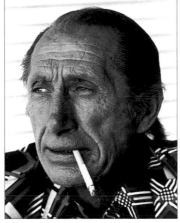

Dusan Popov
German military intelligence (the Abwehr) approached Popov in 1940. He joined their organization but passed secrets to British intelligence. His double-agent codename was Tricycle.

A courier's task is often a dangerous one, as his or her fate is far less important than the information he or she carries. Some agencies have developed concealments that will self-destruct if anyone tampers with them. Although the destruction of the information will not save the courier from being incriminated, it may protect the identity of the agent who gathered it. Some agents begin their careers as couriers, before moving on to other tasks. An example is the Polish agent Maria Knuth, who started in 1948 as a courier in West Berlin, carrying secrets on microfilm.

THE DOUBLE AGENT

These are agents who turn against the intelligence service that originally recruited them and work for another agency, while at the same time making the original agency believe their loyalty has not changed. They may do this for ideological reasons, for personal gain, or to save their lives after being captured. Double agents are a dangerous threat to intelligence operations, as they can be used by their new controllers to feed misleading information to their original employers.

During World War II, Britain's MI5 (see p. 196) set up an organization known as the Twenty, the XX, or the Double Cross Committee. This body clandestinely controlled much of Germany's intelligence-gathering effort in Britain. It went so far as to set up a series of largely fraudulent "German" intelligence networks that reported to the Germans without arousing suspicion, but were in reality under the control of MI5.

Two of the most successful double agents actually volunteered their services to British intelligence during World War II. Dusan Popov (see p. 41) was a Yugoslav who ran a network of three double agents for MI5. He passed misleading intelligence to the German Abwehr.

The other example was also a British agent in World War II – the Spaniard Juan Pujol, codenamed Garbo, who was so successful in deceiving the Germans on behalf of the Allies that he was decorated by both sides!

THE DEFECTOR

A defector is an intelligence officer who abandons his or her original agency and betrays it by giving information to a foreign intelligence service. Some defectors are motivated by ideology, while others act out of fear for their own safety. The latter was the case with Vladimir Petrov, a KGB officer in Australia. In 1954, facing allegations that he had been involved in a plot, he evaded recall to Moscow and turned himself over to the Australian authorities. As soon as they had

Fear of retribution
KGB officer Vladimir Petrov (inset) defected from the Soviet embassy in Australia. In the main picture, KGB men escort his wife to a flight back to Moscow. The Australian authorities freed her, however, and the pair were granted asylum.

Supporting role
Odette Sansom served as a courier for an SOE circuit organizing sabotage in France.

abandoned the KGB, Vladimir Petrov and his wife were granted asylum in Australia, and in return gave valuable information on Soviet espionage activities in Australia. A more recent and dramatic defection was the escape from Moscow of Oleg Gordievsky, a KGB officer who was working for British intelligence. He realized that he was under suspicion, but evaded KGB surveillance. Gordievsky was smuggled out of the Soviet Union by MI6. If they are not under suspicion, however, would-be defectors are often encouraged to remain within their intelligence service to work clandestinely as moles.

KGB defector Peter Deriaban was an example of a defector whose knowledge of his old agency proved useful long after he escaped. He served for years as an adviser to the CIA. In particular, he followed the organization and structure of the KGB and its officers, and lectured on the subject inside the agency.

THE SABOTEUR

The word "sabotage" is French in origin, and refers to the action of a disgruntled workman who destroys machinery by throwing a wooden clog (*sabot*) into it. The destruction of enemy equipment is a frequent objective of sabotage. But there are also more sophisticated forms of sabotage, such as the ingenious but largely ineffective attempt by the Germans in World War II to sabotage the British economy by flooding world markets with counterfeit English banknotes (see p. 34).

Tire slasher and sheath
Saboteurs and special operations personnel used tire slashers to sabotage enemy vehicles.

It was in World War II that saboteurs were most regularly and effectively employed, especially by the British SOE (see p. 30) and American OSS (see p. 32). Both organizations sent teams of officers to assist local resistance groups in campaigns of sabotage. Some of these personnel were trained in the various sabotage methods, others were needed for support roles. The latter was the case with Odette Sansom, who was sent to France by the SOE in 1942 as a courier. She was unwittingly revealed to the Gestapo by a captured member of the resistance and was arrested in 1943.

THE MOLE

Moles are ostensibly employees of one intelligence service who are at the same time secretly working on behalf of a hostile agency. As such, they can be extremely valuable to the intelligence agency that runs them. Provided they have sufficiently high-level access, they

Long-term undercover informer
CIA officer Larry Wu Tai Chin worked as a mole for Chinese intelligence, supplying secret information from the early 1950s until his suicide in 1985.

will be able to supply information on many aspects of their employers' work. People have a variety of motives for becoming moles. Some may do so for ideological reasons, others because of the lure of money. Whatever the case, the double life that they lead is one of extreme stress, often causing such personal problems as alcoholism or irresponsibility with money.

Ring concealment
This World War II ring concealed microdots and radio signaling plans.

The CIA has suffered at least two major penetrations by moles. In one instance, Larry Wu Tai Chin joined the CIA in 1952 and, from early in the 1950s until his death by suicide in 1985, he secretly worked for Chinese intelligence. A recent and well-publicized example of a mole was CIA officer Aldrich Ames (see p. 8 and 194), who offered his services to the KGB in return for money. From 1985 until he was arrested in 1994, he sold a vast number of secrets to the Soviet Union.

THE ANALYST

The information gathered by espionage and technical means forms only a small part of the material that needs to be evaluated by intelligence services. Much of the vast quantity of information that passes through their hands is acquired from publicly available sources. Analysts have the task of combining these diverse elements of intelligence into their written reports and digests. Their output is a potentially valuable aid for military and political decision-makers.

The role of the analyst is unglamorous compared to that of spies who take part in operations, and analysts seldom come to the notice of the public. Without them to provide a usable end product, however, espionage would be much less effective than it actually is. With the current rapid development of information technology (see p. 15), the analysts' role is likely to become still more important.

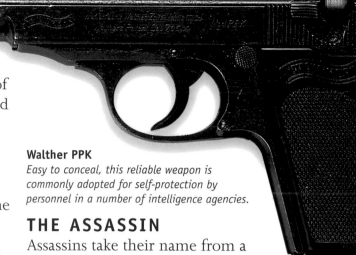

Walther PPK
Easy to conceal, this reliable weapon is commonly adopted for self-protection by personnel in a number of intelligence agencies.

THE ASSASSIN

Assassins take their name from a medieval Muslim sect that exerted its power by murdering the leaders of those who opposed it. The role of the intelligence service assassin is essentially the same. Contrary to common belief, assassinations are not frequently carried out by spies. US Senate hearings in 1976 established that the CIA had never actually participated in the murder of a foreign leader, despite some abortive plans to that end. The CIA is now prohibited by executive order from taking part in assassinations.

By contrast, the intelligence services of the Soviet Union made effective use of assassination to liquidate political enemies. As early as the 1930s they created a special laboratory, the *kamera*, to develop poisons and other assassination tools. Their most prominent victim was Leon Trotsky, one of the founders of the communist state, who was killed in 1940 on the orders of his rival, Stalin.

Later killings included those of two Ukrainian nationalist exiles in Munich by the KGB. These were carried out in 1957 and 1959 by a KGB officer named Bogdan Stashinsky. The device he used was hidden in a rolled-up newspaper and sprayed poison gas in the victim's face, causing death within seconds. At first, there was no suspicion of foul play: even after autopsy the death was not attributed to assassination. Stashinsky revealed all when he defected to West Germany in 1961.

Assignment in Munich
While serving as a KGB officer, Bogdan Stashinsky assassinated two Ukrainian nationalists.

SPIES OF THE FUTURE

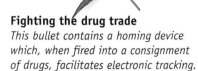

THE FUTURE OF ESPIONAGE will inevitably be affected by changes resulting from the end of the Cold War and the demise of communism in Eastern Europe. In place of the old certainties of superpower rivalry, there is a much more unpredictable world order, made additionally unstable by the forces of nationalism and religious fundamentalism. Spies have a role to play, both in advancing these causes and in countering the new threats that they present. Future spies will also, more often than the spies of today, turn their attention to industrial espionage, crime, terrorism, and the exploitation of new technology.

Fighting the drug trade
This bullet contains a homing device which, when fired into a consignment of drugs, facilitates electronic tracking.

INDUSTRIAL ESPIONAGE

The commercial rivalries between developed nations in the post-Cold War world are likely to increase. In the mercantile wars and technological battles of the future,

Kenji Hayashi
Hayashi was arrested after he was found to have arranged payent for stolen IBM computer secrets in a large-scale industrial espionage operation.

economic spies will be the foot soldiers. There is nothing new about industrial espionage: the Hebern machine (see p. 144) was invented to protect business communications in the early 20th century.

Industrial espionage is particularly prevalent in the field of computer technology. The cost of research and design work means that any company that can steal a fully designed concept can make vast financial savings. In 1981, Kenji Hayashi, a senior engineer for the Japanese company Hitachi, attempted to acquire the details of a new computer disk drive being developed by IBM in the United States.

Hayashi's downfall came when an intermediary, whom he approached in an attempt to acquire the secrets, informed IBM. The matter was investigated by the FBI. Hayashi was arrested after arranging to pay $525,000 for a batch of IBM secrets. He was given a five-year suspended jail sentence and fined $10,000. It was reported that, in settlement of a civil suit brought by IBM, Hitachi paid $300 million in compensation.

Industrial espionage can also be carried out by state agencies. The national intelligence services in some countries, notably France and Britain, have engaged in espionage to help companies in their own countries to compete with foreign companies.

COMBATING CRIME

The fall of communism has created a more unstable world, but has also allowed intelligence services more time to devote to countering the new threats that are emerging. Organized crime is already being targeted. American intelligence agencies are involved in the war against the drug cartels of Central and South America. The agencies in Europe, meanwhile, are alert to the menace of criminals from the former communist bloc seeking to establish themselves in the West.

Intelligence agencies may also be employed to combat new types of technologically based crime. Modern computer codes enable criminals to hide their profits as they move them around the global electronic banking system. Computer microchips have become the world's most valuable black market commodity.

More alarmingly, substances that are required for making nuclear weapons have already been illegally sold from the former Soviet Union. Espionage will certainly play a part in preventing such material from falling into the hands of terrorist groups or being acquired by states that currently lack nuclear weapons.

Christopher Boyce: satellite traitor
While employed by an American satellite communications company, Boyce conspired to sell satellite secrets to the Soviet Union. He received a long jail sentence (see p. 59).

Digital listening devices are already available, too. These have a solid state memory – they record the sound on a silicon memory chip, transmitting it afterward in a burst (see p. 142).

Another improvement in audio surveillance is the use of fiber-optic cables instead of wires to carry signals from microphones. Developments such as these make audio surveillance much harder to detect.

Satellite technology has reached the stage already where it can provide real-time surveillance of a target area, both in pictures and in intercepted radio communications.

SYSTEMS ESPIONAGE

Perhaps the most important influence on the spies of the future will be new developments in computing. Future voice recognition systems will enable automated electronic surveillance to become more sophisticated. New electronic codes will enhance the security of communications, although they will, obviously, make code-breaking a harder task. "Software robots" may cruise the internet public access network, programmed to detect such items as an illicit message between an agent and his controller. And there may be yet more sophisticated "viruses" – destructive programs which, once in the computer operating systems of an enemy, remain dormant until activated in time of war or crisis. While human spies will still be needed, computers will be increasingly important in the gathering and processing of information. And it may be that those who control access to the information will decide who the superpowers of the future will be.

SURVEILLANCE

A number of technological advances are likely to have an influence on the work of the future spy. Video cameras are bound to play a growing part in surveillance. They can already be made smaller than a postage stamp, and images can be enhanced by means of digital manipulation.

Satellite launch
Modern satellites provide immensely detailed intelligence, sending back high-resolution images and intercepting telecommunications worldwide.

Micro video camera
This tiny camera is easy to conceal and can even record pictures through the weave of the user's clothing.

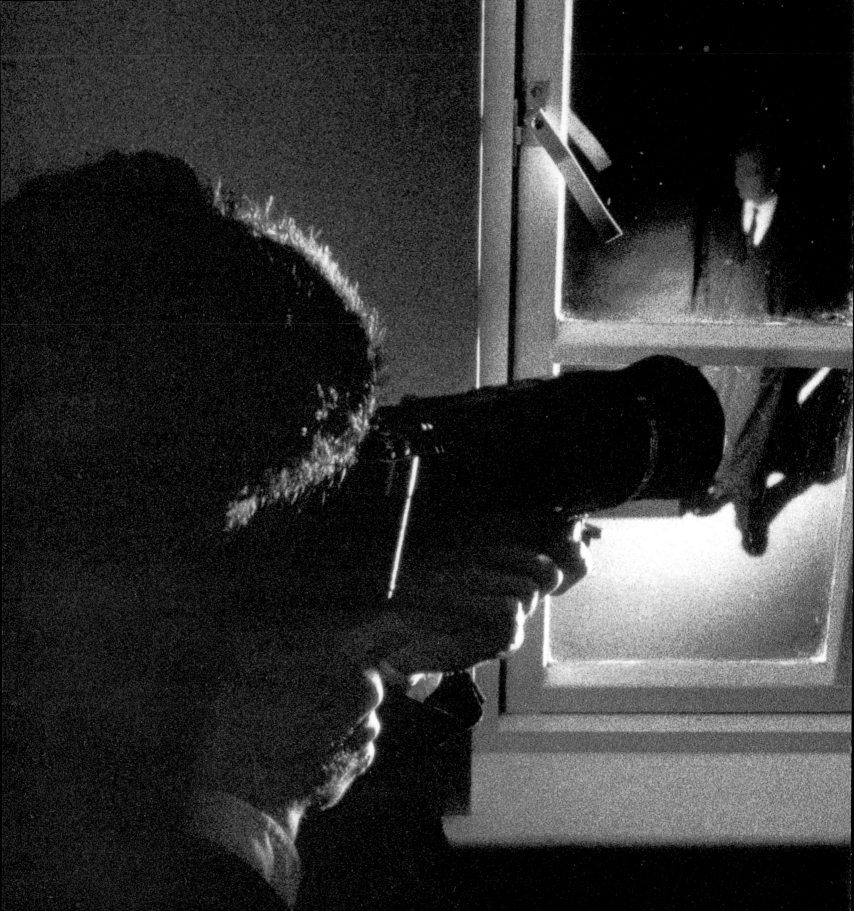

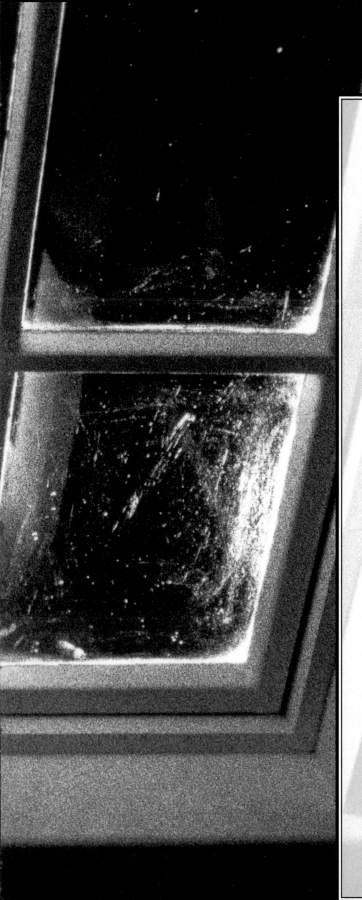

FAMOUS SPYING OPERATIONS

Spying has been part of human activity since time immemorial. Many of the techniques of spying used today were developed in the courts of Renaissance Italy and Elizabethan England. Successive generations of spies and spy agencies have distilled the experiences of the past, learning more sophisticated methods of acquiring and passing information while undermining the ability of the enemy to do the same. In the 20th century, both world wars and the ideological struggle known as the Cold War created an insatiable demand for information. World War II was responsible for the vast Soviet spy networks and the rapid development of cryptography. During the Cold War, the great intelligence agencies – the KGB and the CIA – applied new technologies, such as computers and spy satellites, to espionage. The end of the Cold War did not eliminate the need for spies, but served to increase the scope of their international involvement and the intensity of their conflict. This section of the book covers some of the most important and famous spying operations in the history of espionage.

EARLY ESPIONAGE

Emblem of the Pinkerton Agency
Allan Pinkerton, founder of Pinkerton's National Detective Agency, headed "Pinkerton's Secret Service," which was active in spying for the North during the Civil War.

RULERS AND MILITARY LEADERS have always needed to know the strengths, weaknesses, and intentions of their enemies. Consequently, the trade of spying is as old as civilization itself. Around 500 BC, the ancient Chinese strategist Sun Tzu wrote about the importance of intelligence and espionage networks in his classic book, *The Art of War*. The Bible contains more than a hundred references to spies and intelligence-gathering. Most of the elements of modern espionage, however, originate in 15th- and 16th-century Europe.

Cardinal Richelieu
Richelieu, chief minister to King Louis XIII of France, created the Cabinet Noir intelligence service.

SPIES AT COURT

The political, philosophical, and cultural changes of this period fostered the development of intelligence-gathering. During the 15th century, the principles of polyalphabetic ciphers were laid down; these principles were still in use in the early 20th century. During the 16th and 17th centuries, the European courts became centers of intrigue as rulers strove to maintain and increase their power. The ambassadorial system of diplomacy was established, and ambassadors were expected to combine official duties with espionage and subversion. Intelligence services were created and were used to great effect by such men as Cardinal Richelieu in France (1585–1642) and Sir Francis Walsingham in England (1537–90).

Confederate cipher disk
This substitution disk, which is made of brass, is a type of cipher wheel (see p. 144). It was used by the Signal Service of the Confederacy for secret communications during the Civil War.

THE CIVIL WAR

By the time of the Civil War (1861–65), a number of technological advances, such as the invention of photography, had occurred that changed the methods used to gather and communicate intelligence. The Confederacy may have even used of an early form of microphotography. Telegraphy was used for

Ring revolver
This tiny five-shot weapon, shown with its case and ammunition, was sold under the brand name Le Petit Guardian. *It was made in late-19th-century France.*

the first time in a major war for military communications, in spite of its vulnerability to interception. Aerial photography was also carried out, using hot air balloons.

WORLD WAR I

Early in World War I (1914–18), human spies were seen as the main threat by the public on both sides

Silver dollar concealment
This 19th-century silver dollar could be used to conceal secret messages. The side with the eagle was hinged, and opened when pressed at a point near the rim.

of the conflict. But it was signals intelligence that was to prove far more decisive, and indeed it attained a greater importance than in any previous war. For instance, British Admiralty cipher experts decoded a top-secret German government telegram offering Mexico an offensive alliance against the United States. By subtle use of this discovery, Britain helped to bring the U S into the war on the Allied side (see p. 24). In the US, a cryptology section for military intelligence had been created under Herbert Yardley (see p. 24).

Cheka badge
The Cheka replaced the Okhrana, the old security service of the Czarist regime.

CHANGES IN RUSSIA

Russia's participation in World War I led to the seizing of power by the Bolshevik Party after the 1917 revolution. The party created its own secret police, the Cheka, which conducted a ruthless offensive, called the Red Terror, against opponents of Bolshevism. Once bolshevik power was established, the Cheka extended its activities to foreign countries. After the formation of the Soviet Union in 1923, the Cheka's responsibilities were taken on by various organizations, including the NKVD, which became the KGB in 1954.

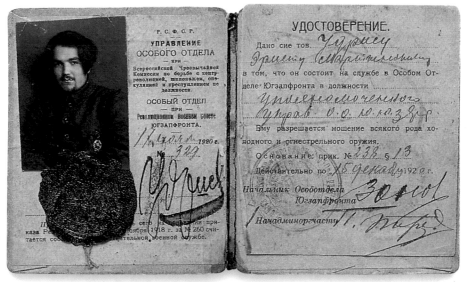

Cheka credentials
The Cheka was founded in 1917. Its name is the Russian-language abbreviation for "Extraordinary Commission for the Struggle against Counter-revolution, Espionage, Speculation, and Sabotage."

Court intrigues

SEVERAL IMPORTANT FEATURES of modern espionage had their origins in the Renaissance, the cultural movement of rebirth and modernization that spread through Europe in the 15th and 16th centuries. In the arts and sciences a new, enlightened age began. But in public life dynamic changes were taking place, and bitter struggles for power and religious authority gave new scope for intrigue and treachery. This was the world observed by writer Niccolò Machiavelli (1469–1527) and dominated by a new class of politicians such as Cesare Borgia (1475–1507).

Niccolo Machiavelli

Machiavelli (1469–1527) was a scholar and writer with an interest in political philosophy. While serving as a diplomat for the Republic of Florence, Machiavelli met Cesare Borgia, whose political subtlety and cunning he later held up as an example to other rulers in his book *Il Príncipe* (*The Prince*). Machiavelli also wrote a book about the art of warfare, in which he emphasized the usefulness of military intelligence.

CESARE BORGIA

By a combination of deceit, charm, and aggression, Cesare Borgia carved out a kingdom for himself in central Italy. Other rulers of the period were just as much in tune with the new political spirit of the age. In the prevailing climate of mistrust, the growing craft of espionage could hardly fail to flourish.

The tools of the trade were already being developed. Impressively complex polyalphabetic ciphers were devised in the 15th century by two scholars, Leon Battista Alberti (1404–72) and Johannes Trithemius, his contemporary. Others, such as Giovanni Soro (d.1544) in Venice, contributed to the science of cryptography (the study of codes and ciphers).

The Renaissance also saw the emergence of the modern nation-state, and it was at the courts of such states that the most important developments in espionage took place. By the second half of the 16th century, states such as France, England, and Spain had set up official structures for the gathering of political and military intelligence at home and abroad. Ministers of state

and diplomats were made responsible for gathering intelligence, and ambassadors abroad were expected to combine their official duties with espionage.

Elizabethan intrigues

An effective intelligence service was maintained in England during the reign of Queen Elizabeth I (1533–1603). As a Protestant nation with a weak army, England was constantly threatened by the Catholic powers, France and Spain. War with either could have proved a disaster for England, so intelligence about their intentions was vital.

Elizabeth herself was unmarried and childless, and there were several foreign princes who wanted to marry her and so gain the throne. Within England, too, she had Catholic opponents who wished to overthrow her and replace her with a Catholic monarch. The security of the Protestant state depended on protecting

the queen from such dangers. In 1573, Sir Francis Walsingham (1537–90) was appointed secretary of state. By skillful use of espionage and counterespionage, he was able to defeat a number of plots aimed at the overthrow of Elizabeth and the restoration of Roman Catholicism.

One possible heir to the English throne was Elizabeth's cousin Mary, Queen of Scots (1542–87). A Catholic, she featured in many political intrigues of the reign, such as the Babington Plot of 1586. This aimed to release Mary, who had been imprisoned in England after being forced to flee Scotland. The principal elements of the plot were an

SPY PROFILE Christopher Marlowe

The English poet and playwright Christopher Marlowe (1564–93) was recruited into the secret service while studying at Cambridge University. In 1587, posing as a Catholic student, he entered a seminary at Rheims in France. Gaining the trust of the Jesuit students, Marlowe learned details of Jesuit plots in England. Marlowe's death in a tavern brawl is believed by many to have been linked to his secret service work.

Queen Elizabeth I
The motifs decorating the Queen's dress in this portrait are emblematic of various aspects of her power. The eyes and ears (inset) symbolize the activities of her secret service.

uprising of the Catholics of England, invasion by an army financed by Spain and the Pope, and the assassination of Queen Elizabeth herself.

At the center of the conspiracy was John Ballard. A priest of the then-militant Catholic order the Jesuits, he was well known to Walsingham's staff. Ballard recruited Anthony Babington, who had formerly acted as a messenger for Mary. Walsingham meanwhile employed a double agent who gained the trust of the conspirators and soon learned how they communicated with Mary.

This correspondence was intercepted and deciphered by Thomas Phelippes, Walsingham's master cryptographer. It contained enough evidence to ensure the arrest and execution of the various plotters and even, on February 8, 1587, of Mary, Queen of Scots.

There were also threats from overseas to the security of the English state. King Philip II of Spain (1527–98) believed that it was his duty to restore England to the Catholic faith. Walsingham sent Anthony Standen to gather intelligence in Spain. Standen gained the help of the Florentine ambassador at Philip's court,

and secured the help, too, of a Flemish courtier whose brother was a servant to the Grand Admiral of the Spanish fleet. In 1587 information from these sources alerted Walsingham to the great fleet, or Armada, that was being prepared for the invasion of England. Using his influence abroad, Walsingham secretly contrived to delay the bank loans Philip needed to finance his expedition. This gave the English time to prepare for the arrival of the Armada, which was duly defeated.

Richelieu and the Cabinet Noir

During the 17th century, the French court became a center of espionage activity. In the early years of the century, France suffered from an overly powerful nobility and from internal religious divisions. It was threatened externally by the power of the Hapsburg family – the rulers of Spain, Austria, parts of Italy, and the Low Countries.

These difficulties were triumphantly overcome by Louis XIII's chief minister, Cardinal Richelieu (1585–1642). Louis himself was an ineffective ruler, with the result that from 1624 to 1642 France was virtually run by Richelieu. One of Richelieu's first acts after being appointed was to set up an intelligence service, known as the Cabinet Noir. This service monitored the activities of the French nobility by intercepting their correspondence.

Using the information gained in this way, Richelieu thwarted plots against the king and strove to establish the absolute power of the monarchy. His greatest successes were in frustrating plots to seize the throne devised by the king's brother, Gaston of Orleans, and the Duke of Cinq Mars.

Cardinal Richelieu
Cardinal Armand Duplessis, Duke of Richelieu, instituted and used a national intelligence service to establish royal absolutism in France.

Richelieu also used agents abroad in support of his policy of weakening the Hapsburgs without involving France in costly wars. They subverted Spain, for example, by encouraging Portugal and Catalonia to rebel against Spanish rule.

The cardinal's machinations helped to bring Sweden into the Thirty Years' War (1618–48) against the Holy Roman Empire. With Germany paralyzed by this conflict, Richelieu was able to seize Alsace for France. By means such as this, his secret service helped to make France a powerful, absolutist nation-state.

American Civil War

DURING THE CIVIL WAR (1861-65), both the Union and the Confederacy were faced with the need for intelligence organizations. Some early attempts were of limited efficiency; but during the course of the war, intelligence-gathering methods improved. The ability of both sides to obtain information from each other was enhanced by the new technologies of the time. Photography, for instance, was exploited for espionage purposes, and an early form of microphotography may have been used.

Allan Pinkerton
Detective agency chief Allan Pinkerton (left), head of the Union secret service, with Abraham Lincoln (center) and General John McClernand.

Secret services

At the outbreak of the war in 1861, neither side had an established intelligence organization. Both the Union and the Confederate forces initially relied upon patriotic volunteers such as Rose Greenhow for intelligence.

Union army commander General George McClellan established a secret service early in the war, selecting a detective, Allan Pinkerton, to be its head. Before the war Pinkerton had owned a detective agency, which had provided security for the railroads. Pinkerton's detectives had limited success as spies, but they established a process of debriefing escaped slaves for information. Conflict arose when another Union commander, General Winfield Scott, started his own security organization, which was led by Lafayette Baker. Baker proved to be less effective than Pinkerton, despite personally spying in the South, disguised as a roving photographer. Both Baker's and Pinkerton's men actively sought out Confederate spies operating in the Union capital of Washington, sometimes arresting each other by mistake.

More efficient regional military intelligence operations were set up by

Belle Boyd, "The Rebel Joan of Arc"
A flamboyant Southern patriot, Belle Boyd (1843–1900) achieved limited success as a spy and courier. After the war she romanticized her activities in a book and enjoyed a long career enacting her espionage work on the stage.

SPY PROFILE | Rose Greenhow

Rose O'Neal Greenhow was an accomplished Confederate agent. A society hostess in Washington, she set up a spy network just before the war began; using her charms, she obtained information from Union politicians and the military. The first battle of the Civil War – at Bull Run – was won by the Confederates aided by information supplied by Greenhow. Even when under house arrest, she continued to gather and pass on information.

obtained daily information by courier from the North. It was only toward the end of the war, in 1865, that an official Confederate secret service was set up.

New technology

Several new methods of intelligence-gathering were used during the war. Photography was so new that few commanders saw it as a threat. Photographers were allowed to take pictures of military defenses and camps, and both sides obtained information in this way. Confederate couriers photographically reduced messages so they could be hidden inside hollow metal buttons. Telegraphy was used for quick communication and both sides devised ciphers for secrecy. Aerial reconnaissance from tethered hydrogen balloons was developed during the war, but it was of limited use because the balloons could be shot down easily.

Confederate cipher disk
Used to provide a substitution cipher for secret communications, this disk was adopted by the Confederate Signal Service Bureau in 1862.

Union commanders in the field, notably that run by Colonel George H. Sharpe for General Ulysses S. Grant.

In the South, Colonel Thomas Jordan and later Major William Norris ran an intelligence-gathering operation that

Doll with secret compartment
There was a great shortage of medicine in the South. Women and children carried medicine in the body of this doll through enemy lines.

The plot to assassinate President Lincoln

In 1865, as the Civil War neared its end, the Confederate secret service devised several plots against Union leaders. Although these plots failed, some key conspirators continued to plot after the official Confederate surrender on April 9, 1865. The most ambitious of these plots was one to assassinate the Union president, Abraham Lincoln, the vice president, and the secretary of war.

John Wilkes Booth, a famous actor, was selected to kill Lincoln, and he shot him as he watched a play at Ford's Theater in Washington on April 14, 1865; the president died later. Booth escaped from the theater, but was later found and shot. A search of his possessions revealed a Confederate cipher device. In popular history Booth is generally considered to have acted alone in his assassination of Lincoln. But he definitely had connections with the Confederate secret service, and questions remain about the group's role.

Abraham Lincoln
This picture shows President Lincoln (1809–65) being shot by Booth, as he sits in a box at Ford's Theater.

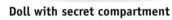

John Wilkes Booth
President Lincoln's assassin, actor John Wilkes Booth (1838–65), had also been involved in an earlier attempt to kidnap the president.

World War I

WORLD WAR I (1914–18) began as a struggle between the great European powers: the Triple Entente of France, Britain, and Russia against the Central Powers of Germany and Austria–Hungary. As the war progressed, more nations were drawn into the struggle. It was during this war that code-breaking (cryptography) began to take on the great importance that it has in intelligence-gathering today.

During the early 20th century, technology for sending long-distance messages made great advances. Telegraph and radio messages, in Morse code, were soon vital to the conduct of war. The intelligence-gathering work of the "agent on the ground," known in the trade as human intelligence, or HUMINT, was joined by a new craft, signals intelligence – later known as SIGINT. In addition to sending and receiving messages, it was now necessary to break the ciphers of enemy nations. Early in World War I, Russia had not learned the importance of this: the first German victory against Russia was the result of German signals intelligence intercepting Russian army signals that had been transmitted in unenciphered Morse code. Some other countries did establish special centers for deciphering

Count Johann Heinrich von Bernstorff
Germany's ambassador in Washington, DC during World War I, von Bernstorff relayed the famous Zimmermann telegram to Mexico.

Concealments for invisible ink
This talcum powder can and dentifrice bottle, full of invisible ink, were seized from German spies captured by the British security service.

messages. For example, the British set up Room 40 of naval intelligence, which was renowned for its deciphering skills.

The Zimmermann telegram

In 1917, German Foreign Minsiter Arthur Zimmermann sent an encrypted telegram to Germany's ambassador in Washington, DC, Count von Bernstorff, informing him that Mexico was to be offered a war alliance with Germany against the United States. The count sent a modified version of the telegram to Mexico City, using the same cipher.

The telegram to Washington was intercepted and deciphered by British code-breakers. The British wanted to tell the Americans about the telegram, but did not want the Germans to know that their cipher had been broken. Admiral Hall, head of the Royal Navy's code-breaking organization, informed the US Embassy in London about the telegram, and the embassy told Washington.

The British suggested that Washington obtain a copy of the telegram sent to

Herbert Osborne Yardley

As a young man, the American Herbert Yardley (1889–1958) gained a reputation for his ability to break codes used by the US State Department, where he worked as an ordinary clerk. After the outbreak of World War I he was commissioned into the US Army and put in charge of the newly formed cryptography section of Military Intelligence (MI8). He devised new codes for use by the US Army and helped to convict a German spy whose secret message had been decoded by MI8.

After the war, Yardley established a permanent department, the American Black Chamber, to assist both the State Department and Military Intelligence with all code and cipher work. (For the difference between a code and a cipher, see the Glossary, p. 200.) Yardley's greatest success came when his cryptography group broke

secret Japanese codes, which enabled the United States to gain significant advantages at the international naval disarmament conference of 1921.

Peace conference credentials
Herbert Yardley led the cryptographic bureau of the US delegation at the 1919 Paris Peace Conference, after the end of World War I.

Mexico from the Western Union Telegraph Company in Washington. That still encrypted copy was relayed to London where it was decoded, with the help of the British, at the US Embassy.

The resulting translation was sent to Washington and leaked to the *New York Times*. The Germans believed that the Americans had obtained an already deciphered version of the telegram sent to Mexico City. This gave the Germans the impression that their cipher was still secure. They had no reason to suspect British involvement. Public indignation over the telegram quickly led to the entry of the United States into the war.

German spies

A fear of German spies spread through Britain and France at the outbreak of World War I. Although some spies were present in both countries, there were actually far fewer than imagined, and most were captured at the beginning of hostilities. One spy who succeeded in evading capture was Jules Silber. He operated in Britain, taking a job in the Office of Postal Censorship and passing censored information to the Germans.

Two Dutch agents who were sent to Portsmouth to spy for the Germans were not so successful. They pretended to be cigar importers and used their orders for cigars as codes for the ships they saw in Portsmouth harbor. These bogus orders were intercepted by the British postal censors, who became suspicious about the quantity of cigars ordered. The spies were captured and executed in 1915.

Mata Hari

Dutch-born Margaretha Zelle (1876–1917) became famous throughout Europe as a dancer under the stage name Mata Hari. She performed a dance which was, by her account, an authentic Hindu temple ritual. Her fame brought her many influential lovers.

Mata Hari briefly took up spying in 1916 when the German consul in Amsterdam persuaded her to use her lovers to acquire information for Germany. He gave her inks with which to send secret messages. It was not long before Mata Hari's amateurish attempts at espionage aroused the suspicions of both French and British intelligence. In spite of this, the French accepted her offer to spy for them. She seduced the German military attaché in Madrid, hoping he would give her information that she could pass on to France.

Mata Hari's end came when she was mentioned in a German secret service telegram from Madrid to Germany. Although referred to as "agent H-21," she was identifiable, and the message was intercepted by the French – it was in a code that they had already broken.

Mata Hari was arrested as a German spy on her return to Paris. She was tried in a French military court, found guilty, and executed by firing squad in 1918.

**MATA HARI IN PRISON
IN FRANCE**

**MATA HARI AS A DANCER BEFORE
WORLD WAR I**

Revolutionary Russia

THE RUSSIAN REVOLUTION of 1917 replaced the feudal government of the Czars with the communist government of the Bolsheviks (the Communist Party). The revolution took place as a result of hardships during World War I and of political pressures for a change in government. The Czarist government had an intelligence and security service called the Okhrana. One of the key tasks of the Okhrana had been to spy on revolutionaries such as the Bolsheviks. After they came to power, the Bolsheviks copied the Okhrana's techniques for gathering information.

Felix Dzershinsky
The Russian secret police was founded by Felix Dzershinsky (seated in center). The huge and powerful organization that he established was to survive for longer than the Soviet Union itself.

EARLY CHEKA BADGE

The Czarist intelligence services had a mixed history. In 1913, military intelligence achieved a major success against the Austro-Hungarian Empire. Important military secrets were acquired from an Austrian army officer, Colonel Alfred Redl. The colonel was secretly homosexual, and the Russians were able to blackmail him into passing Austro-Hungarian war plans to them.

In 1914, on the other hand, it was an intelligence failure that caused the first great Russian disaster of World War I, the defeat at the battle of Tannenberg. Radio signals relating to the deployment of the Russian forces were broadcast in plain Morse code (without the use of a cipher to ensure secrecy). This gave a crucial advantage to the Germans, who were monitoring the broadcasts.

The Okhrana

The Okhrana was more aware of the possibilities of signals intelligence than the military, and it employed spies to assist in code-breaking activities. The organization also had some success in bribing foreign journalists to present a favorable picture of Russia. This helped the Czar to secure war loans from countries allied to Russia.

Cheka credentials
This is the earliest known example of a Russian secret police identification credential. It belonged to a member of the Cheka.

The most effective work of the Okhrana took place in Europe. A system of informers and agents was developed to penetrate revolutionary groups. The information from these networks was so good that Okhrana files are a major source of information on the early history of the Bolsheviks. When the Bolsheviks gained power, they were quick to see the value of the Okhrana's spying techniques and records.

Moscow: the Kremlin
The Kremlin, a walled fortress in the center of Moscow, became the seat of Bolshevik power in 1918; today, it houses Russia's government.

The Cheka

After gaining power in late 1917, the Bolsheviks created their own secret police, the Cheka. Under the command of Felix Dzershinsky (1877–1926), the Cheka immediately set about securing the Bolshevik hold on power. Political opponents of the regime were arrested, imprisoned, or executed. In the face of growing threats to the regime, these actions reached their peak in late 1918. Hostages were taken, concentration camps set up, and torture by Cheka interrogaters officially approved as a tool for extracting information. Combining this extreme ruthlessness with the interrogation techniques of the Okhrana and the prerevolutionary Bolshevik Party's expertise in clandestine activities, the Cheka was able to establish itself as the primary agency for espionage abroad and for counterintelligence at home.

The OGPU

In 1922, with the Bolsheviks firmly in power, the Cheka was converted into the GPU (State Political Directorate), still under Dzershinsky. When the Soviet Union was created in the following year, the GPU became the OGPU (United State Political Administration). The constitution of the Soviet Union charged the OGPU with the mission to "struggle with political and economic counter-revolution, espionage, and banditry." The OGPU, operating from its headquarters at Lubyanka in Moscow, had power over virtually all aspects of Soviet life, and also conducted intelligence operations abroad. It was particularly active against anti-Bolshevik émigrés. Eventually, the organization had 800,000 members. The OGPU remained, under a number of names, a central part of the government of the Soviet Union until 1991.

Silenced OGPU revolver
The 7.62mm Nagant Model 1897 revolver was a standard weapon of both the Imperial Russian and Soviet armies. This special example was used by the OGPU. It had a silencer, here shown removed.

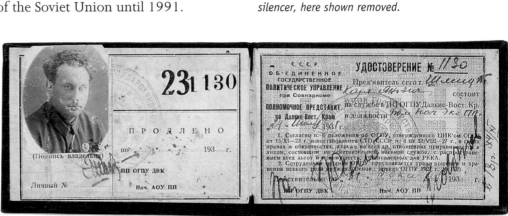

OGPU credentials
In 1923, Felix Dzershinsky's intelligence and secret police organization became known as the OGPU. This organization was the direct forerunner of the later NKVD, MGB, and KGB. After the demise of the communist state in 1991, the KGB was dissolved and its directorates were renamed.

The Trust and Sidney Reilly

The Trust was a deception operation, devised by the secret police chief Felix Dzershinsky (see above). Its purpose was to entice counterrevolutionary émigrés back to the Soviet Union so that they could be killed or imprisoned by the secret police.

Officially called the Moscow Municipal Credit Association, the organization was established in Moscow and had an office in Paris. Its ostensible purpose was to offer support to anti-Bolshevik groups. To gain the trust of the émigré community, Dzershinsky allowed the Trust to engineer the escape of a famous anti-Bolshevik general from Russia. Then, in 1924, the Trust was involved in persuading an émigré leader, Boris Savinkov, to return to Moscow, supposedly to lead a counterrevolution. Once in Moscow, Savinkov was arrested and tortured. Subsequently, he was killed by being pushed down a stairwell in the OGPU headquarters at Lubyanka in Moscow.

In 1925, a British intelligence operative named Sidney Reilly was lured to a meeting with Trust members in Moscow, where he was arrested and forced to write a confession revealing all his Moscow contacts. He was then executed. His body was photographed in the Lubyanka morgue, as proof for OGPU records that he had been captured and killed.

Sidney Reilly
Reilly was targeted by the OGPU because of his work for the British intelligence and his wide range of important Russian contacts.

WORLD WAR II

THE MAJOR COMBATANTS of World War II deployed their intelligence services with varying degrees of success. At the start of war in Europe in 1939, the Soviet Union, Germany, Japan, and Britain had well-established foreign intelligence networks, although the United States did not.

The most extensive networks operated were the Soviet ones, including the west European network under Leopold Trepper. Among other things, Trepper warned of the German invasion of the Soviet Union in 1941. Warnings were sent, too, by Richard Sorge, a Soviet spy in Japan. Unfortunately, Premier Stalin did not trust his own intelligence sources. But there was one message from Sorge that did help significantly, prompting Stalin to move Soviet troops from the east to halt the German advance in the west and prevent the fall of Moscow.

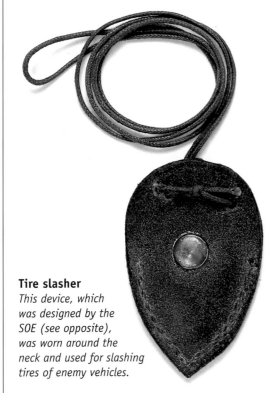

Tire slasher
This device, which was designed by the SOE (see opposite), was worn around the neck and used for slashing tires of enemy vehicles.

AXIS INTELLIGENCE

German espionage efforts were less successful. The intelligence community was split into two rival camps, the Army-controlled Abwehr and the Nazi Party SD. Toward the end of the war, the SD became the dominant force. Germany's intelligence services seriously underestimated the military power of the Soviet Union, and they were completely taken in by Allied deception plans that masked the 1944 D-Day landings. German attempts to establish agents in Britain and the United States, too, were a failure. Furthermore, when good information was acquired by the German intelligence agencies – for example, through the agent known as Cicero (see p. 34) – it was badly mishandled.

Lapel pin
In 1945 the OSS (see opposite) issued this pin to its veterans.

In contrast to Germany, Japan used its intelligence sources well, having gathered intelligence to good effect prior to its successful attacks on Pearl Harbor and on a number

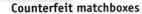

Counterfeit matchboxes
Special operations personnel operating in occupied countries had to have belongings that seemed to be locally made. These matchbox labels and color printing blocks were made for the SOE (see opposite).

Walter Schellenberg
Following the assassination in 1942 of SD head Reinhard Heydrich (see p. 35), Schellenberg (1910–52) took over SD foreign intelligence operations.

of countries in Southeast Asia that were dependencies of European powers. The Japanese also maintained a spy ring in America.

THE WESTERN ALLIES

The British and Americans had to invent intelligence strategies to cope with war against an enemy who seized vast areas of territory. In 1940, European stations of Britain's senior intelligence service, MI6, were all overrun by the Germans. The British created a new service, the Special Operations Executive (SOE). This was the first service that combined intelligence-gathering with clandestine warfare (including support for resistance groups). In 1942, the United States created the Office of Strategic Services (OSS) to play a similar role but with a stronger intelligence-gathering component. Together, and in concert with local resistance groups, the SOE and OSS caused chaos behind enemy lines, in both Europe and Asia.

NEW SKILLS

In terms of influencing the outcome of the war, the intelligence operations that proved to be most effective were those of the Allied code-breakers. British cryptographers broke the ciphers of the German Enigma and its derivatives, while the Americans broke the Japanese Purple cipher. Information thus gathered gave the Allies insight into enemy intentions. This did not guarantee them victory, but it had far-reaching effects on their conduct of the war. For instance, in 1943 it helped to defeat the German submarine fleet, which otherwise would have blocked essential Allied shipping lanes in the North Atlantic.

Cipher machine
Japan produced its own innovations in intelligence codes and ciphers. This is a Japanese rotor-type cipher machine.

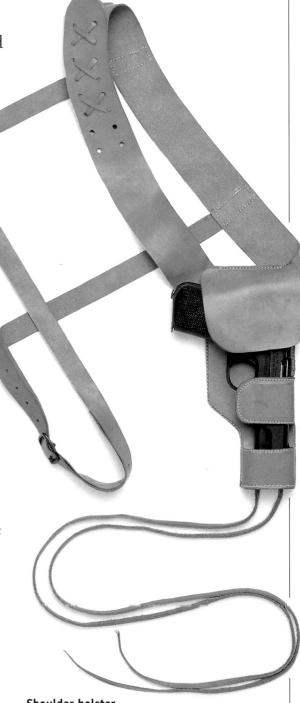

Shoulder holster
Holsters of this type were used by SOE officers who chose to carry a pistol for personal protection. This example contains a Colt .32 pistol.

Special Operations Executive

THE BRITISH SPECIAL OPERATIONS EXECUTIVE (SOE) was founded during World War II in the summer of 1940, after Germany had invaded much of continental Europe. Its task was to equip, train, and help lead resistance groups in areas occupied by the German forces, as well as to take part in aggressive sabotage operations. SOE officers and operatives worked with local resistance groups, coordinating their activities with one another and with the campaigns of the anti-German Allied armies for the liberation of Europe.

All the SOE's recruits were volunteers, and were often dismissed by the more established intelligence services as amateurs, meddling in "cloak-and-dagger" warfare.

SPECIAL FORCES' WINGS

Organization

The SOE was controlled by the Ministry of Economic Warfare, and for most of the war was led by Major General Sir Colin Gubbins. The SOE was divided into separate sections, or "desks," for each country in which operations were planned. Each desk recruited, trained, and operated its own personnel. In action the SOE operated in groups of between two and 30 members. From 1943 on, the SOE cooperated with the American Office of Strategic Services, the OSS 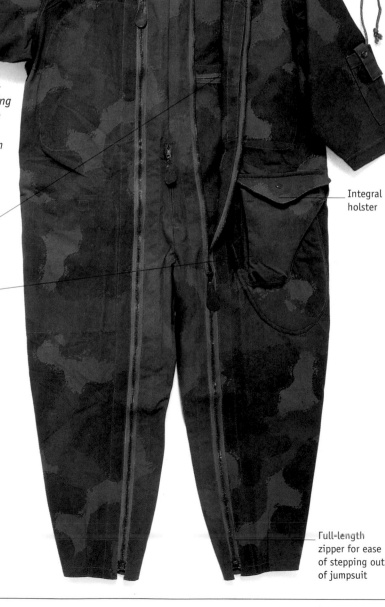(see p. 32).

- Celluloid goggles
- Padded helmet
- Lanyard for knife used to cut parachute
- Retaining strap for helmet
- Integral holster
- Full-length zipper for ease of stepping out of jumpsuit

SOE jumpsuit
Designed for use by covert-action personnel parachuting into occupied territory, the suit provided camouflage, protected the clothing from damage, and had pockets to hold vital equipment.

Opening where spine-protection pad is inserted into pouch

Inner padded pocket for shovel used to bury jumpsuit on landing

SPY PROFILE   Odette Sansom

French-born SOE agent Odette Sansom (1912–95) was sent to southern France in 1942. Her codename was Lise. She served as a courier with an SOE unit led by Captain Peter Churchill. In 1943 they were unwittingly betrayed by a member of the French resistance. Sansom and Churchill were captured and interrogated by the Germans, and sent to concentration camps. Both of them survived their time in the camps and married after the war.

Operations

SOE operatives and officers were sent into enemy territory clandestinely, some landing in aircraft in fields or dropping by parachute, others using submarines and small boats. The SOE's approach was always to cooperate closely with local resistance groups. Together they made sabotage attacks on communications, factories, and power lines to disrupt the enemy. Back in Britain, the SOE set up laboratories to develop equipment for its operatives and officers. Special forms of explosives were created, as were original ways of concealing them, camouflaging them, and controlling their detonation. The SOE laboratories also made special concealable and silenceable weapons. They devised advanced radio equipment that operatives could use to receive messages from headquarters as well as passing back information, for example, on enemy troop movements.

.32-caliber revolver
This weapon was carried by the SOE operative Violette Szabo, who was an excellent shot.

SPY PROFILE **Violette Szabo**

British-born Violette Szabo (1921–45) joined the SOE after her husband, who was an officer in the Free French army, was killed fighting the Germans. Szabo's last mission to France was on June 6, 1944 (D-Day), when she was sent to assist a resistance group. Within days she was captured by the Gestapo (see p. 34) but refused to talk. Szabo was sent to a concentration camp and executed on January 26, 1945.

The risks

Since their work involved resistance and sabotage, SOE operatives were relentlessly hunted by enemy forces. If captured, the operatives risked torture and death. From 1940 until 1944, 393 SOE operatives were sent to work in France – 17 were captured and survived, 104 were killed. Despite such sacrifices, the SOE was never fully accepted by the established intelligence services. Officers of its British rival, the Secret Intelligence Service (MI6), disliked the SOE's policy of combining guerrilla warfare, sabotage, and subversion with more conventional forms of intelligence-gathering.

The SOE nonetheless played a vitally important role in organizing resistance forces and coordinating their operations in support of the Allied invasion of Europe, which finally came in 1944.

The French resistance

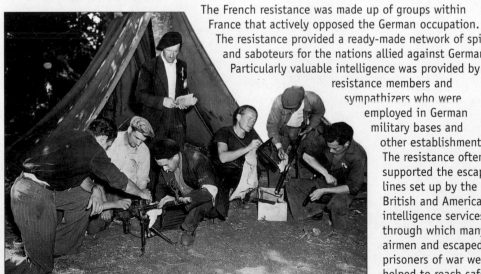

The Maquis preparing their weapons
The first Maquis units were made up of people evading a German forced labor program. Later, the whole French resistance was called the Maquis.

The French resistance was made up of groups within France that actively opposed the German occupation. The resistance provided a ready-made network of spies and saboteurs for the nations allied against Germany. Particularly valuable intelligence was provided by resistance members and sympathizers who were employed in German military bases and other establishments. The resistance often supported the escape lines set up by the British and American intelligence services, through which many airmen and escaped prisoners of war were helped to reach safety. A sabotage campaign was mounted, in which the resistance was

Lapel blade, sheath, and armband
The sheath shows the Cross of Lorraine, symbol of the Free French army, which fought against the Germans from outside France.

aided by the SOE and OSS. This gave rise, in June 1944, to widespread attacks on German transportation and communications in support of the Allied invasion of Europe, the D-Day landings. On August 10, 1944, a series of work stoppages began in Paris that led to a full-scale public revolt against the German occupiers. On August 24, the Allied forces, including elements of Free French armored units, entered Paris. The German garrison surrendered the following day.

Office of Strategic Services

THE OFFICE of Strategic Services (OSS) was created in June 1942, six months after the United States entered World War II. Its director, William J. "Wild Bill" Donovan, had previously held the key intelligence post of coordinator of information, reporting directly to the president. He formed a new service that was truly worldwide in scope. The OSS did not restrict itself to intelligence-gathering; it also waged clandestine warfare, using tactics that were similar to those of the British SOE (see p. 30).

.45-caliber Liberator pistol
This simple, cheap weapon was intended to be supplied in large numbers to resistance fighters. Its role was to capture a better weapon from an enemy soldier.

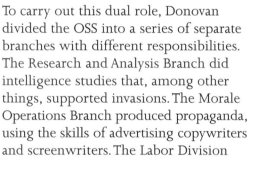

OSS COLLAR INSIGNIA **OSS LAPEL PIN**

To carry out this dual role, Donovan divided the OSS into a series of separate branches with different responsibilities. The Research and Analysis Branch did intelligence studies that, among other things, supported invasions. The Morale Operations Branch produced propaganda, using the skills of advertising copywriters and screenwriters. The Labor Division encouraged subversive activity within trades unions in enemy-occupied Europe, in order to disrupt production and communications systems. Three of the main functional branches of the OSS were: Special Operations (SO), Secret Intelligence (SI), and Counterintelligence (X-2).

Clandestine warfare

The SO branch, modeled on Britain's SOE, supported resistance movements in parts of Europe and Asia. Usually working in groups of between two and 30 people, members of the SO branch operated behind enemy lines. Lines of communications and supply, factories, and airfields were sabotaged.

Secret Intelligence

The SI branch of the OSS established a comprehensive system for the gathering of intelligence. To ensure worldwide coverage, the SI branch was divided into four geographical "desks" dealing with parts of Europe, Africa, the Middle East,

OSS clothing warehouse in London
Clothing such as this German army uniform was taken from prisoners and used by OSS operatives on secret missions in German-occupied territory.

OSS Detachment 101

The first OSS unit created to carry out secret operations was called Detachment 101. Its personnel were trained at an SOE base, Camp X, in Canada. Captain (later Colonel) Carl Eiffler was the commander of Detachment 101 from April 1942 until December 1943. The detachment's mission was to conduct a campaign of sabotage and guerrilla warfare in Burma (now Myanmar) behind Japanese lines. In the fall of 1942, the detachment entered the Burmese jungle and made contact with local Kachin people, who, having suffered badly at the hands of the Japanese, were willing to help the United States. The Kachins were provided with equipment and training by the Americans, and also possessed tribal ambush techniques of their own. Detachment 101 eventually reached a strength of 500, assisted by more than 10,000 Kachins. This combined force caused over 15,000 Japanese casualties.

101 DETACHMENT CAMPAIGN BAR

COLONEL CARL EIFFLER

and Asia. A number of other sections assisted the SI branch in its operations. A Reporting Board analyzed the agents' reports and distributed them. The Ship Observer Unit gathered information on the enemy from seamen's organizations and shipping operators. The Technical Section reviewed technical reports and provided information for Britain, as well as the United States, about matters such as the development of V1 and V2 rockets.

Special equipment

The OSS was supplied with a range of specialized equipment by the Research and Development Division, which was led by Stanley Lovell (see p. 179). Many innovative weapons and devices were produced specially for the OSS. The Liberator pistol was a cheaply made weapon intended for distribution to resistance groups in occupied countries. Special explosives were invented, along with devices for camouflaging them and delaying their detonation. Advanced radio equipment was made for contact between OSS headquarters and operatives in the field. Secret cameras were developed for taking clandestine photographs.

Donovan's achievement

During World War II, the OSS achieved notable successes in both clandestine warfare and intelligence-gathering, and demonstrated the benefits of combining these two major roles in one organization. Nevertheless, its mode of operations was new to the United States and had not yet been wholly accepted. Not only this, but Harry S. Truman, who became US President in 1945, saw Donovan as a political rival and had no reason to keep him on in a top government post. The OSS was abolished in 1945 and its intelligence-

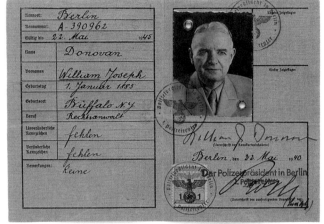

False German identification card
Produced for OSS chief William Donovan, these credentials demonstrate the ability of OSS forgers to create realistic German documents.

gathering role was taken over by the US War Department, while the analysis role went to the State Department. Donovan had hoped that he would be able to set up a postwar intelligence service, but the plan he put forward was reviewed unfavorably by President Truman.

Although Donovan never attained his goal of creating a single, centralized US intelligence service, a variation of his plan did come into being two years after the OSS had been disbanded. This was the Central Intelligence Agency (CIA) (see p. 46). Donovan also left another legacy to US intelligence in the form of several highly experienced OSS veterans who joined the CIA, including William Colby and Richard Helms.

William Egan Colby

During World War II, William Colby (b.1920) served with the OSS in both France and Norway, where he carried out sabotage with local resistance groups (see p. 171). After the war, Colby held posts around the world with the Central Intelligence Agency (CIA). Later, in Vietnam, on leave from the CIA, he headed a key military-intelligence program with the rank of ambassador. Colby was Director of the CIA from 1973 until 1976.

German secret services

DURING WORLD WAR II (1939–45), there were two German intelligence agencies – the Abwehr and the Sicherheitsdienst, or SD. The Abwehr was the intelligence and clandestine warfare section of the armed forces. The SD was controlled by the Schutzstaffel (the SS), an arm of the National Socialist Party (Hitler's Nazi Party), which ruled Germany from 1933 until the end of the war. The role of the SD was to spy on the other Nazi Party members for the SS.

ADMIRAL WILHELM FRANZ CANARIS (1883–1945)

FRONT VIEW

Gestapo warrant disk
Numbered warrant discs were carried by members of the Gestapo as proof of authority for use only when carrying out arrests and house searches.

From 1935, the head of the Abwehr was Admiral Wilhelm Canaris. As a naval officer, Canaris had been involved in undercover work during World War I. When appointed head of the Abwehr, his first task was to establish a working relationship with the SD, as previously there had been very little cooperation between the two agencies. Reinhard Heydrich was the chief of the SD. In 1938, the Geheime Staatspolizei (the Gestapo, the secret state police) and the Kripo (criminal police) came under control of the SD. Heydrich had served as a cadet under Canaris in the navy, and they agreed on a compromise that made the Abwehr responsible for military espionage and all counterespionage, while the SD took responsibility for political intelligence and police work.

Cooperation between the Abwehr and the SD did not last, and Canaris soon expanded the Abwehr in an attempt to become more important than the SD and free himself from Nazi Party control. But he failed to gain the authority he wanted for the Abwehr and, despite some successes, the Abwehr's foreign intelligence operations produced few significant results.

Cicero and Operation Bernhard

Cicero was the codename for Elyesa Bazna (1905–71), the Albanian valet of the British ambassador to Turkey, Sir Hugh Knatchbull-Hugessen. Bazna worked as an agent for the SD between 1943 and 1944. Having stolen the keys to the ambassador's safe, Bazna photographed documents about conferences in Moscow, Cairo, and Teheran and information relating to the impending D-Day invasion of German-occupied Europe. The Germans did not gain much advantage from this information, however, because it was mishandled by the German intelligence services. The SD paid Bazna £300,000 ($1,200,000) in counterfeit notes. These notes had been made as part of a plan – Operation Bernhard – to destabilize the British economy by distributing large amounts of forged currency. The SD used Jewish master forgers from concentration camps to forge the currency, which they did to such a high standard that the forgeries were not discovered until after the war. Bazna's post-war retirement plans collapsed when the forgeries were detected; he sued the German government, without success.

Elyesa Bazna
Years after the discovery of his spying activities, Bazna demonstrated how he had photographed secret documents with a Leica camera.

Counterfeit British 10-pound note
Jewish master forgers in concentration camps were coerced into forging British banknotes, causing the recall of an entire series of currency.

The SD

From 1935 onward, the SD expanded greatly in size and power. Reinhard Heydrich enjoyed the support and patronage of the chief of all German police, Reichsführer SS Heinrich Himmler. Under Heydrich

Operation Anthropoid

On May 27, 1942, Reinhard Heydrich (1904–42), acting Reichsprotektor of Bohemia and Moravia (now the Czech Republic) and head of the SD, was fatally injured in an attack known as Operation Anthropoid. A Czech team, trained by the British SOE (see p. 30), threw a grenade at Heydrich's car as he drove through Prague, inflicting fatal wounds. The attackers were killed after a gun battle a few weeks later. In reprisal for Heydrich's death, the SS razed the Czech village of Lidice and killed all its male inhabitants.

REINHARD HEYDRICH

the SD gradually extended its activities into areas that were supposed to be the preserve of the Abwehr. In 1939 his power was increased when he was appointed head of the Reich Central Security Department (the RHSA). Heydrich gathered intelligence from all sectors of society, even opening an exclusive brothel, known as Salon Kitty, equipped for electronic eavesdropping on its clients. During the war the SD mounted a wide range of operations, some of which – such as Operation Bernhard (see opposite) – were too ambitious to be successful.

The fall of Admiral Canaris

Following the death of Heydrich on June 4, 1942, Canaris became the most important person in the German intelligence services. But he did not have the support of Himmler, who in February 1944 persuaded Hitler to dismiss him. The Abwehr was merged with other intelligence agencies under the RHSA. Canaris was arrested after a failed assassination attempt on Hitler in July 1944, and was executed in April

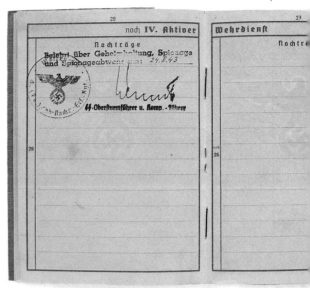

Page from an SD credential
This credential was issued to a member of the SD who had attended a training course on secret work, espionage, and counterespionage.

1945. Himmler was right not to trust Canaris – since 1938 Canaris had been expressing increasingly hostile views toward Hitler and his policies. Canaris was also sending intelligence, via his mistress, to Allen Welsh Dulles, Chief of the OSS Mission, in Bern, Switzerland.

Tuning dial   Crystal socket

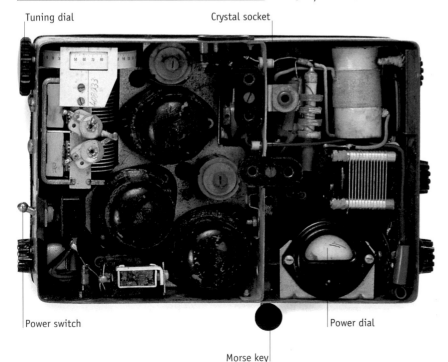

Power switch

Morse key

Power dial

Front cover of radio

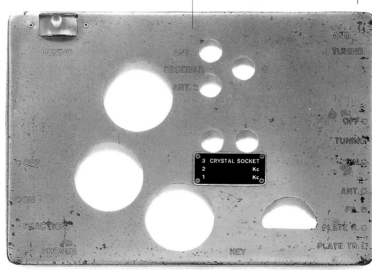

SE 109-3 Abwehr radio
This small battery-powered radio set allowed Abwehr agents in the field to transmit and receive Morse code messages to listening stations. So as not to be incriminating if the set was discovered, any labels on the cover were in English.

Code-breaking

SPIES, DIPLOMATS, military personnel, and others often relied on cipher machines to protect the secrecy of their messages during World War II. Messages enciphered by means of the German Enigma cipher machine (see p. 146) and the Japanese Alphabetic Typewriter 97 were deciphered by code-breakers working in special establishments in both Britain and the United States.

Baron Hiroshi Oshima
Oshima (1886–1975) was Japan's ambassador to Germany during World War II. He sent messages on the broken Purple cipher.

The Purple code

In 1939, the Japanese began using a new cipher machine for sending diplomatic messages. They called it the Alphabetic Typewriter 97, but in the United States it was known by the codename Purple. The Purple machine was a development of an earlier one codenamed Red.

Code-breakers in the US Army Signals Intelligence Service, headed by William Friedman, had already cracked the Red system, and now a team led by Frank Rowlett began work on the new cipher. They were aided by the interception of a message that had been enciphered on both the Red and Purple machines.

This and other intercepted messages were the only information the code-breakers had to help them build their own Purple machine. A breakthrough came when they used stepping switches – part of the telephone technology of the time. By a lucky coincidence, these worked in exactly the same way as the switches in the Purple machine.

By late 1940, Rowlett and his team of US Navy code-breakers were able to construct a Purple machine. Intelligence deciphered using the machine was called Magic. It was so efficient that Japan's

declaration of war – sent to the embassy in Washington a day ahead of the attack on Pearl Harbor to allow time for decipherment – was read by American intelligence before it was presented to the US Secretary of War.

How the Enigma was cracked

In 1939, the British, with Polish help, began investigating the German Enigma cipher machine (see p. 146). The Government had set up a Code and

---

William Friedman

A Russian émigré to the US, William Friedman (1891–1969) was the author of a series of pioneering papers that set out the main principles of modern cryptography. Friedman's wife, Elizabeth, was also an expert cryptographer, and sometimes they collaborated. In 1929, Friedman was appointed the civilian head of the US Army Signal Intelligence Service. In the 1930s, he was a pioneer in the use of machines for code-breaking. After World War II, his work culminated in the formation of the US National Security Agency (see p. 46), an organization that specializes in signals intelligence and cryptography.

Switching unit

Housing for stepping switch

Stepping switch removed from housing

Purple cipher machine
In this Japanese device, two electric typewriters were connected via two switching units. Plain text typed into one of the typewriters would emerge from the other in the Purple cipher.

Enigma cipher machine
Early models of the Enigma machine had three rotors, but this one has four. The rotors, complex internal wiring, and changing setup produced a cipher that the Germans considered unbreakable.

Bletchley Park, England
At this country house, and in prefabricated huts on its grounds, over 1,000 people worked during World War II to break German ciphers.

Alan Turing

A mathematical genius, Alan Turing (1912–54) played a leading role in the breaking of the Enigma ciphers. At the age of 24, Turing had written a paper that set out the principles by which modern computers work. During World War II, Turing was set to work at the Government Code and Cipher School at Bletchley Park. While there, he conceived the idea behind Colossus, the first electronic computer in the world. The computer helped British code-breakers to meet the challenge presented by the new, more complicated German cipher machine, the 10-rotor Geheimschreiber (see p. 147).

Cipher School, which in 1939 moved to Bletchley Park, a short distance outside London, where a community of mathematicians, linguists, and creative thinkers in other disciplines worked at first on breaking the Enigma ciphers, and later on breaking other enemy ciphers.

The chief problem they faced was to discover the key settings that had been selected when setting up each Enigma machine for its daily use. A further problem was that the equipment itself differed between the various German organizations that used it.

"Bombes"

Before the war, Polish code-breakers had developed a machine called a "bomba" that had successfully deciphered some of the Enigma messages. Unfortunately, the Germans were continually making the Enigma more complicated.

At Bletchley Park, new versions of the bomba, now called "bombes," were developed. At first, these failed to keep pace with the increasing complexity of the Enigma cipher. The mathematician Alan Turing then added 26 electrical relays that speeded up the process of deciphering a message.

Even then, success was achieved only by means of educated guesswork. Using a process of hypothesis and experiment, code-breakers were able to deduce the wording of the part of the message that spelled out the key settings in use.

Mathematician Gordon Welchman developed a procedure known as traffic analysis, which made it possible to sort messages according to the organizations that sent them. This would identify the type of Enigma machine used.

Naval Enigma signals were broken from 1941 to 1945, partly with the help of captured machines and documents, yielding vital information for Britain.

Ian Fleming
James Bond's creator, Fleming (1908–64) worked for British naval intelligence in World War II. He was involved in plots to steal Enigma documents.

Soviet spy networks

DURING WORLD WAR II, the top priority for Soviet espionage was to help defend the Soviet Union against its enemies, Japan and Germany. From the 1930s, Soviet Military Intelligence's Fourth Department (formerly and again later called the GRU) set up spy networks in Japan and Europe. The largest of these was in Western Europe, run from Brussels and later Paris. It was nicknamed the Red Orchestra (*Rote Kappelle*) by German counterintelligence.

The Red Orchestra was headed by Leopold Trepper and had agents at high levels throughout enemy civil and military structures. It was, however, often frustrated by the poor quality of its clandestine radios, which meant that sometimes the network had to depend on vulnerable human couriers. The network suffered badly from German counterintelligence: the Germans captured important messages from Moscow that led them to identify key members of the network; they

Schulze-Boysen
Soviet agent Harro Schulze-Boysen (1909–42, left) was an officer in the German air force. This picture was taken at the German air ministry.

Leopold Trepper
Nicknamed "Big Chief," Trepper (1904–83) went to Brussels in 1938 to launch and operate the Red Orchestra. He later moved to Paris.

The Red Orchestra

The Red Orchestra was the part of the the Soviet spy network that covered Western Europe. It was led by Leopold Trepper and conducted its business under the cover of the Foreign Excellent Raincoat Company. All units reported to Moscow, but not all were in contact with one another. After Trepper's arrest by the Gestapo in 1942, the Red Three unit was the most productive element of the Red Orchestra. This unit was run by Alexander Rado and operated from Switzerland. Its most important agent was Rudolf Rössler (codename Lucy). Today, the Red Orchestra is studied as a classic example of a Soviet intelligence network.

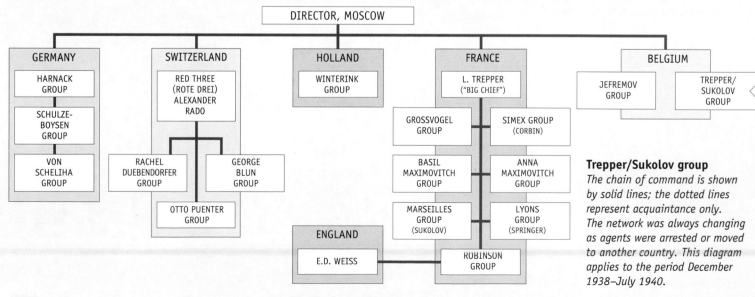

Trepper/Sukolov group
The chain of command is shown by solid lines; the dotted lines represent acquaintance only. The network was always changing as agents were arrested or moved to another country. This diagram applies to the period December 1938–July 1940.

Richard Sorge

This Soviet stamp shows Sorge (1895–1944) with a Hero of the Soviet Union's star.

also captured the cipher used for messages from Brussels. Another difficulty was that the Soviet leader Josef Stalin distrusted some of the sources used by the Red Orchestra. For this reason, not all of the information that the Red Orchestra sent to Moscow from Western Europe was believed by the Soviet authorities.

Unheeded warnings

When the Germans invaded France in 1940, Trepper moved to Paris. He went into business as a contractor for the German army. Intelligence that he gathered from sources in the German army, enabled Trepper to forewarn Stalin of Hitler's plan to invade the Soviet Union in June 1941 but, like other warnings, this was ignored. Warning of the attack also came from two other

Soviet agents in Germany, Harro Schulze-Boysen and Arvid Harnack. They sent German secrets to Moscow by radio, until their arrest and execution in 1942. Trepper himself was arrested soon afterward. He managed to trick the Germans into believing that he was a double agent. He escaped in 1943, and lived out the war in hiding.

Richard Sorge

Long before Japan entered the war in 1941, Moscow feared a Japanese invasion. The Fourth Department sent Richard Sorge, a spy who was half German, to Tokyo in 1933. Posing as a German journalist, Sorge befriended the German military attaché in Tokyo, Eugene Ott, and a Japanese

Hotsumi Ozaki
Recruited by Sorge in 1930, Ozaki gathered intelligence from Japanese political circles.

journalist named Hotsumi Ozaki. In July 1941, Sorge learned from these sources that Japan was more inclined to begin its military campaign in Southeast Asia than to attack the Soviet Union.

If it were true, this information would enable some Soviet armies to be moved from defensive duties on the Soviet Union's eastern borders and used to fight the Germans attacking Moscow. Josef Stalin did not believe it, however, just as he had disbelieved Sorge's warning of Germany's attack in May 1941. Only later in 1941 was Stalin ready to believe Sorge's information about Japan, when signals intelligence confirmed it. Stalin was then able to move more troops from the east to halt the German invasion. Sorge was arrested and executed in 1944.

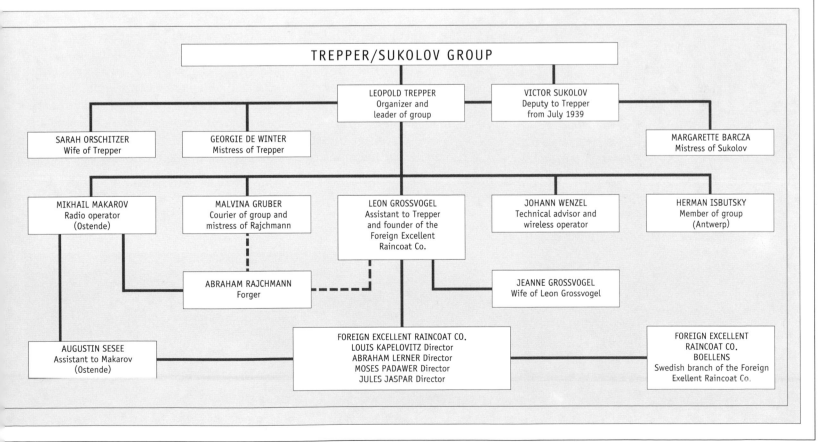

TREPPER/SUKOLOV GROUP

- **LEOPOLD TREPPER** — Organizer and leader of group
- **VICTOR SUKOLOV** — Deputy to Trepper from July 1939
- **SARAH ORSCHITZER** — Wife of Trepper
- **GEORGIE DE WINTER** — Mistress of Trepper
- **MARGARETTE BARCZA** — Mistress of Sukolov
- **MIKHAIL MAKAROV** — Radio operator (Ostende)
- **MALVINA GRUBER** — Courier of group and mistress of Rajchmann
- **LEON GROSSVOGEL** — Assistant to Trepper and founder of the Foreign Excellent Raincoat Co.
- **JOHANN WENZEL** — Technical advisor and wireless operator
- **HERMAN ISBUTSKY** — Member of group (Antwerp)
- **ABRAHAM RAJCHMANN** — Forger
- **JEANNE GROSSVOGEL** — Wife of Leon Grossvogel
- **AUGUSTIN SESEE** — Assistant to Makarov (Ostende)
- **FOREIGN EXCELLENT RAINCOAT CO.** — LOUIS KAPELOVITZ Director, ABRAHAM LERNER Director, MOSES PADAWER Director, JULES JASPAR Director
- **FOREIGN EXCELLENT RAINCOAT CO. BOELLENS** — Swedish branch of the Foreign Exellent Raincoat Co.

Japanese intelligence

DURING WORLD WAR II, Japan's intelligence organization had several elements. Abroad, embassies played a key role coordinating intelligence-gathering. Within Japan, the Tokko – a special bureau of the Tokyo police force – was responsible for domestic counterintelligence. The armed services also had their own intelligence sections, with the military police (Kempei Tai) covering counterintelligence activities in territories occupied by the Japanese.

Admiral Yamamoto
Yamamoto (1884–1943) planned the attack on the Pearl Harbor base of the US Pacific Fleet, making use of intelligence obtained from a Japanese spy.

The Tokko was formed in 1911 with the purpose of suppressing "subversive thoughts" and defending Japan's strictly regulated political system. It did much to prevent the rise of communism in Japan in the years after World War I.

Counterintelligence

By 1932, the Tokko had become Japan's chief internal counterintelligence organization. It was divided into four sections: the first monitored left-wing political activists; the second maintained files on the right wing; the third section watched foreign residents and embassies; and the fourth monitored friendly embassies, like that of Germany.

The domestic responsibilities of the Kempei Tai were officially limited to matters concerning members of the armed services. However, the right-wing military movement that dominated Japanese politics used the Kempei Tai to intimidate opposition politicians, arresting those who campaigned against the political order of the time as "terrorists." During the war, the power of the Kempei Tai was enhanced by the patronage of the prime minister,

Hideki Tojo (1884–1948), who had been one of its officers early in his career. In territories occupied by Japan during the war, such as parts of China and Southeast Asia, the Kempei Tai operated with extreme ruthlessness, gaining a brutal reputation similar to that of the Gestapo in Germany (see p. 34).

Achievements and failures

Immediately after the Japanese capture of Singapore in February 1942, the Kempei Tai arrested hundreds of Chinese Singaporeans, whom it considered to be security risks, and executed them at night on beaches near the city center. Later, in 1944, naval Kempei Tai units were responsible for hunting down and executing a team of saboteurs from Allied countries, who had attempted to raid Singapore Harbor (see p. 123). Despite the zeal of Japanese counterintelligence efforts, a major spy ring working for the Soviet Union managed to flourish in Tokyo in the late 1930s and early 1940s. This spy network, created by Richard

The attack on Pearl Harbor
A Japanese naval officer in Hawaii provided intelligence on American ship movements until hours before the attack on December 7, 1941.

Consul-General Nagao Kita
As Japanese consul-general in Honolulu, Hawaii, Kita provided the enciphering facilities for the naval spy Takeo Yoshikawa.

Sorge (see p. 39), passed a great deal of highly important information to Moscow before it was discovered in 1941. One reason for Sorge's great success may have been that the Tokko was overburdened by the enormous volume of meaningless reports that it received from overeager informants.

Intelligence in the Pacific

During the months before Japan's entry into World War II, Japanese army intelligence established its agents throughout Southeast Asia, as part of what was known as Organization F. Meanwhile, Japanese naval intelligence scored a major success in securing information on the US Navy base at Pearl Harbor in Hawaii, which Japan intended to attack. In March 1941, Japanese naval ensign Takeo Yoshikawa traveled to the Hawaiian islands under an assumed

Purple cipher machine
The Japanese diplomatic service used the Purple machine to encode correspondence (see p. 36).

Sabotage balloons

Throughout World War II the continental United States lay outside the range of bombers from either Germany or Japan. Nevertheless, the Japanese brought the United States under an unusual kind of aerial bombardment. Between 1944 and 1945, some 6,000 balloons bearing incendiary charges were launched from Japan.

The balloons were carried by the prevailing winds, and dropped their charges over the heavily forested northwest of America. At least 369 balloons completed the 6,000-mile (9,700-km) journey. The only fatalities, however, were a family of seven, who were killed by a single balloon.

Japanese sabotage balloon
The Japanese used balloons carrying incendiary devices to bombard the United States. They were wind-borne, and were primarily intended to cause forest fires.

name. From then until Japan's surprise attack on the base on December 7, 1941, he sent weekly reports on the dispositions of American warships. Yoshikawa was familiar with the organization and structure of the American Navy. He possessed no code of his own but sent his messages through diplomatic channels, under the signature of Japanese Consul-General Nagao Kita. American code-breakers could read the coded Japanese diplomatic mail, sent by cable (see p. 36), but the cable authorities in Hawaii, for reasons never explained, did not pass on the relevant cable traffic to the American authorities. Yoshikawa's last message was transmitted just 12 hours before the Japanese began their attack on Pearl Harbor.

Intelligence in Europe

Another Japanese intelligence operation was run from Spain, a neutral country. This group was the TO network, which gathered intelligence on Allied shipping from agents in the United States and elsewhere. The coordinator of TO was Yakichiro Suma, who held the rank of a minister in the Japanese embassy in Madrid. Intelligence from TO was used by the Germans as well as the Japanese.

SPY PROFILE   Dusan Popov

Dusan "Dusko" Popov (1912–81) was a Yugoslav double agent, ostensibly working for the Abwehr (see p. 34) but actually controlled by the British. In 1941, the Abwehr sent him to the US with a list of questions, including some about Pearl Harbor. Popov gave the list to FBI director J. Edgar Hoover, but the Americans took no action regarding Pearl Harbor. As a result, the significance of this interest in the US Navy base was overlooked.

COLD WAR

U-2 spy plane
Introduced in 1956, the U-2 operated at such a high altitude that it was out of range of the Soviet aircraft and missiles of the time.

THE PERIOD OF CONFRONTATION between East and West that ran from 1945 until the fall of communism in the early 1990s is known as the Cold War. At the very beginning of this period, the Soviet Union's former wartime allies in the West were shocked to discover the extent of Soviet espionage activity that was directed against them. The United States responded by creating its own foreign intelligence organization, the Central Intelligence Agency (CIA). Later, the National Security Agency (NSA) was set up as a central body responsible for signals intelligence and cryptography. Counterintelligence within the United States remained the responsibility of the Federal Bureau of Investigation (FBI).

National Security Agency emblem
America's NSA is responsible for information security, foreign signals intelligence, and cryptography.

HUMAN INTELLIGENCE

The divided city of Berlin was in the forefront of espionage operations in the Cold War. Surrounded by the Soviet sector (later East Germany), it became an international center of intelligence activity. One of the most notable incidents was the digging of a tunnel by the CIA and MI6 to intercept a cable carrying military communications to Moscow (see p. 44).

The capture of Berlin in 1945 had given the Soviet state intelligence organization, the NKGB (which later became the KGB), control of Nazi records. This enabled the NKGB to blackmail many West German citizens into becoming spies. The secret police files of other states also provided blackmail material, as in the example of the Czech spy known as Anna (see p. 48).

The Soviet Union was also successful in operating a number of spies in Britain. Notable among these were George Blake, Gordon Lonsdale and his network of agents, and, most damagingly, the five members of the Cambridge ring (see p. 197). Most of these early Soviet spies were motivated either by ideology or

**MICRODOT READER
(ENLARGED 1.5 TIMES)**

**MICRODOT FILM
(ACTUAL SIZE)**

Microdot film and reader
During the Cold War, microdots were much used to convey intelligence in a miniaturized form. They can be read only under powerful magnification.

by the threat of compromise. Later, however, the KGB found that the lure of money was the easiest way to recruit agents. The two most important KGB agents to be exposed in the United States in recent times, John Walker and Aldrich Ames, both offered their services for money. Ames operated as a mole inside the CIA, while Walker sold secrets from within the US Navy.

SPIES IN THE SKY

Another major element of the Cold War was the arms race, a contest for nuclear weapons supremacy between East and West. In this struggle the CIA found that its existing techniques for intelligence-gathering were inadequate for assessing the nuclear strength of the Soviet Union. This led to the development of the U-2 spy plane, which was able to conduct high-altitude photographic reconnaissance. Besides flying over the Soviet Union, the U-2 was used in 1962 to monitor developments on the island of Cuba, revealing the presence of Soviet medium-range nuclear missiles. This precipitated the Cuban Missile Crisis, the most dangerous event of the Cold War, resolved only by a firm American stance.

Another technological race arose from the Soviet Union's launch of the first satellite in 1957. By 1961, satellites were being used for photographic reconnaissance, although the early technology necessitated jettisoning the film for recovery and development on Earth. In 1976 the Americans began using digital technology, which enabled satellites to beam high-definition images back to Earth as soon as they were taken. Such developments in technology have become a prime target for espionage.

Soviet stamp
This postage stamp commemorates 50 years of Soviet security services.

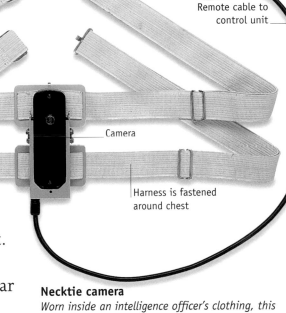

Control unit in pocket

Remote cable to control unit

Camera

Harness is fastened around chest

Necktie camera
Worn inside an intelligence officer's clothing, this KGB camera took photographs through a fake tiepin. It was operated by a remote shutter release that was concealed in the pocket.

KGB gas gun
Developed during the Cold War for assassinating political opponents of the Soviet regime, this weapon emitted cyanide gas, capable of causing almost instant death.

Berlin: spy city

THE GERMAN CITY OF BERLIN occupied a unique position during the Cold War years that followed World War II. After the end of the war, the victorious Allies – the United States, Britain, France, and the Soviet Union – divided Germany into zones of occupation. The old capital, Berlin, was similarly divided into four zones, even though it was surrounded by the Soviet zone of occupation, which became the German Democratic Republic, or East Germany.

Reinhard Gehlen
A German intelligence officer during World War II, Gehlen (1902–79) worked for the Americans after the war. He became head of the West German intelligence service.

The Soviet Union soon sealed off its own zone from Western interference. Within the Soviet sector, the MGB (state security) and GRU (military intelligence) operated without restriction, confiscating German industrial machinery, even whole factories, to be sent back to provide jobs in Soviet towns. German scientists were rounded up and made to work for Soviet industry.

Intelligence activity

Meanwhile, agents were recruited to begin spying in the West. Captured Nazi records provided plenty of material with which to blackmail potential agents. West Germans with relatives in the East could also be coerced, by threats to their families, into

French sector | **US sector**
British sector | **Soviet sector**

A divided city
Isolated within Soviet-occupied territory, later to become East Germany, Berlin was divided by the wartime Allies into four zones of occupation. The arrow shows the position of the Berlin tunnel, used to tap into Soviet military communications.

assisting the Soviet Union. As a result, between 1950 and 1969 a total of 2,186 agents were convicted of espionage in West Germany, and 19,000 admitted espionage but were not prosecuted.

The head of the West German Foreign Intelligence service for most of this period was Reinhard Gehlen. During the war, he had headed the section of

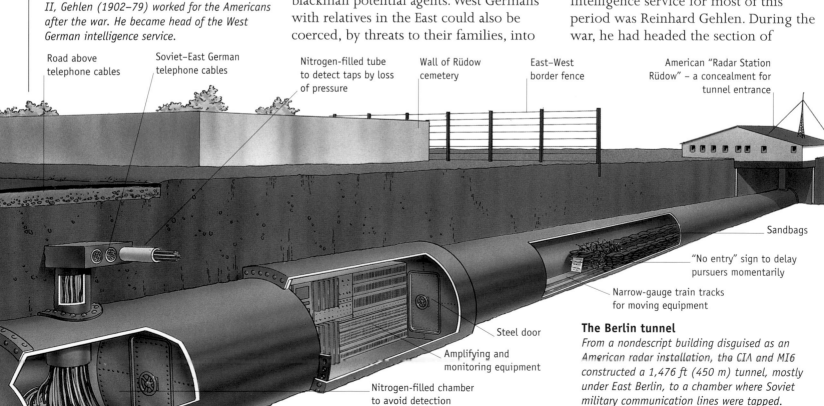

The Berlin tunnel
From a nondescript building disguised as an American radar installation, the CIA and MI6 constructed a 1,476 ft (450 m) tunnel, mostly under East Berlin, to a chamber where Soviet military communication lines were tapped.

Road above telephone cables

Soviet–East German telephone cables

Nitrogen-filled tube to detect taps by loss of pressure

Wall of Rüdow cemetery

East–West border fence

American "Radar Station Rüdow" – a concealment for tunnel entrance

Sandbags

"No entry" sign to delay pursuers momentarily

Narrow-gauge train tracks for moving equipment

Steel door

Amplifying and monitoring equipment

Nitrogen-filled chamber to avoid detection

Checkpoint Charlie
This famous crossing place in the Berlin Wall was the site of several successful escapes from the East, some failures, and a dangerous confrontation between American and Soviet tanks in 1961.

German military intelligence responsible for the Soviet Union. He surrendered to the Americans in 1945 but persuaded them to employ him and his staff as spies in return for files and names gathered by his wartime espionage network.

In 1949 Gehlen was appointed head of the new German Federal Intelligence Service (later the West German Foreign Intelligence Service – BND). Gehlen remained in this position until 1968, when his reputation was tarnished by the discovery of double agent Felfe (see p. 129) among his headquarters' staff.

Underground interception

One of the Cold War's most ambitious intelligence operations was mounted in Berlin in 1954 by the CIA and Britain's MI6. From just inside West Berlin, the CIA dug a tunnel 1,476 ft (450 m) long to reach a point directly beneath the underground telephone lines by which the Soviet military HQ in East Berlin communicated with Moscow. MI6 then tapped into these lines. The tunnel functioned for a year before it was found by East German repairmen. The intelligence gathered was mainly about the disposition of Soviet army units. Had the Soviets planned an invasion of the West, the tap might have provided a warning.

In later years, it emerged that the KGB spy George Blake (see p. 191) had warned his controllers about the tunneling operation. However, the controllers did not inform the GRU in order to protect Blake from being exposed as a mole.

The Berlin Wall

On August 13, 1961, the East German police began building a fence between East and West Berlin. This grew into a 96 mile (155 km) concrete structure with watchtowers and minefields, encircling all of West Berlin. Roads controlled by army checkpoints were allowed through the wall. On October 27, 1961, at the American Checkpoint Charlie, a confrontation took place over Soviet attempts to deny American representatives access to the Eastern zone. For 16 hours American and Soviet tanks faced each other across no-man's-land, until the representatives were finally allowed through.

Lipstick pistol
This KGB 4.5mm single-shot firing device was found in the purse of an East German spy arrested in West Berlin.

US security agencies

AFTER WORLD WAR II, the United States established a number of new organizations to meet the Cold War intelligence threat. The main three, the Central Intelligence Agency (CIA), the National Security Agency (NSA), and the Defense Intelligence Agency (DIA – see p. 58) were concerned with collecting and analyzing foreign intelligence. A fourth key organization, the Federal Bureau of Investigation (FBI), was already in charge of counterintelligence within the United States. Only one other country had a larger security system than America – the Soviet Union (see p. 38). But in intelligence-collection systems the United States had the edge.

CIA CREST

Apart from these major American security organizations, there are also many other agencies of the United States government that are responsible for aspects of security. While some are often in the public eye, others operate in the closest possible secrecy.

Federal Bureau of Investigation

Established in 1909 as part of the US Department of Justice, the FBI became a national agency in 1934. Since 1939, it has been the primary organization responsible for the various aspects of domestic counterintelligence: it is charged with detecting and neutralizing all espionage, sabotage, and other clandestine activities carried out within the United States by hostile foreign intelligence services. The Washington Metropolitan Field Office of the Bureau has been involved in resolving a number of major spy cases, including the very damaging Walker case (see p. 54). The FBI works closely with the CIA, which is responsible for counterintelligence overseas. The CIA has no powers of arrest, and cooperates with the FBI to deal with traitors and spies within CIA ranks. Since the arrest in 1994 of SVR mole Aldrich Ames (see p. 190) in the CIA, the FBI and CIA have cooperated even more closely with each other.

Central Intelligence Agency

Created under the National Security Act of 1947, and based on a concept formulated in 1944, the CIA is made up of several directorates. The Directorate for Operations is responsible for the clandestine collection of all foreign intelligence, and for counterintelligence gathered from outside the United States. The Directorate of Intelligence is responsible for the analysis of intelligence and the production of

J. Edgar Hoover
Hoover (1895–1972) directed counterintelligence during World War II, and tried in vain to bring foreign intelligence-gathering under FBI control.

FBI emblem
This is an emblem from the FBI headquarters in Washington, DC. The FBI is part of the US Department of Justice.

Allen Welsh Dulles
An OSS veteran and Director of the CIA from 1953–61, Dulles (1893–1969) ran covert operations in Iran and Central America, as well as the disastrous Bay of Pigs operation in Cuba.

finished reports. The CIA also has a Directorate for Science and Technology, which is comprised of various offices. (The Office of Technical Service is described on p. 113.) Several offices provide administrative services. The Office of SIGINT Operations assists the NSA in gathering signals intelligence (see below). The Foreign Broadcast Information Service (FBIS) is an office of the CIA that monitors radio broadcasts and television stations around the world and produces transcripts of broadcasts, some of which are available to the media and the public. In the past, the National Photographic Interpretation Center provided the United States intelligence community with analysis of overhead reconnaissance photographs, taken

NSA CREST

either from satellites or aircraft. The analysis of photographs is now carried out by the National Imagery and Mapping Agency (NIMA), which is not part of the CIA.

National Security Agency

The NSA was established in 1952 and has three main areas of activity. The first is information security, which means the protection of all national security systems and information, including computer systems. The second is the collection of foreign signals intelligence (often called SIGINT). The NSA's third area of activity is the creation of codes and ciphers for use by US national intelligence agencies and the military. The NSA also attempts to break the codes and ciphers of foreign powers.

Air America

On the surface, Air America was a normal American commercial airline; but it was in fact covertly operated by the CIA to support its operations throughout Southeast Asia. It evolved from a little-known organization, Civil Air Transport (CAT), which had been formed in China in 1946 to support American covert operations. At its peak during the Vietnam War (1961–75), Air America ran the world's largest commercial fleet of aircraft. Its pilots were often ex-military personnel, attracted by generous wages. They flew a variety of aircraft in support of CIA operations, sometimes (in great secrecy) carrying agents across national borders. One group, using U-2 and SR-71 jets, flew secret reconnaissance missions from Thailand. Air America was sold after the war and operates simply as a small-scale air charter company.

EMBLEM WORN BY AIR AMERICA PILOTS

Air America in action
At the end of the Vietnam War in 1975, the Southern capital, Saigon, finally fell to North Vietnamese forces. Here, some South Vietnamese intelligence officers are being evacuated by an Air America helicopter from the residence of the CIA Deputy Chief of Station in Saigon.

Codename Anna

ANNA WAS THE CODENAME given to the Czech spy Alfred Frenzel. A member of the Czech Communist Party in the 1930s, Frenzel went to England as an agent of the Czech government in exile when Germany invaded Czechoslovakia in World War II. At the end of the war, Europe was divided into a "democratic" West and an eastern bloc of countries dominated by the Soviet Union. Frenzel emigrated to the newly created state of West Germany, where he eventually became a member of parliament.

Czechoslovakia, in the meantime, became a communist state. The new state intelligence service (Statni tajna Bezpecnost or StB), examined the files of the prewar military intelligence and political police, and found information on Frenzel's past activities.

In West Germany, Frenzel had now been appointed to the parliamentary defense committee, which was responsible for the reestablishment of the West German armed forces, and for their future role in NATO.

The StB investigators saw that Frenzel's position could be exploited and sent his file to the head of StB's First Directorate, known as I Sprava. This body was in charge (under the control of the Soviet KGB) of foreign intelligence gathering. I Sprava decided to recruit Frenzel as a spy and assigned the task to StB Major Bohumil Molnar in Vienna.

Intelligence coup
Alfred Frenzel (1899–1968) became Czechoslovakia's most important spy in West Germany during the late 1950s, operating under the codename Anna.

Recruiting the spy

In April 1956, Frenzel was visited by an old friend who had become an employee of the Czech government. He offered Frenzel a job working for the Czech government and threatened to expose Frenzel's past political and criminal record if he refused. In addition, he made certain threats regarding the safety of Frenzel's wife, who was visiting Prague at the time. Forced to agree, Frenzel traveled to Vienna for a meeting at which he received 1,500 West German marks and was given

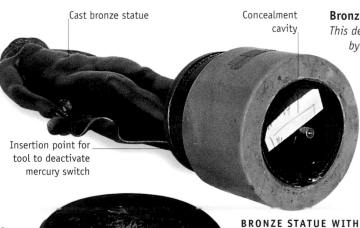

Cast bronze statue

Concealment cavity

Insertion point for tool to deactivate mercury switch

Base

BRONZE STATUE WITH BASE REMOVED

Bronze statue container
This device was made in Czechoslovakia by the StB's Technical Directorate. To open it, a mercury switch must be deactivated; otherwise an explosive charge will destroy the contents.

MERCURY SWITCH

FILM CONTAINER

BRONZE STATUE

Battery film container
This battery could power a torch, but could also be used to hide film. If the battery container was not opened correctly, the film was destroyed by acid.

the codename Anna. In July he put his signature on a document that showed that he had links with the StB. Having signed this, Frenzel was now trapped: the Czechs would be able to blackmail him if he did not spy for them.

Frenzel began to pass information to his handlers, including a copy of the entire West German defense budget. In return, he was promised a large salary, to be paid into a Czech bank account, and a villa and car in Czechoslovakia should he eventually choose to defect. Frenzel also received money for each batch of information he provided. Subsequent batches included West German Air Force plans, and details of new American and and German aircraft and missiles. In September 1959, control of Anna was passed to a new StB officer operating as an illegal (see p. 201) under the assumed

name of Franz Altman. For transporting secret information, Altman used a range of containers that had been disguised as everyday objects by the StB's Technical Directorate, known as IX Sprava. The containers were designed in such a way that their contents would be destroyed if tampered with.

The unmasking of Anna

Altman's method was to pass his disguised containers to Czech diplomatic couriers, who would carry them, with all Frenzel's information, out of West Germany. In October 1960, the West German counterintelligence service, the

Bf V, started to watch Altman after the tax authorities became suspicious of him. This led to the discovery of his role as a spy. Altman was arrested while trying to leave the country with six rolls of film in a fake baby powder can. The can had to be disarmed before opening (see below).

When developed, the film revealed photographs of secret documents that were traced back to Frenzel: he had failed to cover the reference numbers when photographing them. He was arrested and given a 15-year sentence, but was exchanged for four West German spies in a swap five years later. He died in Czechoslovakia in 1968.

Film container in a baby powder tin
An internal electrical circuit had to be turned off before this container could be opened, otherwise it fired a flashbulb, which would ruin the film.

Straightened paper clip inserted to deactivate the device

Container for powder surrounded by protective wax paper

Switch

Battery

Flashbulb

Film holder

Switch

DEVICE INSIDE CAN

Vaser

Wund

u. Kind

Pude

biologisch wirks
milder Fettpuder
Schutz und zur P
empfindlicher H

BABY POWDER CAN

House of spies

NUMBER 45 CRANLEY DRIVE, a small bungalow in the west London suburb of Ruislip, provided the technical support for a Soviet spy network. The head of the network was Konon Trifimovich Molody, alias Gordon Lonsdale. As a KGB "illegal" officer without embassy protection, Lonsdale reported directly to Moscow and operated under a legend (see p. 194). He arrived in London in 1955 and, using KGB funds, set up a slot-machine leasing company which, as he later claimed, was so successful that it generated a profit for the KGB. For six years, Lonsdale lived the life of a well-to-do businessman and surrounded himself with beautiful women.

At the same time, Lonsdale ran a network of agents in Britain. He did not recruit agents himself but used those who had already been recruited. The Cohens, for example, had been active as Soviet agents in New York. Houghton had been recruited by Polish intelligence.

The Krogers

The couple who lived apparently normal lives at 45 Cranley Drive were Lona and Morris Cohen, operating under the alias of Helen and Peter Kroger. They provided Lonsdale with the technical support that he needed to pass on his intelligence information to the KGB headquarters in Moscow. The Krogers ran a small business as antiquarian book dealers, and this provided them with opportunities to smuggle microdots hidden in the books that they bought and sold internationally. They sent these books to various addresses abroad, from which they were then forwarded to the Soviet Union. The Krogers' radio and burst transmitter (see p. 142) were reserved for urgent communications with Moscow.

45 Cranley Drive, Ruislip
This unremarkable bungalow, in a residential London suburb, was the Krogers' home and base for Lonsdale's communications with Moscow.

HELEN AND PETER KROGER

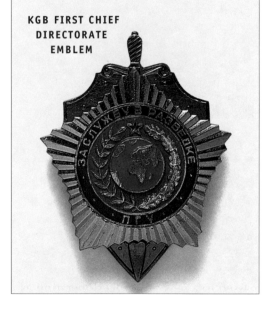

KGB First Chief Directorate

The KGB was divided into a number of directorates, the most prominent of which were the First Chief Directorate, commonly known as the FCD, and the Second Chief Directorate, which was in charge of domestic security. The FCD was responsible for overseas operations, and had several subdirectorates. Directorate T gathered scientific and technical intelligence. Directorate K infiltrated foreign intelligence services and was in charge of the security of Soviet embassies. Directorate S was the office that ran Soviet illegals (see p. 194) worldwide, including Konon Molody, whose alias was Gordon Lonsdale.

KGB FIRST CHIEF DIRECTORATE EMBLEM

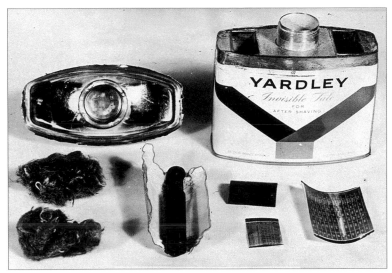

Talcum powder can concealment
The British security services MI5 and Special Branch discovered this concealment after searching the Krogers' bungalow. Inside the can of talcum powder were hidden radio communication schedules recorded on microfilm.

ETHEL ELIZABETH "BUNTY" GEE

HARRY FREDERICK HOUGHTON

Spy gadgets

The Krogers' bungalow contained the espionage equipment needed to support Lonsdale's spy network. In a space under the kitchen floor, entered by a hole just large enough to crawl through, an agent's radio and burst transmitter were kept. Microfilm was hidden in a can of talcum powder, while one-time pads and signal plans were concealed inside a flashlight battery (see p. 154 for a similar form of concealment) and a cigarette lighter. A box of face powder held a tiny microdot reader (see p. 157). The Krogers also had false passports, thousands of dollars, and equipment to make microdots.

Betrayal of the ring

The Lonsdale spy network was finally broken when the British security service MI5 (see p. 196) received information from a Polish defector. MI5 placed the so-called Portland spies under watch, and this led them to Lonsdale and subsequently to Helen and Peter Kroger.

The Portland spies were Harry Houghton, a clerk at a weapons research establishment in Portland, England, and his lover, Ethel Gee, a file clerk who also had access to secret

information. In return for money, these two passed Lonsdale details of NATO plans, naval maneuvers, and a new submarine-detection system. On January 7, 1961, Lonsdale was arrested as he received a package of information from Houghton and Gee, who were also arrested soon afterward.

At his trial, Molody refused to reveal his identity. His legend as Lonsdale, prepared by the First Directorate of the KGB, was flawless except for one detail. The real Lonsdale had been circumcised at birth, whereas Molody had not.

Molody and the Krogers were jailed, but Molody was freed in a spy swap in 1964. Houghton and Gee were given 15-year sentences. They were married after their release. Molody probably controlled other spies, but their number and identities are not known.

Searching the Krogers' cellar
This trapdoor led to a small cellar beneath the kitchen at 45 Cranley Drive. A search carried out by MI5 personnel revealed the KGB agents' radio and burst transmitter attachment used by the Krogers to send urgent messages to Moscow.

SPY PROFILE | Konon Molody

Russian-born Konon Molody (1924–70) lived in the US from 1932 to 1938, where he learned English. In 1938 he went to the Soviet Union and joined the NKVD (see p. 27). Molody went to Canada in 1954, where he adopted the identity of Gordon Lonsdale, a dead Canadian. He moved to London in 1955 and became a highly successful businessman, a cover for his espionage activities. He is believed to have controlled many agents, but only four were arrested.

U-2 spy aircraft

CONVENTIONAL INTELLIGENCE-GATHERING by the Americans in the early 1950s had failed to provide effective monitoring of the Soviet Union's growing nuclear capability. The Soviets tested their first nuclear bomb in 1949, and Moscow was building jet bombers that were believed to be capable of attacking the United States. Aerial photographs providing clear information about the new Soviet military threat were urgently needed, and in late 1954 the CIA commissioned the design and construction of an advanced spy aircraft that could be used to obtain them.

Krushchev inspects U-2 wreckage
Soviet Premier Krushchev (in light suit) examines equipment salvaged from the wreckage of Powers' aircraft after it crashed in Soviet territory.

The new spy aircraft, the U-2, was designed to photograph Soviet military installations from a very high altitude. Operating at over 80,000 ft (24,000 m), the U-2 was immune from attack by all the Soviet interceptors and antiaircraft missiles of the early 1960s. The U-2 Hycon Model 73C camera that was carried in U-2s was capable of recording details as small as 12 in (30 cm) across, and the 73B Pan Camera, also carried by U-2s, could take more than 4,000 pictures in the course of a single mission. The aircraft looked much like a motorized glider. It had a wingspan of 79 ft (23.5 m), and was powered by a single engine. Operating at high altitudes where there was little oxygen, the U-2 risked engine failure through lack of oxygen, known as a "flame-out." To relight the engine, the pilot would have to glide down to an altitude where there was more oxygen.

Operation Overflight

The first U-2 unit to be formed was the 1st Weather Reconnaissance Squadron (Provisional). By 1960, ten U-2s were operational, all under the cover of an organization called the National Advisory Committee for Aeronautics, which was supposedly engaged in meteorological research. The U-2 missions were codenamed Operation Overflight and flew from bases in the United Kingdom, Turkey, and Japan. Although the Soviet Union knew of the violations of its airspace, it was unwilling to admit publicly that its fighter aircraft and antiaircraft missiles were incapable of stopping them. Once the U-2 reconnaisance had established that the Soviet bomber threat was imaginary, attention was switched

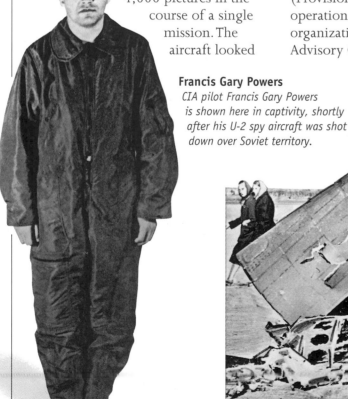

Francis Gary Powers
CIA pilot Francis Gary Powers is shown here in captivity, shortly after his U-2 spy aircraft was shot down over Soviet territory.

A crashed U-2
Russian citizens examine the wreckage of Francis Gary Powers' U-2 after its crash near Sverdlovsk, 700 miles (1,120 km) east of Moscow in the Ural Mountains.

U-2 in Moscow
The wreck of Powers' U-2 was put on public display to embarrass the Americans. Here, residents of Moscow inspect the wreckage.

to the Soviet Union's nuclear missile program. Information on this was needed by US President Eisenhower before attending the Paris Summit with Soviet Premier Krushchev. Eisenhower consulted the CIA director, Allen Dulles, who assured him there was no chance of a U-2 pilot being captured alive. On May 1, 1960, confident that neither the U-2 nor the pilot would fall into Soviet hands, Eisenhower authorized a flight over the Soviet intercontinental ballistic missile test center at Tyuratam.

Powers crashes

The mission was flown by CIA pilot Francis Gary Powers. Powers took off from Peshawar in northern Pakistan, intending to fly over the missile test sites, as well as over other military and industrial areas, and land in Norway. Near the Soviet city of Sverdlovsk, his U-2 suffered an engine flame-out that forced him to descend to an altitude low

enough for him to relight his engine. This brought the aircraft within range of a newly developed type of Soviet antiaircraft missile, the SA-2.

One of the missiles fired went off close to the aircraft, causing the fragile wing of the U-2 to buckle and sending the aircraft into a spin. Powers was thrown from the aircraft before he could set its self-destruct mechanism. He parachuted to safety and the U-2 crashed. However, the aircraft's systems remained intact and were available for the Soviets to inspect. Believing that the U-2 and its pilot had been destroyed, the US government announced that

U-2 spy aircraft
Powered by a single jet engine, the U-2 had a wingspan of 79 ft (23.5 m), optimizing its performance at extreme altitudes.

an aircraft on a weather reconnaissance mission had been lost after it had strayed into Soviet airspace. Krushchev then revealed that Powers was in Soviet hands and had admitted aerial espionage, catching the Americans in a very embarrassing lie. The Paris Summit ended in disarray, to the Soviet Union's political advantage. Powers was found guilty of espionage at a Moscow trial; he was later exchanged for a KGB spy in American hands (see p. 196).

U-2s and the Cuban missile crisis

During the early 1960s, the CIA focused on gathering intelligence from Cuba because it had a communist government that was on friendly terms with the Soviet Union. On October 14, 1962, a U-2 spy aircraft photographed evidence of the installation of Soviet missiles near Havana, the Cuban capital. The missiles appeared to be medium-range nuclear SS-4s, easily capable of reaching the United States. On October 22, President Kennedy announced a maritime quarantine of Cuba, to prevent further stockpiling of missiles. Tension between the United States and the Soviet Union escalated, reaching a peak on October 27, when a U-2 flying over Cuba was shot down. There was the prospect of war. However, on October 28, the Soviet Union announced that it would withdraw the missiles. U-2 missions were later flown to verify this withdrawal.

Airfield in Cuba with 21 Soviet bombers

Closer shot confirms identity of bombers

Soviet bombers in Cuba
U-2 pictures proved that not only missiles, but Soviet Il-28 nuclear bombers were present in Cuba, well within range of the United States.

Walker spy ring

THE KGB'S MOST IMPORTANT SPY in the United States in the 1970s was John Anthony Walker, Jr. He was a chief warrant officer in the US Navy who had access to naval secrets, and decided to become a spy because he needed money after a series of business failures. Walker made his first contact with the KGB in early 1968 by asking to see "someone from security" at the Soviet embassy in Washington, DC. He had calculated correctly – the Soviets were willing to reward him, as they did in similar cases, with cash payments.

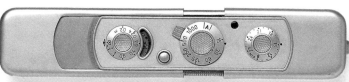

Walker's Minox camera
In the course of his long career as a spy, Walker photographed so many secret documents that his Minox C camera wore out.

John Walker
As part of his cover, Walker espoused a variety of anticommunist political causes and joined fringe groups such as the Ku Klux Klan (KKK).

Walker took with him a month's key settings for the KL-47 cipher machine used at the US Navy's command center for Atlantic submarine forces, where he worked. Announcing that he had easy access to such settings, Walker demanded $1,000 per week. He was given some cash in advance and, at a later meeting, received $5,000 in return for a series of cipher key settings' cards. Walker was also given a Minox camera (see p. 88) to copy secret documents and cipher material.

Dealings with the KGB

During the next 17 years, Walker gave the KGB more cipher key cards as well as various technical manuals. These items enabled the Soviets to obtain important naval secrets, including the movements of the American nuclear submarine fleet. Besides this, the Soviets gained advance knowledge of American bombing raids on North Vietnam in the early 1970s.

The KGB gave Walker a rotor reader with which to analyze the inner wiring of US Navy cipher machine rotors. They also trained him in espionage tradecraft at a series of secret meetings in Austria. In the US, Walker seldom met his KGB handler personally, but used a series of dead drops (see p. 160) to pass over information and receive payment.

Family and friends

When Walker saw his access to secret material ending because of his imminent retirement from the navy, he drew his family into the spy ring. He recruited his brother Arthur and his son Michael, who was serving in the navy. John Walker also recruited his friend Jerry Whitworth, a navy communications specialist.

Rotor reader

Walker was given this device by the KGB to trace the internal wiring of the rotors used in the US Navy's KL-47 cipher machine. Walker removed the rotors from the KL-47 and placed them over the disk of the rotor reader. Contacts inside the disk sent signals through the rotor reader's internal circuitry to light up numbers on a display board. Walker was taught how to interpret these numbers so as to work out the internal wiring of the cipher rotors.

The KGB already had lists of the key settings of the KL-47, as these had been stolen by Walker. Knowledge of both the key settings and the internal rotor wiring enabled the KGB to decipher some of the US Navy's radio messages.

KL-47 ROTOR MOUNTED ON READER

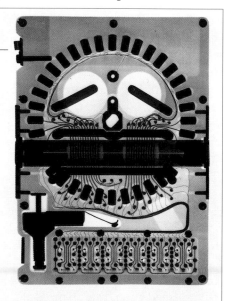

X-RAY OF READER SHOWING WIRING

The Vienna procedure

Once Walker was established as an agent, the KGB avoided direct meetings with him in the United States for security reasons. Instead he was instructed to travel abroad, usually to Vienna (or sometimes to Hong Kong), for training, instructions, and payment from his KGB case officer.

Vienna was often used for such purposes by the KGB, because of both its status as an international city and the neutrality of its counterintelligence service. To direct him to his meetings, Walker was given maps and written instructions. Complex routes were used in order to give the KGB time and opportunity to detect whether Walker was under surveillance.

Along his route he was watched by KGB agents with body-worn surveillance radios (see p. 130). All likely frequencies were monitored for signs of any unusual activity by Austrian counterintelligence or the CIA, which operated from the American embassy. If any of the KGB agents involved noticed anything suspicious, the meeting would be aborted. Walker was given backup instructions for an alternative meeting in case this happened.

The instructions and map shown here were used on a trip Walker made to Vienna in 1978. It is known that during the course of a 40-minute meeting with his handler he received money and instructions, and handed over cryptographic secrets stolen by his accomplice Jerry Whitworth.

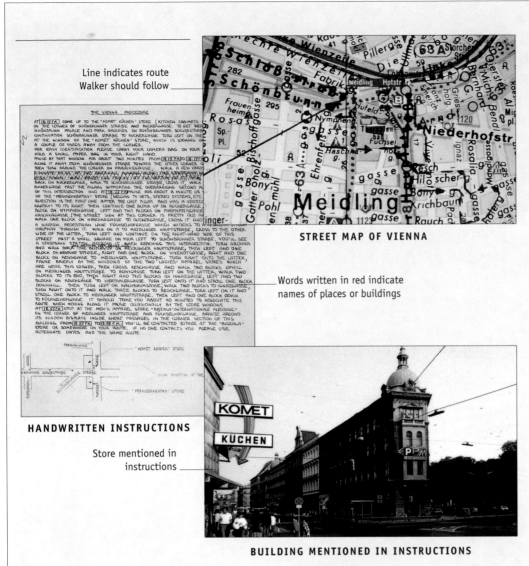

Line indicates route
Walker should follow

STREET MAP OF VIENNA

Words written in red indicate
names of places or buildings

HANDWRITTEN INSTRUCTIONS

Store mentioned in
instructions

BUILDING MENTIONED IN INSTRUCTIONS

Walker's wife knew for many years that he was a spy, but she kept silent. After the couple divorced, she eventually did inform the FBI. One evening in 1985, FBI personnel followed John Walker to a dead drop site outside Washington, where Walker left a package of secret material obtained from his son.

The FBI intercepted this material, missed a chance to pick up the KGB handler, and arrested Walker later that evening at a nearby hotel.

John Walker was sentenced to life imprisonment; his accomplices also received prison terms. What the ring's activities had cost the US in terms of security remains beyond calculation.

**MICHAEL WALKER:
CODENAME S – ON ACTIVE
SERVICE IN THE US NAVY**

**ARTHUR WALKER:
CODENAME K – ELDER
BROTHER OF JOHN WALKER**

**JERRY WHITWORTH:
CODENAME D – NAVY
COMMUNICATIONS EXPERT**

East German foreign intelligence

HVA CREST

EAST GERMANY'S FOREIGN intelligence service was called the Hauptverwaltung Aufklärung, or HVA. It was created in 1952 by the Ministerium fur Staatssicherheit (MfS), East Germany's State Security Ministry, popularly known as the Stasi (see p. 91). Throughout the Cold War, the HVA served East Germany for the primary purpose of preventing surprises, especially military surprises, against the state or its Eastern bloc allies. In this respect, the HVA was a highly effective organization, and its director for over 30 years, Markus Wolf, was one of the most successful spymasters of the Cold War.

Lens
Film
Winding socket
FILM CASSETTE
Shutter release
Film-winding and shutter release lever
CAMERA

Venus document camera
In 1986, the final subminiature document camera was produced for the HVA, using the Minox film format and a uniquely designed 150-shot cassette. The tiny camera could be operated with one finger.

The newly formed HVA recognized that its fledgling service lagged behind the experienced West German intelligence service, led by former Nazi General Reinhard Gehlen. To compensate, the HVA developed innovative techniques to target people who had access to the secrets that it wanted to know.

Through experience, the HVA learned that a lowly US Army sergeant in NATO or a technical employee in the Ministry at the West German capital Bonn could provide a larger quantity of higher-quality secret information than a senior government official or senior military officer. Such "lowly" agents were also easier to control and less demanding.

Recruiting and positioning agents

In HVA colleges, recruiters were taught how agents could be found by focusing on and exploiting human needs and weaknesses. Many of these were of a sexual nature; for example, someone could be blackmailed into becoming an agent after being secretly photographed with a prostitute.

However, the HVA found that the best way to recruit was to offer money. In some cases, the money was needed to pay debts or maintain a gambling addiction, but in most cases the lust for money was the main motivation for most of the people recruited by the HVA.

Among the HVA's principal successes was the positioning of agents inside the government in West Germany. In addition, the HVA carried out spying operations against the United States and other NATO countries, and foreign military forces stationed in Germany.

In 1974, Gunter Guillaume, the personal assistant to West German Chancellor Willy Brandt, was unmasked as an HVA agent. Guillaume had access to the government's most secret documents, and the revelation of his spying activities led to the collapse of the West German government when Brandt resigned.

The Romeo method

The HVA initiated a policy of instructing its male agents sent to the West on spying assignments to look for future wives and lovers from among government secretaries and others with access to secrets. This simple plan, later known as the "Romeo method," worked with great effectiveness, much to the detriment of NATO and the West German government in Bonn.

Technical support

The HVA had its own technical group that worked with the OTS, the technical service for all of the MfS, to support its

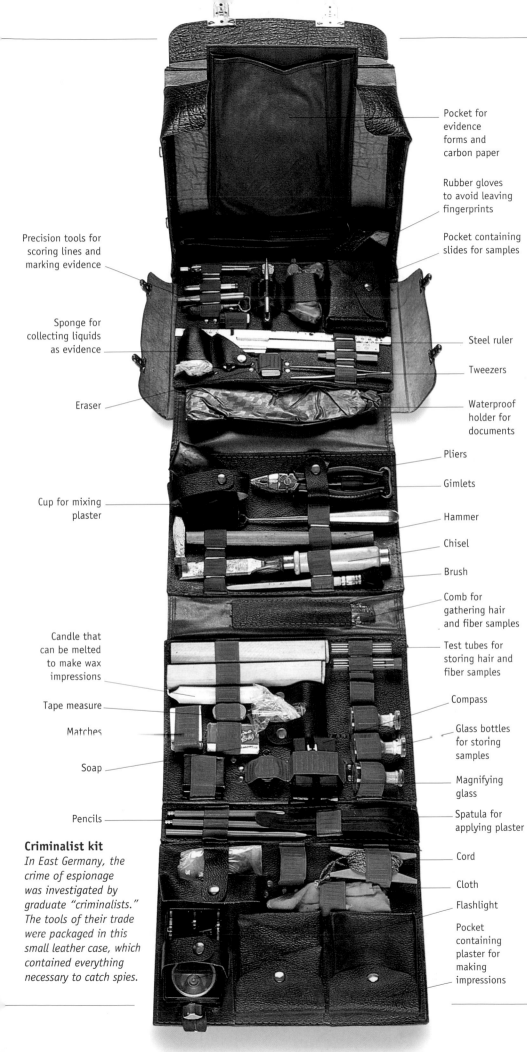

Pocket for evidence forms and carbon paper

Rubber gloves to avoid leaving fingerprints

Pocket containing slides for samples

Precision tools for scoring lines and marking evidence

Sponge for collecting liquids as evidence

Steel ruler

Tweezers

Eraser

Waterproof holder for documents

Pliers

Cup for mixing plaster

Gimlets

Hammer

Chisel

Brush

Comb for gathering hair and fiber samples

Candle that can be melted to make wax impressions

Test tubes for storing hair and fiber samples

Tape measure

Compass

Matches

Glass bottles for storing samples

Soap

Magnifying glass

Pencils

Spatula for applying plaster

Cord

Cloth

Flashlight

Pocket containing plaster for making impressions

Criminalist kit

In East Germany, the crime of espionage was investigated by graduate "criminalists." The tools of their trade were packaged in this small leather case, which contained everything necessary to catch spies.

agents and clandestine operations with specialized technology. For example, technicians developed a unique method of secret communication in which HVA agents in West Berlin could call a local telephone number and have their messages automatically transmitted across the Berlin Wall by means of an embedded infrared voice-link that was impossible to intercept.

Specialized cameras were developed for the HVA. Silent subminiature cameras could photograph 150 documents on a single film cassette. Uranus microdot cameras (see pp. 152, 153) were part of a communication system that allowed agents to send and receive documents photographically reduced to less than 1 x 1 mm in size.

The skill of the technical specialists working within the HVA enabled many of its agents to remain undetected long after the collapse of East Germany and the end of the Cold War.

Cold War poster
This poster warned of the presence of spies in West Germany. The modified Minox camera in the center of the poster was unique to the MfS.

Spying from space

THE LAUNCH OF THE FIRST man-made satellite, by the Soviet Union in 1957, opened up new opportunities for intelligence-gathering. A camera on a satellite could carry out surveillance of any part of enemy territory that lay beneath its orbit. The first spy satellite was launched by the Americans in 1961. For 15 years, pictures from a satellite took longer to reach the analyst than those from a spy plane, although, of course, they could cover a far greater area. All this changed in the 1970s, when digital technology made pictures immediately available.

American satellite image
KH-11 satellite image of a Soviet aircraft carrier under construction. A US naval intelligence analyst was jailed for releasing this image.

The early satellites had to jettison their film in a container to be retrieved and flown to a processing point, often over long distances. This process was known as "bucket dropping" and was so slow that the Arab-Israeli Six-Day War of 1967 was over before the first satellite photographs of it reached Washington. Satellites were for strategic (long-term) surveillance, while tactical (day-to-day) observation was done by spy planes.

The KH-11

The Americans initiated a top secret program to produce better satellites. The result, the KH-11 satellite, became operational in 1976. It was different from earlier models in that it carried no film. Instead, it beamed its images in digital form to ground stations as soon as they were taken. In addition to making pictures rapidly available for analysis, this system has other advantages. The digital

images are capable of extremely high definition. From its orbit 200 miles (322 km) above the Earth, the KH-11 could resolve detail as small as 6 in (15 cm) across. The images can then be enhanced further by computer manipulation. At America's National Photographic Interpretation Center, a library of visual

The US National Reconnaissance Office (NRO)

This office was officially declassified as a secret organization in 1992. President Eisenhower established the NRO in 1961 in recognition of the new intelligence dimension promised by satellites. The NRO manages the US Photographic and Electronic Listening Satellites Program and the US Airborne Reconnaissance Program. Its powerful computers analyze data and were used in the Gulf War (1990–91) to identify Iraqi weapons systems.

The Rhyolite satellite
This American telecommunications interception satellite was very advanced for its time, the mid-1970s. It targeted the Soviet Union and China, eavesdropping on secret communications traffic and providing intelligence on ballistic missile tests. The 1,500 lb (680 kg) satellite had a large antenna dish, which was capable of picking up "leaked" transmissions from Earth over 22,000 miles (35,000 km) away. These were then relayed back down to a ground station for analysis.

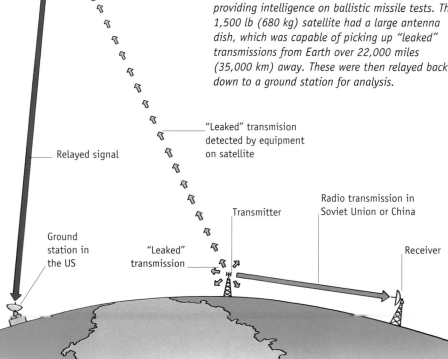

Satellite in Earth orbit

Antenna dish

Relayed signal

"Leaked" transmission detected by equipment on satellite

Ground station in the US

"Leaked" transmission

Transmitter

Radio transmission in Soviet Union or China

Receiver

Soviet satellite image
The CIA obtained this Soviet satellite image of Washington, DC, and its own headquarters; the image was later displayed in an agency internal poster.

interpretation keys is maintained. An intelligence analyst can check a satellite image against the visual keys in order to recognize a major weapons system.

A satellite codenamed Lacrosse was launched in 1988, using radar to "see" through clouds. It was joined in 1989 by an infrared version. Both satellites have "night vision." With these capabilities, satellites continue to be the chief means of monitoring Strategic Arms Limitation Treaties between the United States and the Soviet Union (and now Russia).

Satellite spies

Inevitably, satellite technology became the target of espionage, and its secrets have to be closely guarded. American agencies do not release their satellite images for public use until the pictures have been modified to reveal as little as possible of the technology involved.

A major spy scandal did, however, occur in the United States in 1977, which showed that security in some satellite companies was not tight enough. The scandal concerned a pair of self-taught and somewhat amateurish, though mercenary, spies: Christopher Boyce and his childhood friend Andrew Lee.

Through the influence of his ex-FBI father, Boyce had obtained a job with TRW, the company that produced and operated the Rhyolite satellite for the CIA. The Rhyolite was a spy satellite that monitored Soviet and Chinese secret telecommunications.

Boyce's job was in a top-secret office, known as the Black Vault, where he helped to coordinate communications between TRW, the national intelligence agencies, and the satellite monitoring stations. Security in the Black Vault was so lax that Boyce found he had easy access to classified material.

Lee's role was to make contact with the KGB. He would travel to Mexico City, and sometimes as far as Vienna, to sell the information to the Soviets. The material he sold concerned, among other things, the Rhyolite program, the KH-11 satellite, and various ciphers.

The pair were brought to trial after Lee was arrested by the Mexican police for suspicious activity outside the Soviet embassy. He was carrying a pocketful of satellite secrets on strips of Minox film.

Christopher Boyce

Christopher Boyce (b.1953) took a job with the American satellite company TRW and used it to obtain information about America's satellites. The information he and Lee sold to the KGB alerted the Soviet Union to the vulnerability of its military communications to eavesdropping by American satellites. Arrested in 1977, Boyce was sentenced to 40 years, escaped, and received 20 more years on recapture.

Andrew Daulton Lee

Andrew Lee (b.1952) is a documented example of a spy whose motive was to find money to pay for his drug habit. In 1975 he began to sell satellite secrets, provided by his friend Christopher Boyce, to the KGB. Lee traveled to Vienna and Mexico City to carry out these transactions. After his arrest in Mexico, he was handed over to the FBI. Lee was tried and sentenced to life imprisonment in the United States.

Camera pod from a spy satellite
A Soviet camera pod lies on the ground in Kazakhstan, after its film has been extracted for processing. Soviet satellites relied on cameras that used conventional film long after the Americans introduced digital transmission.

POST-COLD WAR SPYING

F ORMER CIA DIRECTOR James Woolsey stated that with the end of the Cold War the great Soviet dragon was slain. He wryly noted, however, that in its place intelligence services were now facing a "bewildering variety of poisonous snakes that have been let loose in a dark jungle; it may have been easier to watch the dragon." These days, the superpowers face an array of threats from around the globe that sap their resources and dilute their effectiveness.

CHANGING FACE OF ESPIONAGE

Spying is more prevalent today than at the height of the Cold War. One reason for the increase is that espionage is now a greater necessity for many nations to survive. Blurring of traditional roles of friends and foes is another factor – there are friendly nations but no friendly intelligence services. At the same time, the superpowers' growing reliance on new technologies has made them more vulnerable in several ways. The infrastructure is more difficult to protect and the increasing use of satellites and electronic spies instead of human intelligence sources, also known as HUMINT, leaves gaps in intelligence gathering.

ESSENTIAL ESPIONAGE

The necessity for espionage grows as the gap between the superpowers and other countries increases; stealing economic and military information becomes the only way for many countries to compete. Conversely, the need to invest in counterintelligence becomes essential as nations strive to protect their own secrets and deny their use to others.

FRIEND OR FOE

The major superpowers always collected intelligence and attacked the ciphers, or

FAPSI crest

Russia's FAPSI – federal agency of governmental communication – is responsible for the security of all encrypted and government communications, as well as intelligence gathering in the sphere of special communications. The organization operates intercept stations around the world.

Robot S-C electronic 35mm camera

The Robot S-C camera is specially designed for surveillance and security missions, as well as for document reproduction. Its tiny size makes it easy to camouflage for operational use.

David pen

As well as functioning as a writing pen, this Czech device called "David" could secretly photograph a dozen documents. The pen's end cap unscrewed to reveal the lens.

codes, of their friends as well as their enemies. The national interests of former friends and foes are now being redefined in terms of competing economic interests. Cultural and historic friendships between nations continue to fade as they are replaced by trading partnerships and other interdependent economic relationships. The importance of spies and counterspies is increasing as a nation's first line of defense.

DIGITAL WORLD

The internet and computers have altered the ways in which spies collect and communicate information to their handlers. "Agent communication" is no longer seen as the point of greatest vulnerability to a spy. Spies now employ wireless burst communications, encrypted messages, and digital dead drops in ways that place security and counterintelligence forces on the defensive. The principle of asymmetrical warfare dictates that a weaker opponent attack a stronger opponent at their point of greatest vulnerability. Intelligence services identify and exploit the weaknesses of stronger countries, whose information infrastructure has become more vulnerable with every new technological advance. Superpowers expand networked systems at a faster rate than they protect them, leaving them vulnerable to exploitation and attack by cyber-spies.

HUMAN SOURCES MUST BE DEVELOPED

Satellites can show exactly what an enemy is doing, but they cannot show what they are thinking or planning. Western nations must reverse the trend toward reliance on technology to gather intelligence and refocus on recruiting human sources (HUMINT). Only an agent inside a terrorist cell can prevent a future occurrence similar to the tragedy of September 11, 2001.

GRU badge
Russia's military intelligence service is called GRU. Since the collapse of the Soviet Union in 1992, the importance of GRU's foreign intelligence gathering operations has increased.

OTS 50th-anniversary poster
The CIA's Office of Technical Service (OTS) has been equipping and training America's spies for over half a century. The organization's motto is, "Imagine what is possible and then prepare to be amazed."

Neocet surveillance camera
The electrically operated Neocet is the successor to the KGB's long-serving F-21 surveillance camera. The Neocet can be camouflaged in a variety of concealments.

Russian foreign intelligence

AS THE SOVIET UNION COLLAPSED AND the KGB was dismembered, the PGU, or First Chief Directorate, was reborn as the SVR (Foreign Intelligence Service) in December 1991. Its first director, Yevgeniy Primakov, would report directly to the Russian president and oversee a vast global intelligence network. Although initially reduced in size, the SVR refocused its resources against its main opponent, the US, and continued to rebuild its strength under Russian President Vladimir Putin. The end of the Cold War did not reduce confrontations between intelligence services, but only served to intensify the conflict.

SVR CREST

Birth of the SVR

Until the dissolution of the Soviet Union, the KGB had been its "sword and shield" and the PGU (First Chief Directorate), its "eyes and ears." Operating from a secret headquarters on the outskirts of Moscow (Yasenevo), the PGU gathered intelligence globally on every country considered important by Soviet leaders.

In late 1991, the PGU became an independent agency reporting directly to the Russian president and was eventually renamed the SVR (Foreign Intelligence Service). Still operating from Yasenevo, the new SVR was intended to be free of a historical legacy in which intelligence reports were always filtered and altered to reflect the current perceptions of Soviet leadership. Its initial director, Yevgeniy Primakov, briefed the new Russian president, Boris Yeltsin, for the first time using only the facts.

Despite Yeltsin's support, the SVR was hemorrhaging experienced intelligence officers to the emerging Russian private sector and lacked the financial resources even to house its employees adequately. During this time of chaos, the SVR shrank by an estimated 30 to 40 percent and was forced to consolidate its intelligence-gathering activities by eliminating coverage of many smaller countries. Even this step, however, did not produce surpluses of intelligence officers or money, since it was also forced to increase its coverage of the Baltic States and members of the Former Soviet Union (FSU) that were now turning toward NATO and the West.

Early SVR strategy

Using a strategy unchanged since the heated days of the Cold War, Primakov focused his available resources against the US, which remained the primary global adversary. Relationships between the SVR and CIA reached a post-Cold War low in February, 1994, when CIA intelligence officer Aldrich Ames (see p. 190) was unmasked following a nine-year career as a mole in which he betrayed the CIA's

SVR headquarters buildings
The headquarters of the SVR is located on Moscow's outer ring road at Yasenevo. The architecture was influenced by the design of the original headquarters of the CIA in Langley, Virginia.

Hidden SVR radio receiver

In 1999 an SVR radio receiver was recovered from a secret KGB cache outside the Swiss town of Befaux. KGB defector Vasili Mitrokhin had revealed the presence of booby-trapped KGB caches of espionage equipment throughout Europe. Using Mitrokhin's instructions, the Swiss federal police located the Swiss cache near a small chapel just outside Befaux buried 3 ft (1 m) deep beneath a large stone. An attempt was made, unsuccessfully, to deactivate the booby trap. Nevertheless, the cache was recovered. Apart from the radio receiver, it contained a burst (cipher) encoder. An unknown number of caches in deteriorating condition remain buried throughout Europe.

CHAPEL OUTSIDE BEFAUX, SWITZERLAND

EARPHONE

KGB cache
The first landmark to the booby-trapped cache was a small chapel on the edge of the woods outside Befaux, Switzerland.

BOOBY-TRAPPED CACHE

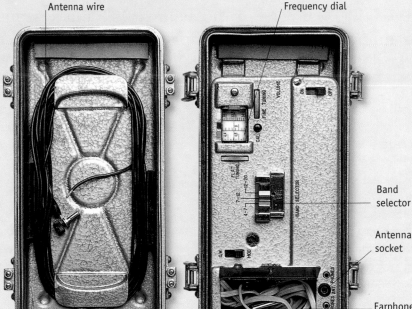

Antenna wire

Frequency dial

Band selector

Antenna socket

Earphones

LID OF RECEIVER

RADIO RECEIVER

---

human assets in Moscow and its most sensitive operational secrets.

In 1996, Primakov was promoted to Minister of Foreign Affairs and replaced by his First Deputy, Vyacheslav Trubnikov. Trubnikov inherited an intelligence service focused on three main areas: understanding US intentions as they operated against Russian interests in FSU states; the increasing threat of Islamic fundamentalism; and the troubles in Yugoslavia. Additional intelligence was needed for Russia's role in the fight against international terrorism, international crime, and drug trafficking.

Growing strength of the SVR

In the late 1990s, the authorized strength of the SVR grew to 15,000 and was further bolstered with additional resources following the election of former intelligence officer Vladimir Putin as the new Russian president in late 2000. Accurate intelligence was seen as essential to President Putin if Russia was to regain its prominence in the international arena, and the SVR was still considered among the world's best intelligence services.

HUMINT (human intelligence) has always been a strength of the SVR and often compensates for its continuing lack of resources for technology and satellites; human spies are less expensive, and frequently more effective. The arrest in 2001 of FBI Special Agent Robert Hanssen (see p. 64) as a Russian/Soviet mole since 1979 removed any lingering doubt that the intelligence conflicts of the Cold War had abated. The SVR has been quick to identify and foster "anti-Americanism" among countries in the European Union as a motivation for recruitment but still relies on money as the primary lure for new recruits.

Major General Yuri Kobaladze
An accomplished intelligence officer, Kobaladze was head of the SVR's press office in the 1990s. He gave many public interviews and was well known for his skill in managing the press and media.

Hanssen spy case

THE MOST IMPORTANT FBI EMPLOYEE to spy for Russia was Robert Hanssen (b. 1944). A onetime Chicago policeman, Hanssen joined the FBI in 1976, and soon took advantage of his top secret clearance status to sell sensitive classified information to Russia and the former Soviet Union for money and ego satisfaction. He was finally arrested by the FBI in 2001 after leaving a package containing highly classified information at a prearranged site, or dead drop, near his home in Vienna, Virginia.

FBI field office emblem
Hanssen worked for the Washington field office for several years; this FBI element later played a key role in his arrest.

In 1979, Hanssen walked into the offices of AMTORG, the trade organization in Manhattan that provided cover for Soviet military intelligence (GRU) and offered to sell government secrets. In order to establish his credibility, Hanssen betrayed one of America's most important GRU moles, Major General Dmitri Polyakov, whose codename was "Tophat." (Polyakov was eventually executed by the Russians for his spying activities)

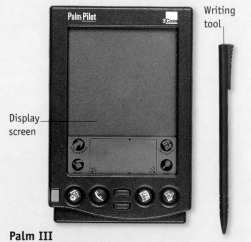

Robert Phillip Hanssen
Hanssen held key counterintelligence positions at the FBI and, as a result, had direct access to many highly classified documents.

Hanssen "gives up" spying

A year after Hanssen had started spying, his wife, Bonnie, came across nearly $20,000 in their house and confronted him. Hanssen maintained that he had sold only "worthless information" but vowed to stop. He severed contact with the GRU, confessed to his priest (Hanssen had converted to Catholicism), and told Bonnie the ill-gotten money had been given to charity. At this time, the FBI knew nothing of Hanssen's betrayal.

In 1981, Hanssen accepted a postition with the Intelligence Division's budget unit at FBI Headquarters in Washington, D.C. He was now privy to financial details about the supersecret programs run by not only the FBI, but also the CIA, National Security Agency, and Defense Intelligence Agency. Hanssen performed well but was not promoted as rapidly as his peers; his dissatisfaction grew. In September 1985, to advance his career, he accepted a promotion to field supervisor in the Intelligence Division of the FBI in New York City. Even with his larger salary, Hanssen felt under financial strain since he now had a family of six children to support. Financial worries, coupled with career dissatisfacton, made Hanssen decide to sell secrets to the Soviets for money once again.

Selling secrets to the KGB

In October 1985, Hanssen sent a letter to the KGB, offering his services. Signing the letter "B," Hanssen established his credibility by betraying three KGB officers secretly working for the FBI (Sergei Motorin, Valery Martynov, and Boris Yuzhin – Motorin and Martynov were executed and Yuzhin imprisoned), for which he asked to be paid $100,000. Henceforth, pausing only briefly in the early 1990s, Hanssen received $1.4 million dollars in cash and diamonds over the next 17 years for revealing details of highly classified counterintelligence programs. The scope of the secrets

Digital spying

Hanssen used computers to support his work as a spy. In 1988, he mailed a disk to the KGB that appeared to be blank but contained a hidden message. By using a procedure called 40-track mode, he had reformatted the disk to have slightly less capacity than usual so that secret messages could be concealed in the "lost area."

Hanssen wrote letters to the SVR (the KGB's successor) on his home computer and kept copies on a removable 8MB Versa memory card hidden in his briefcase. He used a Palm III handheld computer to schedule appointments with the SVR. On February 5, 2001, the FBI secretly searched Hanssen's Palm and found "Ellis" scheduled for February 18; agents waited there to arrest him.

Palm III
Hanssen could easily carry the compact Palm III in his briefcase. He later asked the SVR for a Palm VII, which could use wireless internet connectivity.

Writing tool

Display screen

Hanssen's final dead drop

At 4:34 p.m. on February 18, 2001, Hanssen drove to Crossing Creek Road, not far from his residence on Talisman Drive in Vienna, Virginia. He parked the car and walked across the road to the entrance of Foxstone Park. On the dark-red wooden post that supported the entrance sign he placed a small strip of white adhesive tape to indicate to the SVR that he was "loading" the dead drop site. An SVR officer driving down the road would spot the tape as a "signal" and arrange for the drop to be "cleared." Similar procedures are used by spies around the world to transfer money and materials without ever having to meet each other.

With the signal in place, Hanssen walked into Foxstone Park along the trail to dead drop "Ellis," which was located beneath the first footbridge over the meandering Wolftrap Creek. He carried with him a slim package that contained seven secret FBI documents and an encrypted letter to the SVR on a computer disk, all wrapped in a black plastic trash bag. The package was placed in the drop site – on a rusted beam beneath the footbridge – invisible to anyone who did not know precisely where to look. Retracing his steps, Hanssen reappeared from the woods nine minutes later. As he crossed the road and approached his car, he was arrested by the FBI, who had had him under surveillance for many months. The FBI had even secretly purchased the house across from Hanssen's, where they had set up an observation post to monitor his activities.

DEAD DROP SITE "ELLIS"

SATELLITE VIEW OF AREA

HANSSEN'S RESIDENCE

SIGNAL SITE IN FOXSTONE PARK

Hanssen gave away to the KGB and SVR (the KGB's successor) was catastrophic to American national security interests. Included were technical programs for gathering intelligence on the Soviets in the US, agent names, and more than 6,000 pages of classified documents.

Only five weeks before retirement, on February 18, 2001, when his access to marketable secrets would end, Hanssen sensed he was under FBI surveillance. Nevertheless, he continued his espionage activities, leaving a final package at dead drop "Ellis" in Foxstone Park, Vienna, Virginia (Hanssen had by this time

been reassigned to Washington, D.C.). Observed by the FBI, he was arrested. He later pleaded guilty and received a life sentence without the possibility of parole, avoiding the death penalty only by agreeing to reveal all that he had done. Bonnie was allowed a pension.

Money for Hanssen
In payment for Hanssen's "Ellis" drop, the SVR had left a package containing $50,000 in cash at a second drop site.

Boris Yuzhin
KGB officer Yuzhin was one of the FBI agents that Hanssen betrayed in order to establish his credibility.

Counterterrorism

TERRORISM, OR THE PURSUIT of political ends through violence and intimidation, has a history as long as that of espionage. During the second half of the 20th century, however, the phenomenon became more widespread and more dangerous. As a consequence, countering terrorism has come to absorb a large proportion of the efforts of the world's intelligence and security services. Counterterrorist work involves many different types of activity, including human intelligence, direct action, and the use of linked computer networks and powerful databases.

The role of human intelligence

To combat terrorism, governments require accurate intelligence regarding the plans and intentions of terrorist groups. To acquire such information, security services must gather human intelligence from inside the terrorist organizations. This may be achieved through spies who are members of the intelligence services, or through informers recruited from the ranks of the terrorists themselves or from the community within which they operate. The use of such individuals has

formed an important part of the British strategy against terrorist groups in Northern Ireland, which is conducted under the overall control of MI5. The Israeli agency responsible for internal security, Shin Bet, has also made much use of spies and informers in infiltrating Palestinian terrorist organizations.

Direct action

Occasionally, intelligence services have taken direct action against terrorists. Operatives of Israel's Mossad have been

WMD Operations Unit crest
The WMD (Weapons of Mass Destruction) Operations Unit of the FBI receives incident information and provides technical assistance during a suspected or actual chemical, biological, or nuclear incident.

active over the years in the assassination of Arab terrorist suspects. Their most notable feat took place in 1988, when they penetrated a heavily guarded house in Tunis to assassinate Abu Jihad, a leading figure in the Palestinian liberation movement. Other countries

Ramzi Yousef

On February 26, 1993, Ramzi Yousef attacked New York City's World Trade Center in an unsuccessful attempt to topple both towers. Two years later, he would flee a hideout in Manila, leaving behind a laptop computer that contained encrypted files outlining a plot to blow up 11 US commercial aircraft in a single day. Yousef was arrested in Pakistan and, in 1998, he was sentenced to life in prison in the United States.

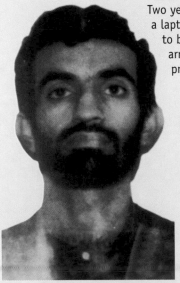

RAMZI YOUSEF

WORLD TRADE CENTER AFTER 1993 ATTACK

have been less eager to take such obviously traceable action. However, there have been cases where proxy organizations have been employed to kill terrorist suspects. For example, during the 1980s, the Spanish security services assisted in the creation of Grupos Antiterroristas de Liberación (GAL), which murdered a number of people suspected of membership of the Basque separatist terror group ETA. There has also been criticism of the CIA's activities in El Salvador and Guatemala during the 1970s and 80s, where it is accused of involvement with right-wing "death squads," responsible for killing many left-wing revolutionary suspects.

Tactics in the 20th century

The end of the Cold War during the final decades of the 20th century made terrorism more unpredictable than ever before. This effect was aggravated by the creation of the internet.

Terrorist groups are able to use the worldwide web to add a truly global dimension to their activities. Terrorist cells employ the internet to communicate with each other in secrecy. Encrypted messages carrying instructions or maps can be posted on existing sites, and their origins are effectively untraceable. Internet communication may also be used by terrorists to launch cyber-attacks on electronic data held by those whom they identify as their enemies. As a consequence, security agencies must find ways to monitor these communications; however, the vast scale of the internet makes this task very difficult.

The internet works in many ways to the advantage of terrorists. However, security services have been aided in their hunt for terrorists by digital technology that permits the creation of linked computer networks, powerful databases, and the use of artificial intelligence.

A further threat that has risen to prominence recently is the possibility that a terrorist group might launch a biological, chemical, or even nuclear

Yehiya Ayyash
Called the Engineer, Ayyash belonged to a Palestinian terrorist organization and was a skillful bomb-maker. On January, 5, 1996, he was killed by an explosive device planted in his mobile phone. The Israeli security service Shin Bet was widely blamed.

attack in pursuit of its goals. All these things are possible in theory although, thankfully, not so easy to put into practice. However, intelligence agencies are very aware of the need to forestall attacks by such "weapons of mass destruction," especially the necessity of preventing fissionable material, capable of being made into a nuclear device, from falling into the wrong hands.

September 11, 2001

The terrorist attack on the United States on September 11, 2001, marked the dawn of a new era in counterterrorism. Over 3,000 people lost their lives when hijacked airliners were crashed into the World Trade Center in New York City and into the Pentagon building in Virginia.

The perpetrators were members of the extreme Islamic organization al Qaeda, who were at that time operating covertly from several countries and, more openly, from Afghanistan. The goal of al Qaeda is to rid Muslim countries of Western (and particularly American) influence. The scale of the attack was unprecedented in the annals of terrorism. As a direct result, there arose an international commitment to wage a "war on terrorism," which would involve both intelligence services and conventional forces. For the world's security and intelligence services, this means that counterterrorist operations have become central to their role.

Al Qaeda training manual

A manual produced by al Qaeda that passed into American hands contains chilling evidence of the Islamic extremist organization's goals. The 11-volume manual provides instructions on the best ways to kill thousands of people and spread fear in the United States and Europe by attacks against targets "with high human intensity," such as skyscrapers, airports, and packed football stadiums. It also urged actions against Jews in every country, by attacking their organizations, institutions, clubs, and hospitals.

Al Qaeda manual

The manual exposed
On December 6, 2001, Attorney General John Ashcroft displayed the al Qaeda training manual in testimony before the US Senate.

Digital espionage

DIGITAL TECHNOLOGY has made it possible for intelligence agencies to gather and analyze vast amounts of information. However, the wide availability of the personal computer and the internet have changed the ways that spies operate and brought new challenges for intelligence. For example, whereas government code-breakers were once able to intercept and break most enemy ciphers, the ready availability of advanced encryption software now strains even the most advanced supercomputers. In addition, as the superpowers become increasingly reliant on networked systems so they become more vulnerable to digital spies and sabotage.

Supercomputers
Powerful, super-fast computers with massive storage capacities enable intelligence agencies to analyse vast amounts of information quickly.

Gathering information

Satellites that could produce electro-optical digital images were first used in the 1970s. The images could be beamed to ground stations as soon as they were taken, making them immediately available for analysis. More recently, such image-collecting spy satellites have been joined by "ears in space," satellites that are capable of eavesdropping on all forms of communication signals and transmitting them back to terrestrial stations. The increasing use of radio frequencies for the transmission of telephone and computer data makes these listening satellites capable of collecting ever larger amounts of information. With speech recognition software, the satellites are able to filter out unnecessary pieces of information and recover messages that incorporate specified keywords being communicated by both friends and foes.

More than 50 years ago, an intelligence officer observed that 90 percent of everything spies need to know is openly available. The internet has become the repository of the information needed to fuel the economies of the world's superpowers and the analysts of intelligence services. The keys to this "fountain of knowledge" are high-speed internet access, advanced networking, and massive computer power to analyze billions of bits of data in order to discover the secrets hidden inside.

Powerful internet browsers are even now traveling through cyberspace into the computers and networks of both the suspecting and unsuspecting in order to record their secrets. In the immediate future, a clever computer programmer will unleash "cyber-agents" to recover more vital information in a day than a thousand fictional James Bonds could recover in a lifetime.

Recruiting spies

Convicted KGB spy John Walker noted after his arrest that the defenses of the United States were constructed to protect against enemies from outside, not from the treachery of Americans within. Purchasing secrets from traitors still remains an extremely effective and profitable means of intelligence collection. Hostile intelligence services

Menwith Hill monitoring station

Menwith Hill, Yorkshire, England, is one of the world's most sophisticated communications monitoring posts. It employs more than 1,000 Americans belonging to the US National Security Agency (NSA) and 600 British staff working closely with the UK's GCHQ (Government Communication Headquarters). With its dozens of satellite receivers housed inside huge white domes, the site is thought to be the center for Project Echelon, a global system for intercepting all email, phone, fax, and telex communcations. Its massive computers can lock onto conversations or messages for analysis if certain key words (such as terrorist) are used.

Digital steganography

Steganography is the science of hiding messages. While cryptography attempts to scramble a message in a systematic manner so that it can only be read by the intended recipient, steganography hides the message in a way that conceals the fact it even exists. Microdots are forms of steganography, as is secret writing. Modern digital steganography can combine the two techniques by encrypting (systematically scrambling) the message and then hiding it to conceal its existence. Messages or images can be hidden inside any form of digital media including graphic images, websites, and recorded music.

Innocent-looking image containing "secret" image ready to be emailed

ORIGINAL IMAGE

IMAGE TO BE HIDDEN

COMBINED "HARMLESS" IMAGE

traditionally relied on intuition and informants to identify people who could be recruited as spies. Excessive personal debt, substance abuse, and failed careers were often the first indicators of weaknesses that could be used as levers for recruitment. Digital spies can now carry out computerized checks on the internet to uncover spending habits, debt loads, medical records, and job-change patterns in order to identify potential recruits. By using the internet as a spotting tool, the efforts of intelligence services can be focused on a small pool of potential recruits who have existing weaknesses waiting to be exploited.

Communicating

A spy operating in hostile territory was most vulnerable not when stealing secrets, but rather when attempting to communicate them to his handler. The internet has reduced this area of vulnerability for the spy. The use of chat rooms, internet auction sites, and innocent-appearing web pages makes it easy to send and receive coded messages and instructions. Advanced encryption techniques may be combined with

digital steganographic techniques for embedding messages or images into a scan, or a voice or music recording. Even the most powerful computers strain under the power required to analyze trillions of individual pieces of data for patterns that may indicate the presence of an embedded message.

Analysis

Espionage analysts have always worked behind the scenes in order to convert many individual pieces of information

Phil Zimmermann
Zimmermann is the creator of Pretty Good Privacy (PGP), the world's most advanced encryption software. The use of encryption by terrorists and spies presents new challenges for security agencies.

collected from sources around the world into a useful intelligence product – information that political and military leaders need so that they are able to make better decisions. Today's analysts rely increasingly on technology. Powerful computers, supplemented by artificial intelligence programs, neural networks, and three-dimensional databases are used to collate information from all sources in order to discern patterns and make predictions. Nevertheless, the ability to collect intelligence is growing faster than our abilities to create a usable intelligence report from a mass of seemingly unrelated information.

Counterintelligence

Digital technology works in many ways to the spy's advantage, but it can also be used effectively by counterspies. For example, the internet makes it much easier to establish the true identity of a spy who has adopted a cover or legend (see p. 194). It enables a vast range of personal information to be quickly checked by searching sources such as local property tax records and professional association memberships.

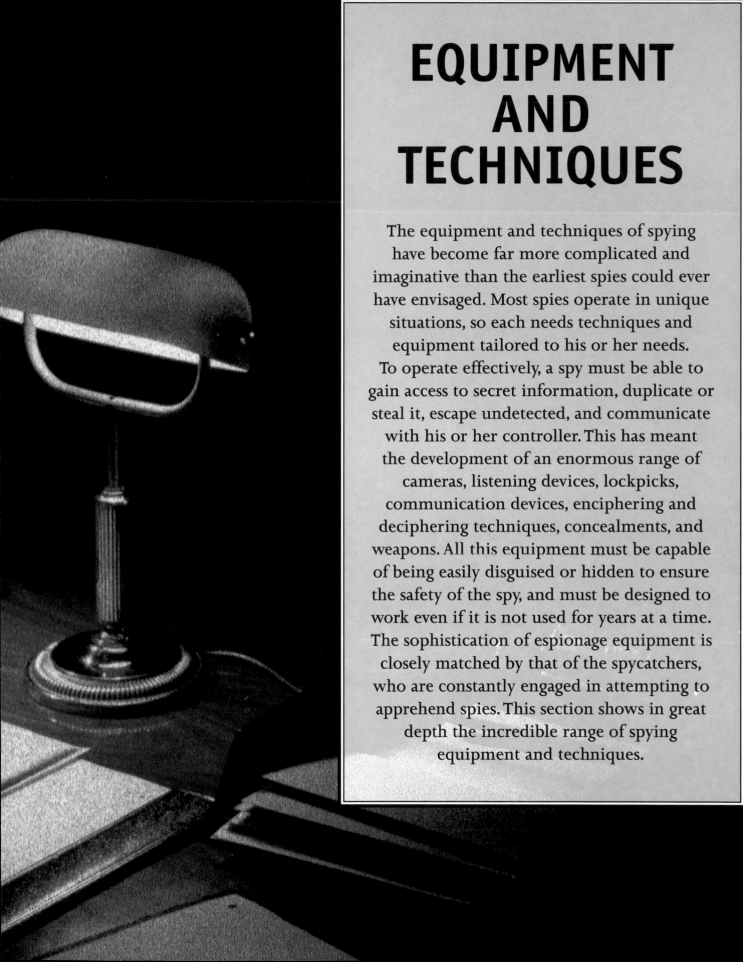

EQUIPMENT AND TECHNIQUES

The equipment and techniques of spying have become far more complicated and imaginative than the earliest spies could ever have envisaged. Most spies operate in unique situations, so each needs techniques and equipment tailored to his or her needs.

To operate effectively, a spy must be able to gain access to secret information, duplicate or steal it, escape undetected, and communicate with his or her controller. This has meant the development of an enormous range of cameras, listening devices, lockpicks, communication devices, enciphering and deciphering techniques, concealments, and weapons. All this equipment must be capable of being easily disguised or hidden to ensure the safety of the spy, and must be designed to work even if it is not used for years at a time. The sophistication of espionage equipment is closely matched by that of the spycatchers, who are constantly engaged in attempting to apprehend spies. This section shows in great depth the incredible range of spying equipment and techniques.

CAMERAS

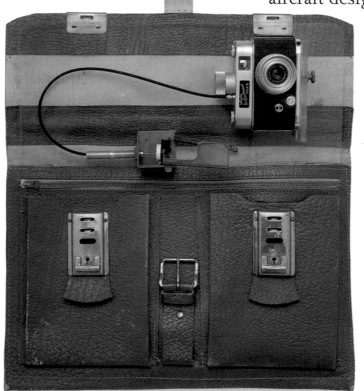

SINCE ITS INVENTION in 1827, photography has played an increasingly important role in intelligence-gathering and espionage. Spies use cameras for taking photographs of people; places such as airfields or other military installations; and objects from bridges to military equipment and from aircraft designs to documents. To be most effective, a spy may need to avoid taking photographs openly. In these cases, a small, easily concealed camera capable of taking high-quality pictures is needed. The intelligence services use three main types of camera, each suited to a specific requirement.

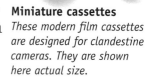

Miniature cassettes
These modern film cassettes are designed for clandestine cameras. They are shown here actual size.

SUBMINIATURE CAMERAS

Small enough to carry in the pocket, subminiature cameras can be adapted for a variety of uses. In addition to general photography, most are suitable for surveillance photography and document copying. To make them easier to conceal, some have no viewfinder, and must be aimed instinctively. The most famous and successful subminiature camera is the Minox, which was first made in Latvia in 1938. Although the Minox was not originally intended for use in espionage, its excellent lens, small size, and quality of construction made it eminently suitable. A line of accessories devised for Minox cameras enables them to be used in concealments or for document photography, and the brand has been widely used by intelligence services. Other brands of commercially produced subminiature cameras include the Echo 8 cigarette-lighter camera and the Steineck wristwatch camera, both used in the Cold War. During World War II, intelligence services, unable to obtain enough Minox cameras, developed their own cameras, notably the matchbox cameras of the French secret service and the OSS (see p. 32).

Photo-surveillance briefcase
A Robot camera is concealed in a briefcase for surveillance use. The camera has to be aimed instinctively — without the use of a viewfinder — while the case is held under the user's arm.

Minox film canister
First produced in 1938, the Minox camera used preloaded cassettes of film providing 50 exposures.

CONCEALED CAMERAS

Spies often need cameras that will enable them to take photographs without being detected. Cameras may be hidden inside an object such as a handbag, or strapped to the body, with the lens hidden behind a fake tiepin or button. With the latter, pictures are taken by means of a remote shutter release hidden in a pocket. Two commonly used concealed cameras were the Soviet F21 and the West German Robot. Both were developed from a pre-World War II German design, and used spring-driven motor winding mechanisms. Many concealments have been devised, some by Soviet and Western intelligence agencies and some by the Robot factory itself (see p. 80).

KGB surveillance camera
Designed to be concealed in the hand, or worn by the spy in a body harness, this camera was operated by pressing the actuating rod.

Steineck ABC wristwatch camera
This camera could take six pictures, under the pretense of checking the time.

COPY CAMERAS

A special class of cameras exists for the task of photographing documents. They are often custom-made, but commercial copy cameras are available, with special accessories. A standard camera can be used when necessary, but skill and practice are needed to obtain acceptable images. Most intelligence services issue special copy camera kits, housed in unobtrusive boxes or attaché cases, which can be used by agents who do not have specialized photographic skills. The KGB developed a miniature copy camera the size of a Minox film cassette for smuggling past security checks. Later, the same agency issued a "brush" camera that is swept across documents like a hand-held photocopier, photographing as it goes.

Czech copy camera
Used for document photography by personnel of the Czech security agency StB, this camera was housed in an anonymous-looking wooden case.

Concealed cameras I

SPIES USE CONCEALED CAMERAS for covert photography. The camera may be hidden under a spy's clothing, or disguised as another object. While some subminiature cameras have only one fixed disguise, there are concealed cameras that may be disguised in a number of ways. For example, the Tessina, Robot (see p. 80), and F21 (see p. 82) each have a special line of concealments. Standard cameras can be used clandestinely if equipped with special attachments like the vehicle nationality plate (left) with one-way glass in the "A" through which pictures can be taken.

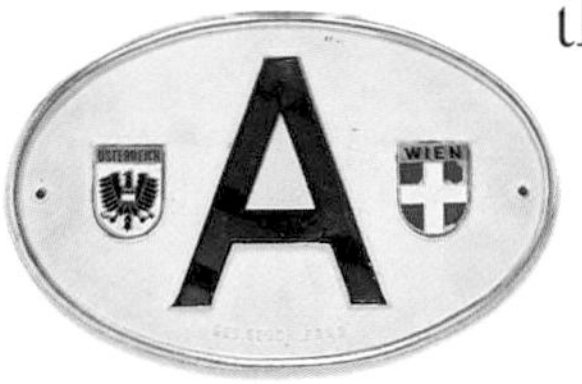

VEHICLE PLATE CONCEALMENT

Modified Leica lens cap

The word "Leica" has been cut out of this standard camera's lens cap. Pictures can be taken through the cutout while the lens cap is on and it appears as

Cutout

MODIFIED LENS CAP

Shutter release button   Lens

STANDARD LEICA CAMERA

Tessina camera in cigarette packet

The world's smallest motor-driven 35mm camera, the Swiss Tessina fits in a cigarette pack (this should be a brand recognized in the country where it will be used). An internal frame holds the lens aligned with tiny holes in the pack. The shutter release is pressed through the pack, to take up to 10 pictures before rewinding is necessary.

Internal metal frame

Tiny holes

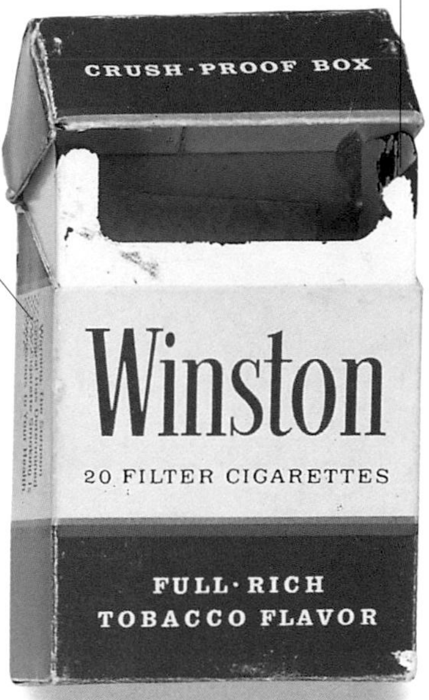

CIGARETTE PACK CONCEALMENT

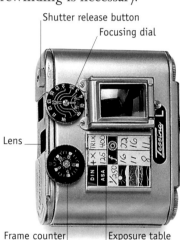

Shutter release button

Focusing dial

Lens

Frame counter   Exposure table

TESSINA CAMERA

Tessina camera concealed in book

The tiny Tessina camera may alternatively be hidden inside a cutout section of a book. Pictures can be taken through the side of the book by applying pressure to the cover, and thereby operating a shutter release plate.

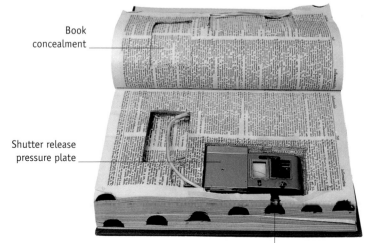

Book concealment

Shutter release pressure plate

Opening for lens

Toychka 58-m necktie camera

This KGB camera was designed to be strapped to a spy's body and take pictures through a special tiepin. There are two identical-looking tiepins, one for use with the camera and a standard one for everyday use. A spy would wear the standard tiepin regularly, so that people would become used to seeing him wearing it. The special tiepin would be worn with the camera when he needed to take pictures. The camera is spring-wound and almost silent.

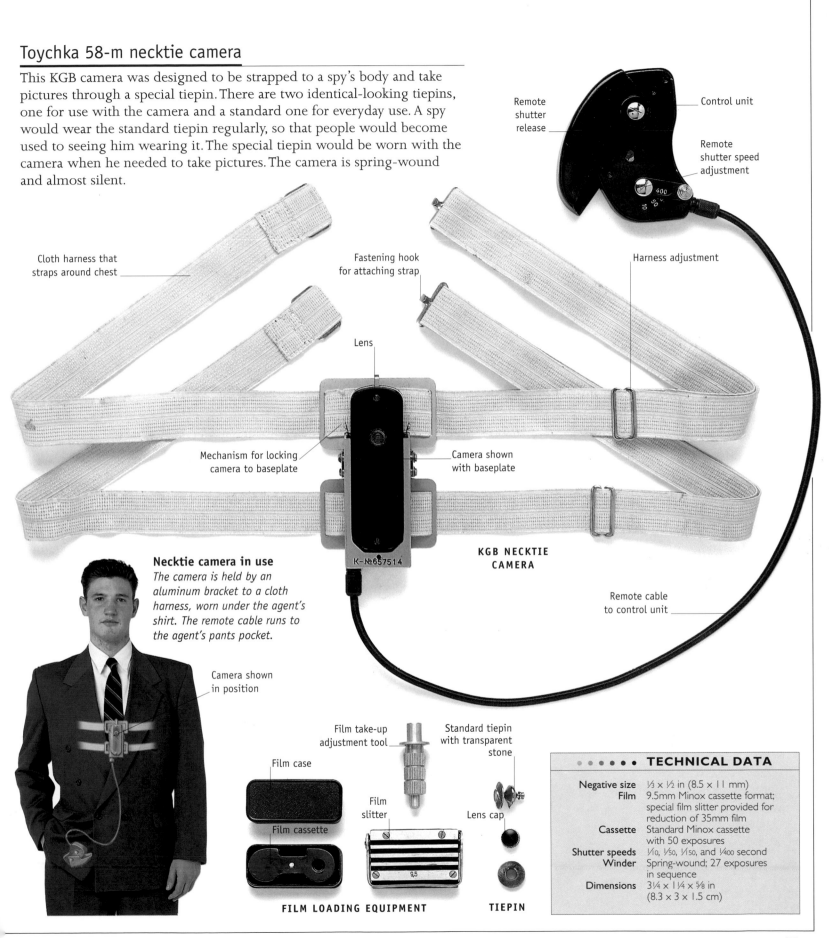

Remote shutter release

Control unit

Remote shutter speed adjustment

Cloth harness that straps around chest

Fastening hook for attaching strap

Harness adjustment

Lens

Mechanism for locking camera to baseplate

Camera shown with baseplate

KGB NECKTIE CAMERA

K-№657514

Remote cable to control unit

Necktie camera in use
The camera is held by an aluminum bracket to a cloth harness, worn under the agent's shirt. The remote cable runs to the agent's pants pocket.

Camera shown in position

Film take-up adjustment tool

Standard tiepin with transparent stone

Film case

Film cassette

Film slitter

Lens cap

FILM LOADING EQUIPMENT

TIEPIN

	TECHNICAL DATA
Negative size	$\frac{1}{3} \times \frac{1}{2}$ in (8.5 × 11 mm)
Film	9.5mm Minox cassette format; special film slitter provided for reduction of 35mm film
Cassette	Standard Minox cassette with 50 exposures
Shutter speeds	$\frac{1}{10}$, $\frac{1}{50}$, $\frac{1}{150}$, and $\frac{1}{400}$ second
Winder	Spring-wound; 27 exposures in sequence
Dimensions	$3\frac{1}{4} \times 1\frac{1}{4} \times \frac{5}{8}$ in (8.3 × 3 × 1.5 cm)

Concealed cameras II

Button concealment with Minox III camera

In the 1950s, this special East German concealment was sewn inside a coat to allow covert photographs to be taken through the center of the button by using a hidden Minox camera. A remote shutter release triggered the camera.

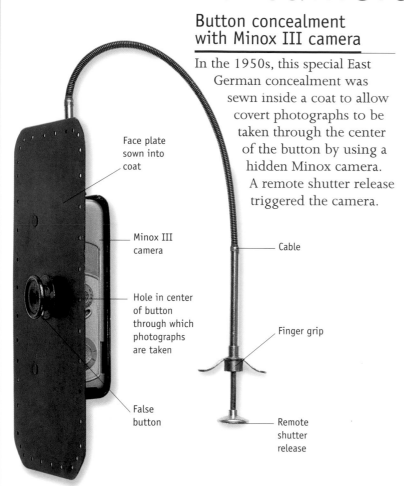

Face plate sown into coat

Minox III camera

Hole in center of button through which photographs are taken

False button

Cable

Finger grip

Remote shutter release

Glove concealment for modified Minox

The Stasi (see p. 73) made this glove concealment for a modified Minox camera that can be used with one hand. The camera is hidden in the glove so that its lens lines up with a hole in the leather. Pressing the spring-rod releases the shutter and then advances the film.

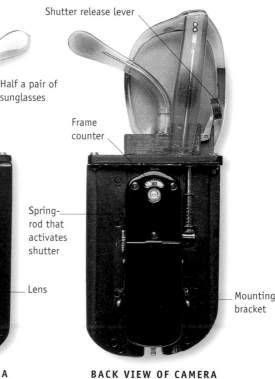

Hole in leather for lens

GLOVE CONCEALMENT

Spring-rod

Viewer

Focusing dial

Shutter speed dial

MINOX CAMERA

Sunglasses case concealment

The surveillance department of the Stasi (see p. 73) created this intriguing concealment. Inside a false sunglasses case is hidden a KGB Toychka surveillance camera. Half a pair of sunglasses in the case adds to the illusion that masks the presence of the camera. The operator would carry the case in one hand and take pictures by pressing a lever on the side of the case. A spring-driven winder inside the camera allowed many photographs to be taken without having to remove the camera from its case to wind the film.

Mesh over lens

CAMERA IN CASE

Half a pair of sunglasses

Lens

FRONT VIEW OF CAMERA

Shutter release lever

Frame counter

Spring-rod that activates shutter

Mounting bracket

BACK VIEW OF CAMERA

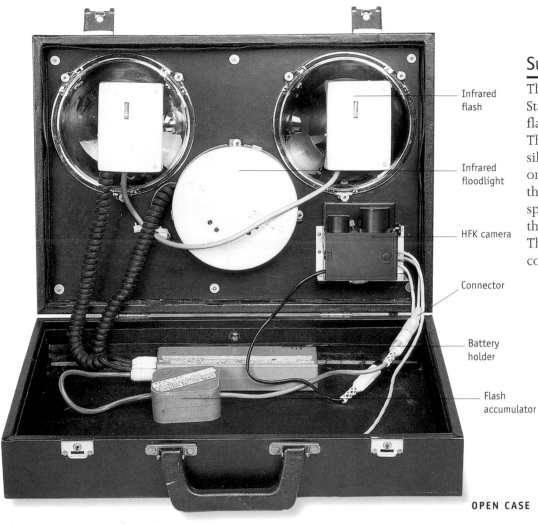

Infrared flash

Infrared floodlight

HFK camera

Connector

Battery holder

Flash accumulator

OPEN CASE

Surveillance attaché case

This surveillance briefcase, made by the Stasi (see p. 73), can take infrared (IR) flash photographs in complete darkness. The internal Zeiss HFK camera, with a silent electronic shutter, photographs onto IR film through a small opening in the attaché case. The case is covered in a special fabric that allows IR light to pass through but appears opaque to the eye. The infrared flashes through the case's covering are invisible to the human eye.

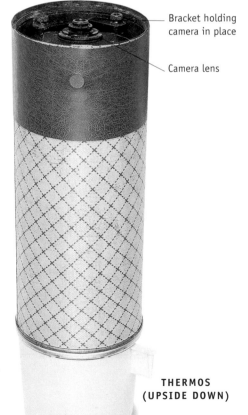

Opening for lens

CLOSED CASE

Thermos concealment

The KGB modified this functioning thermos to conceal an F21 camera (see p. 82). The thermos would be carried by a member of the 7th Directorate (KGB's surveillance team) on the street or inside a factory to secretly photograph an unsuspecting target. The F21's spring-driven winder allowed multiple photographs to be taken rapidly.

Frame counter

Winder

Shutter speed knob

Shutter release

Camera body

Mounting bracket

Aperture bracket

CAMERA IN BASE

Lens opening

THERMOS(1925)LIMITED
THERMOS
BRITISH MADE
LONDON

BASE COVERING WITH LENS OPENING

Bracket holding camera in place

Camera lens

THERMOS (UPSIDE DOWN)

Concealed cameras III

Beobachtungskomplex II through-the-wall camera

The Stasi (East Germany's state security ministry) produced this specialized camera during the 1980s for clandestine photography in hotels. Selected rooms were modified by building a camera port into the wall that was preaimed at the bed or sitting area. The lens tube of the camera would be inserted into the prepositioned port before or after the guests had registered. Fewer than 100 of these surveillance cameras were produced.

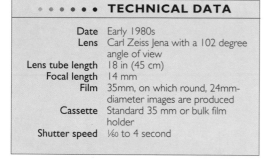

•••••• **TECHNICAL DATA**	
Date	Early 1980s
Lens	Carl Zeiss Jena with a 102 degree angle of view
Lens tube length	18 in (45 cm)
Focal length	14 mm
Film	35mm, on which round, 24mm-diameter images are produced
Cassette	Standard 35 mm or bulk film holder
Shutter speed	1/60 to 4 second

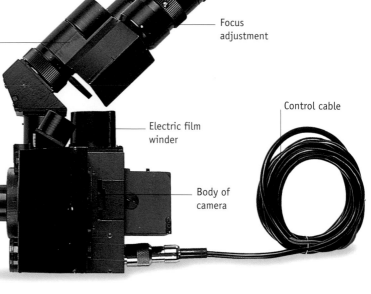

Eyepiece

Focus adjustment

Binocular attachment facilitates viewing through camera into room on other side of wall

Control cable

Electric film winder

Lens tube

Body of camera

Cuckoo-clock concealment

This cuckoo clock has been modified by adding a camera port and concealed lens opening above the number 12 on its face. When mounted, the clock would mask a through-the-wall camera, such as the one shown above.

Pinhole lens opening in middle of cuckoo door

CLOCK FACE

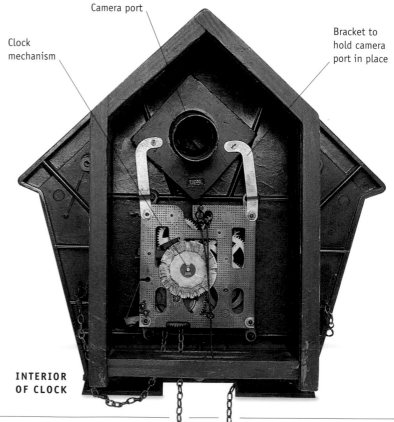

Camera port

Clock mechanism

Bracket to hold camera port in place

INTERIOR OF CLOCK

Through-the-wall viewing kit

Made by the KGB, this kit comprises a viewer and optical tubes for the surveillance of a targeted meeting or hotel room. The tubes go through a wall as far as a pinhole opening on the other side. By using the viewing tubes, the operator would know when to trigger a remote camera.

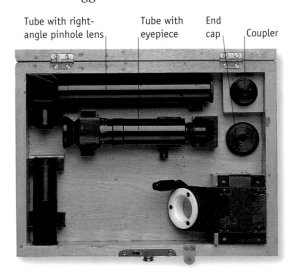

Tube with right-angle pinhole lens   Tube with eyepiece   End cap   Coupler

Ankle or forearm concealment

This Minox concealment is designed to be strapped underneath the operator's clothing on the ankle or forearm. During a spying operation, the camera would be pulled from the concealment and photographs taken. Afterward, by releasing the camera, it would automatically retract back underneath the clothing to leave the operator with empty hands.

Retractor

Strap for attachment to forearm or ankle

Camera holder

Minox camera

Antenna depressed to operate camera

Radio with F21 camera

This small radio was used to conceal a KGB F21 surveillance camera (see p. 82). The camera took pictures through an opening in the back of the radio and was actuated by pressing the antenna. The F21's spring motor enabled the camera to take multiple photographs without rewinding.

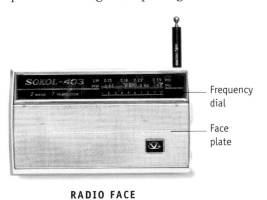

SOKOL-403   LW 0.15 0.18 0.22 0.39 Mc
2 BAND 7 TRANSISTOR   MW 0.63 0.67 0.90 1.50 Mc

Frequency dial

Face plate

RADIO FACE

Carrying strap

External power socket

Concealed opening for lens

RADIO IN CASE

Film back   Aperture adjustment   Shutter release   Film winder

INTERIOR OF RADIO SHOWING CAMERA

Robot camera

THE ROBOT CAMERA, dating from 1934, was powered by a spring-driven motor that allowed successive pictures to be taken without the user having to wind on manually. It was used in World War II by the German air force to provide proof of destroyed targets and by the German intelligence service (see p. 34). In the early years of the Cold War, spies in both the communist bloc and in the West used it because, with no need for hand winding between photographs, it could be used in a variety of concealments.

(see p. 34)

TECHNICAL DATA

Date	1969
Lens	Xenon 40 mm f1.9
Negative size	About 1 x 1 in (24 x 24 mm)
Film	Standard 35 mm or special film, depending on application; 50 exposures
Shutter	Rotating shutter, ¼ to ⅟₅₀₀ second plus B
Motor	Double spring-wound
Options	Special silent, slow-winding model available from factory

Robot star 50 camera

The Star 50 was the last Robot model to evolve from the World War II design. It could take 50 pictures and the short focal length of its lens meant good depth of field, making sharp pictures possible.

Shutter release button

Viewfinder (not used in covert operations)

Lens

Shutter speed dial

Handbag concealment kit

The Robot factory owners were aware of the different intelligence applications of its line of cameras, and made kits that enabled them to be installed in a variety of objects. This kit allows the user to hide a Robot Star 50 inside a handbag. The hidden camera takes the photographs through a decorative metal ornament, of which a wide selection was available from the manufacturer.

Remote shutter release, placed out of sight

Cable

Attachment holds camera lens to bag

Solenoid switch for remote operation of shutter

Internal frame to hold camera inside bag

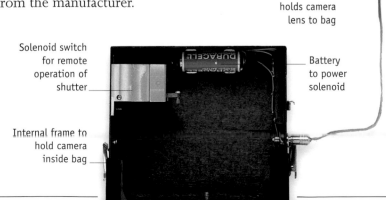

Battery to power solenoid

Solenoid

Internal frame

Battery

Remote shutter release

Metal ornament hides the opening for the camera's lens

METAL ORNAMENTS

Handbag concealment
The Robot concealment kit could be installed in a variety of bags. Care was taken to select a type of bag that was commonly carried in the intended country of use and that was also strong enough to support the camera.

Photo-surveillance briefcase

This briefcase, with its concealed camera, was used during the 1950s and 1960s for photo-surveillance operations by the United States intelligence services. Intelligence officers would carry the briefcase under one arm and take photographs at right angles to the way they were facing. Since the viewfinder could not be used, a great deal of practice was needed to take accurately framed photographs. The officer had to learn instinctively how to position the briefcase correctly in order to photograph the desired subject. The camera is operated by pressing the shutter release lever through the briefcase.

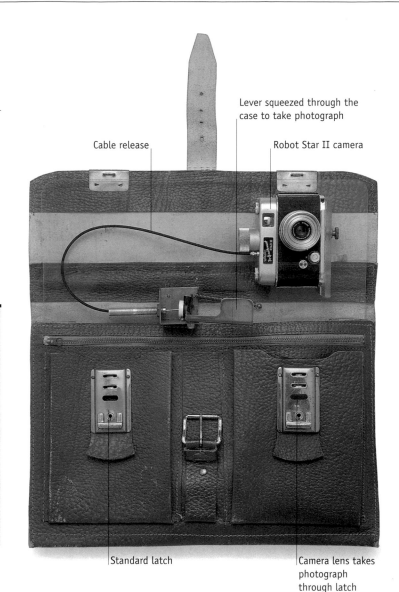

Lever squeezed through the case to take photograph

Cable release

Robot Star II camera

Standard latch

Camera lens takes photograph through latch

SPY PROFILE · Philip Agee

In 1968 Philip Agee, a CIA officer, resigned. In a book published in 1975, he exposed details of every CIA officer and operation that he had ever encountered during his 12-year career. Agee denied cooperating with any hostile agencies, but former KGB officers revealed he had worked with the KGB. Under surveillance after resigning, Agee was secretly photographed by means of a Robot camera hidden in a briefcase.

Waist-belt surveillance camera

A waist-belt concealment lets a Robot camera take photographs through a false button. It was intended for the unobtrusive surveillance of people. Spare buttons were provided, so that all the buttons on the user's coat could be replaced and would match the false one.

False button mounted in front of the camera lens

Front piece of belt hides camera

Hole over camera lens

Belt strap

Hook

Hook hole

Cable release

False button

Surveillance camera in position
When the Robot camera is worn on a waist belt hidden under a coat, it is virtually impossible to detect.

Robot Star II camera

Back piece of belt supports camera

F21 concealed camera

BELT BUCKLE CONCEALMENT

THE SMALL, LIGHTWEIGHT F21 camera was adapted from the German Robot camera (see p. 82) in 1948 by the KGB. The F21 was used for surveillance photography; it could take several pictures in quick succession with a spring-driven winder, and it had many concealments, so spies could use the camera in a wide variety of different situations. A version of the F21, the Zenit Model MF1, has been sold commercially without concealments since the end of the Cold War.

Lens aperture adjustment lever

Remote shutter release

POCKET REMOTE CONTROL UNIT FOR F21

Cable to concealed camera

F21 camera and accessories

The F21, with lenses, accessories, and concealments, makes a versatile kit for clandestine photography. Its small size (it is shown here full size) and quietness make it unobtrusive. Because it has no viewfinder, it must be aimed instinctively.

Winder

Frame and film counter adjustment

Shutter release

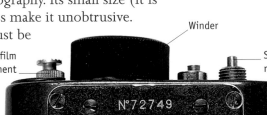

N°72749

ALTERNATIVE FACEPLATE AND LENS FOR CAMERA

Lens

F21 CAMERA

• • • • • •	**TECHNICAL DATA**
Lens	28 mm f2.8
Focusing range	10 ft (3 m) to infinity
Negative size	About ¾ x 1 in (18 x 24 mm)
Film	Standard issue, 21 mm
Cassette	14–100 frames, depending on thickness of film
Shutter speeds	1/10, 1/30, 1/100 second
Dimensions	3 x 1⅝ x 2⅛ in (77 x 41 x 55 mm)
Weight	6⅜ oz (180 g)
Temperature range	−4 °F to 131 °F (−20 °C to 55 °C)

Special F21 camera

Winder

Shutter release

N°72652

Lens

Wooden block

F21 UMBRELLA CONCEALMENT (INTERIOR)

Jacket concealment

The jacket shown here is one of many styles used with the F21 by Soviet intelligence services. A faceplate attached to the F21 carries a false button that covers the lens. The camera is suspended inside the lining, while the false button protrudes through a hole in the front of the jacket. When the remote shutter release – held in a pocket – is gently squeezed, the center of the false button opens briefly to allow a photograph to be taken.

POSITION OF F21 CONCEALMENT

False button protrudes here

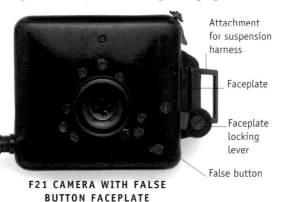

Attachment for suspension harness

Faceplate

Faceplate locking lever

False button

F21 CAMERA WITH FALSE BUTTON FACEPLATE

Facing adapts button for use on a different jacket

NORMAL BUTTON

ALTERNATIVE FACING FOR FALSE BUTTON

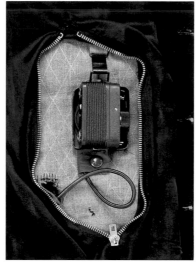

INSIDE VIEW OF F21 CONCEALMENT

Camera case concealment

A spy would wear this camera case around the neck as though the camera was not being used. But inside, an F21 was mounted sideways to take pictures at right angles to the front of the case. As the spy pressed a button, a flap opened and a picture was taken.

Strap

Metal frame

Pulley operating flap

Location of flap

Location of shutter release button

35mm camera case

F21 camera mounted sideways

Opening in umbrella fabric for lens

Umbrella concealment

It was possible for a spy to take pictures through a tiny hole in an inconspicuous object such as an ordinary telescopic umbrella without attracting any attention. The F21 camera was mounted in a shaped wooden frame that fitted inside the umbrella, with the camera lens aligned with a hole in the umbrella cover. A spy would carry the umbrella in his hand and take a photograph by pressing the shutter release through the umbrella fabric.

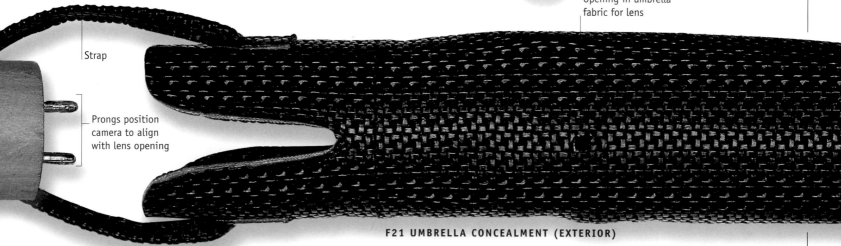

Strap

Prongs position camera to align with lens opening

F21 UMBRELLA CONCEALMENT (EXTERIOR)

Subminiature cameras I

SUBMINIATURE CAMERAS are a class of pocket-sized cameras that use small film sizes, often 16mm or 9.5mm. They are useful for gathering photographic intelligence, and many are built into an outer casing that disguises the camera as a different object. To ensure that the disguise is effective, certain features of normal cameras, like the viewfinder, may be omitted. Spies may need a considerable amount of training to use subminiature cameras because pictures have to be taken surreptitiously, and often under very difficult circumstances. Intelligence agencies sometimes have subminiature cameras specially made for their own use. On other occasions they use models that are available commercially and are suitable for espionage photography.

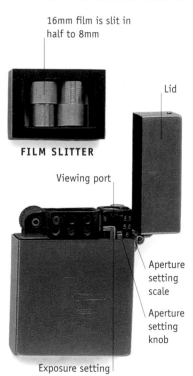

WORLD WAR II FRENCH MATCHBOX CAMERA

Wristwatch camera

The Steineck ABC camera was made to resemble a wristwatch. It uses a circular piece of film with six exposures. Pictures can be taken while pretending to check the time.

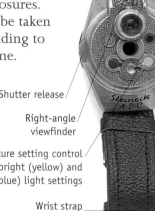

Lens

Shutter release

Right-angle viewfinder

Aperture setting control with bright (yellow) and dim (blue) light settings

Wrist strap

Cigarette lighter camera

Designed in Japan in 1951, the Echo 8 cigarette lighter camera was once the smallest commercially available camera in the world. It was housed inside a working cigarette lighter. This concealment made it ideal for use in social or business settings, where a cigarette lighter would not attract attention. To use the camera, the spy just needed to flip up the top and light a cigarette while aiming the camera at the subject.

16mm film is slit in half to 8mm

Lid

FILM SLITTER

Viewing port

Aperture setting scale

Aperture setting knob

Exposure setting lever

CIGARETTE LIGHTER CAMERA

How the camera was used
This picture is from a contemporary instruction manual. The lens, shown as a dot, has been made more clearly visible for instruction purposes.

Milox TI-246 camera

The Milox camera was first produced in 1968 at the Meopta camera works in Prerov, which is now in the Czech Republic, and used for surveillance photography. The unique optical design of this thin camera allowed it to be used in a variety of concealments, such as a small handbag.

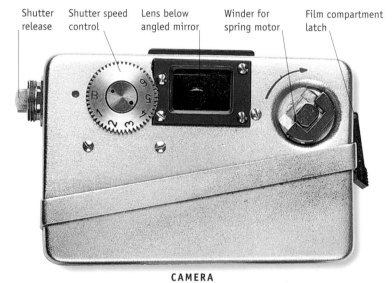

Shutter release

Shutter speed control

Lens below angled mirror

Winder for spring motor

Film compartment latch

CAMERA

Film cassette

Aluminum case

FILM CASSETTE IN CASE

Ajax-8 surveillance camera

This KGB surveillance camera was used from 1949 up until the 1980s. It was designed to be aimed instinctively while concealed in the hand. It could also be worn flat against the body in a body harness, enabling photographs to be taken through a fake button or brooch. The shutter is released and the film is advanced when the thumb lever is pressed.

Pinhole camera

This tiny KGB camera (shown actual size) from the 1980s utilizes a 19th-century photographic principle: each of its four chambers has a pinhole aperture for a lens, making it possible to photograph close-up and distant objects without focusing.

Shutter speed control

Focus scale

Connecting point for body harness

Cast metal casing

Thumb lever

Pinhole aperture

Screw to open pinhole lens

PINHOLE CAMERA

KGB TEST PHOTOGRAPH TAKEN WITH A PINHOLE CAMERA

Matchbox camera

The Kodak company developed this 16mm camera for use by the OSS (see p. 32) during World War II. It was made in the shape of a matchbox and could be camouflaged by adding a matchbox label appropriate for the country in which it was to be used.

Lens opening

Shutter release

Lens opening

Label glued to housing

CAMERA

CAMERA WITH MATCHBOX LABEL

Subminiature cameras II

Cigarette-case-and-lighter camera

A German document camera from the 1950s and '60s is concealed here inside a European-style combination cigarette case and lighter. The small camera uses a Minox-format cassette. When hidden in the lighter, the camera could be carried through a security checkpoint without being detected. Specialized cameras in concealments such this were made in small numbers exclusively for intelligence services.

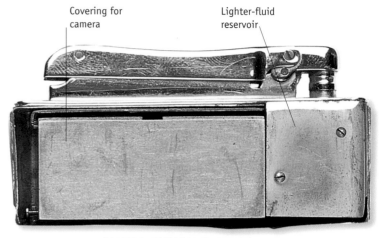

Covering for camera

Lighter-fluid reservoir

CAMERA CONCEALED IN LIGHTER

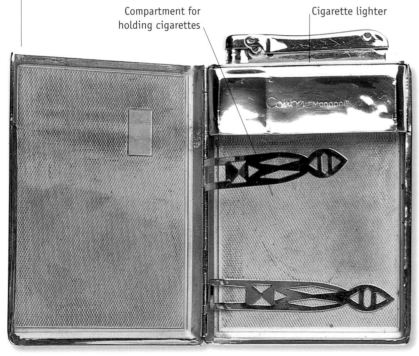

Compartment for holding cigarettes

Cigarette lighter

CIGARETTE HOLDER AND LIGHTER

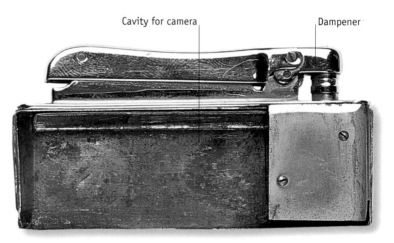

Cavity for camera

Dampener

LIGHTER WITHOUT CAMERA

Svouk lighter camera

Produced in the 1970s, this precision working cigarette-lighter camera had its own special 6mm film. The camera was used for photographing documents through a pinhole opening in its base. The camera was one of three in the Svouk series, which were designed by the KGB's 11th Optical Laboratory in Moscow.

Cigarette lighter

Leather cover hiding camera

Opening for lens in base of lighter

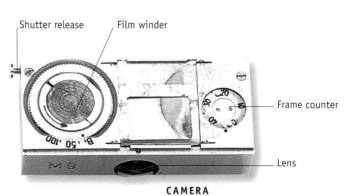

Shutter release

Film winder

Frame counter

Lens

CAMERA

COVERING FOR CAMERA

Tropel cameras and concealments

The lighter, key fob, and pen below conceal tiny CIA Tropel cameras. These objects were in turn hidden in the fake rock. KGB officer Boris Yuzhin, a mole for the CIA, lost his cigarette lighter in the Soviet Consulate in San Francisco in 1981. When found, it was discovered to contain a Tropel camera.

Camera lens

Unscrewed end of pen

Lens opening in lighter

Camera lens

Pen cap

LIGHTER Key

PEN

FOB AND KEY

Concealment cavity

Fake rock surface

FAKE ROCK CONCEALMENT

Zvouk glue-stick camera

This KGB glue stick (which is now dried out) conceals a Zvouk copy camera in its base. Photographs were taken by lifting the camera 12½ in (30 cm) above a document and, while holding the stick's base, rotating the body a quarter-turn. The camera could photograph 30 documents onto a cassette loaded with black-and-white 6mm film.

Camera body

Lens opening

FILM CASSETTE

GLUE STICK

CAMERA IN GLUE STICK

BASE OF GLUE STICK

Side of binoculars used for observation

Side of binoculars attached to camera

Clamp for attaching binoculars

Minox camera

Tripod

Minox camera with attached binoculars

For photographing distant objects, the Minox could be attached to a binocular eyepiece. The operator would use one side of the binoculars for observation and quickly take pictures, through the other side of the binoculars, of any target of interest.

Minox camera

EARLY FILM CASSETTE CASE

THE MINOX SUBMINIATURE CAMERA, in its various models, was for years the world's most widely used spy camera. It was originally manufactured in 1938 in Riga, capital of Latvia, as a commercial camera, but it was soon apparent that the small size, precision, and flexibility of the Minox made it ideal for clandestine photography. It is suitable both for general use and for close-up work, such as taking photographs of documents, and can take 50 pictures without reloading. Models produced since the end of World War II were equipped with very high resolution lenses which, when used with better-quality film, allowed a tremendous amount of detail to be obtained from the tiny negatives. With its many accessories, the Minox could be adapted for a wide range of intelligence uses, and it stayed in widespread use until the end of the Cold War in the early 1990s.

Demonstrating the Minox
American KGB spy John Walker (see p. 54), following his arrest, shows how he used his Minox C camera with its measuring chain.

Model B Minox and accessories

Produced from 1958 to 1972, this was the most widely used of all Minox cameras for intelligence purposes. It was the first model to have a built-in light meter. Since it did not need batteries, it could be hidden for long periods before use.

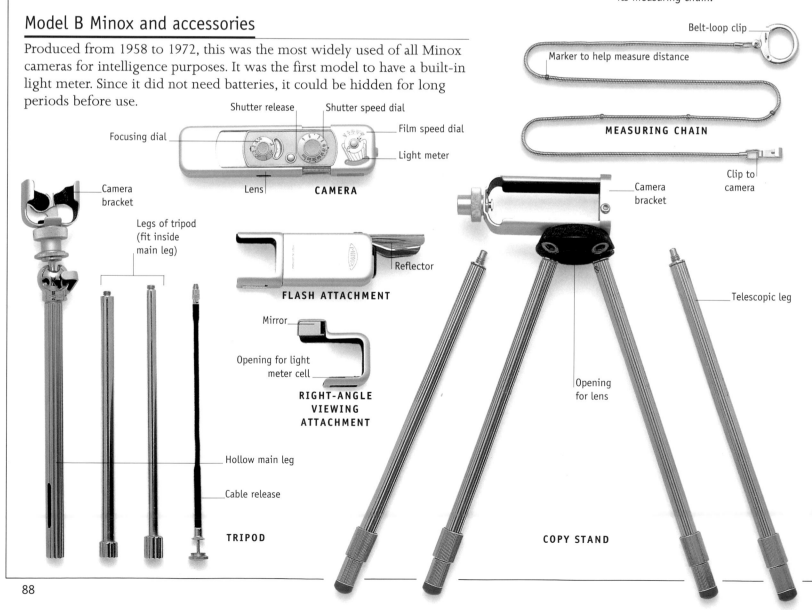

Shutter release

Shutter speed dial

Film speed dial

Focusing dial

Light meter

Lens **CAMERA**

Belt-loop clip

Marker to help measure distance

MEASURING CHAIN

Clip to camera

Camera bracket

Legs of tripod (fit inside main leg)

Camera bracket

Reflector

FLASH ATTACHMENT

Telescopic leg

Mirror

Opening for light meter cell

RIGHT-ANGLE VIEWING ATTACHMENT

Opening for lens

Hollow main leg

Cable release

TRIPOD

COPY STAND

Daylight developing kit

With Minox's miniature developing tank, spies could process their film in full daylight. The tank is the size of a small soda can and uses tiny quantities of chemicals, poured in through a lightproof opening.

Lightproof opening for chemicals

Thermometer

Thermometer case

PROCESSING THERMOMETER

NEGATIVE VIEWER

Groove for film

Cassette holder

DAYLIGHT DEVELOPING TANK

Riga Minox enlarger

Early Minox enlargers were designed to produce small prints from the tiny negatives. Since World War II, improved enlargers have been developed, which make bigger prints from the higher resolution film now available.

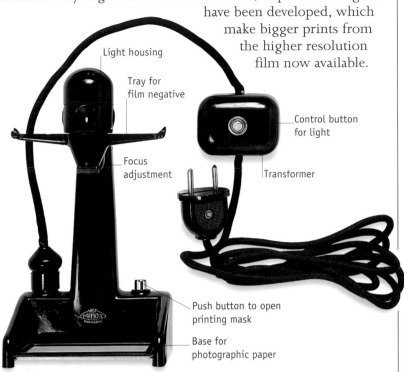

Light housing

Tray for film negative

Focus adjustment

Control button for light

Transformer

Push button to open printing mask

Base for photographic paper

Riga Minox camera

The original Minox camera was made in Riga, Latvia, and was seen as a marvel of technology when it first became available in 1938. During World War II, the intelligence agencies found it difficult to acquire enough Minox cameras for their espionage activities. This top view of the camera is shown actual size.

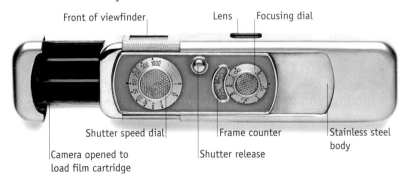

Front of viewfinder

Lens

Focusing dial

Shutter speed dial

Frame counter

Stainless steel body

Camera opened to load film cartridge

Shutter release

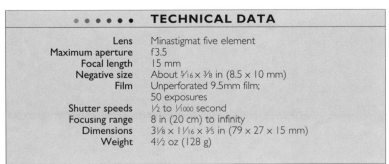

••••••	**TECHNICAL DATA**
Lens	Minastigmat five element
Maximum aperture	f3.5
Focal length	15 mm
Negative size	About ⁵⁄₁₆ × ³⁄₈ in (8.5 × 10 mm)
Film	Unperforated 9.5mm film; 50 exposures
Shutter speeds	½ to ¹⁄₁₀₀₀ second
Focusing range	8 in (20 cm) to infinity
Dimensions	3⅛ × 1¹⁄₁₆ × ³⁄₅ in (79 × 27 × 15 mm)
Weight	4½ oz (128 g)

The Minox inventor

The Latvian engineer Walter Zapp (b.1905) wanted to create a portable camera that would fit easily in the palm of the hand and yet take high-quality, spontaneous pictures. During the 1930s, Zapp developed a mechanism that met these very strict size requirements. In 1938, the first Minox camera was produced in Riga, Latvia. It used film one-quarter the size of standard 35mm film and could hold film cassettes loaded with 50 frames. Although Zapp had developed the Minox to be used for general photography, the camera soon became highly sought after by intelligence agencies around the world for use in espionage photography.

Early Minox design team
The 1937 design team that produced the first Riga Minox, with Walter Zapp at the center.

Copy cameras I

SPIES OFTEN HAVE just a few moments in which to copy secret documents. They may have stolen the documents and need to replace them before the documents are missed, or they may have access to them in an office that is empty only for short periods. Normal cameras can be used for document photography but they require care and time to take good-quality pictures. Intelligence services have developed special portable copy cameras that are quick, easy, and reliable to use. Copy cameras can be either miniaturized or disguised: a fine example of the latter is the KGB rollover camera that is disguised as a notebook (see p. 92).

Yelka C-64 copy camera

This equipment was designed for the KGB and operates on a wide range of electrical voltages, including that of car batteries. It is simple to use and produces good pictures. The Yelka was built with hinges that enabled it to be folded down when not in use. The whole unit, when folded, fits inside its own base (its copy stand), which is about the size of a large book. The example shown here was used by personnel in East Germany's intelligence agency, the Stasi.

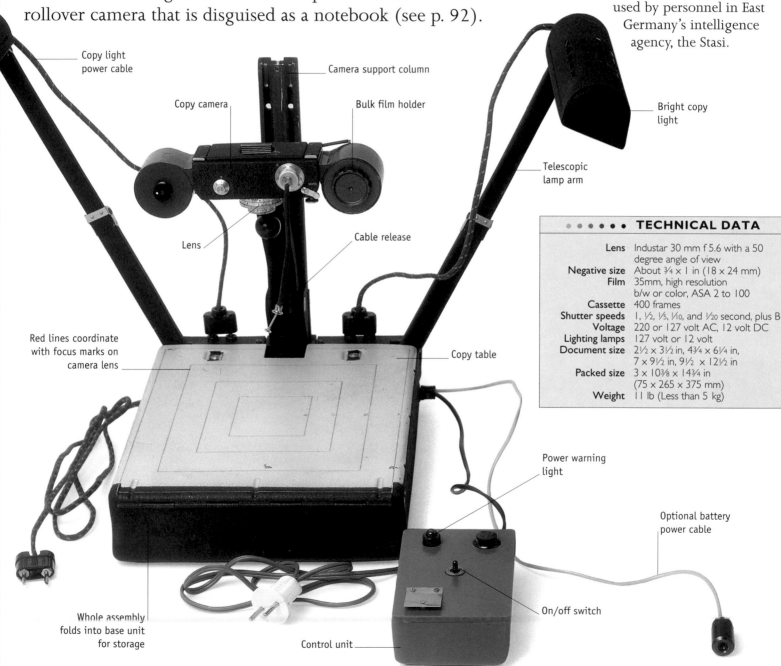

Copy light power cable

Camera support column

Copy camera

Bulk film holder

Bright copy light

Telescopic lamp arm

Lens

Cable release

Red lines coordinate with focus marks on camera lens

Copy table

Power warning light

Optional battery power cable

Whole assembly folds into base unit for storage

On/off switch

Control unit

	TECHNICAL DATA
Lens	Industar 30 mm f 5.6 with a 50 degree angle of view
Negative size	About ¾ × 1 in (18 × 24 mm)
Film	35mm, high resolution b/w or color, ASA 2 to 100
Cassette	400 frames
Shutter speeds	1, ½, ⅕, ⅒, and 1/20 second, plus B
Voltage	220 or 127 volt AC, 12 volt DC
Lighting lamps	127 volt or 12 volt
Document size	2½ × 3½ in, 4¾ × 6¼ in, 7 × 9½ in, 9½ × 12½ in
Packed size	3 × 10⅜ × 14¾ in (75 × 265 × 375 mm)
Weight	11 lb (Less than 5 kg)

Das Ministerium für Staatssicherheit

East Germany's State Security Ministry was usually known as the Stasi – short for its official German title (above). In effectiveness, it was second only to the KGB among Soviet bloc intelligence organizations. The Stasi's principal responsibility was to monitor the activities of East Germany's own citizens. After the collapse of East Germany in 1989, the German public was astonished to learn the extent of surveillance that had been going on in their midst.

Stasi lapel pin
Stasi officers watching a public meeting or demonstration wore lapel pins to identify themselves to each other and to informers. This Stasi pin, shown twice real size, has a revolving disk that can display four different identifying colors.

Attaché case copy camera

An attaché case forms the concealment for this American copy camera. When the case is opened, the copy lights fold out into position and operate with either electricity or batteries. The modified fixed-focus 35mm camera uses nylon gears for silent operation. This type of attaché case copy camera has been used by a variety of American intelligence organizations.

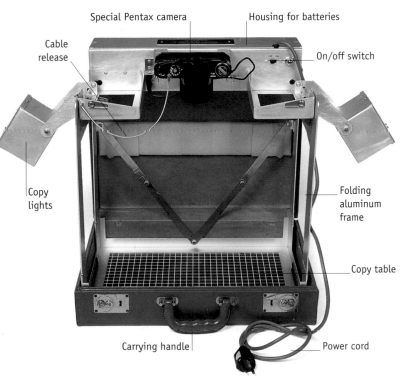

- Special Pentax camera
- Housing for batteries
- Cable release
- On/off switch
- Copy lights
- Folding aluminum frame
- Copy table
- Carrying handle
- Power cord

Copy camera kit

The components of this copy camera kit, designed for the Czech intelligence service (known by its Czech initials StB), could be quickly assembled from the small case in which they were usually carried. Colored marks on the legs correspond to focus settings on the camera.

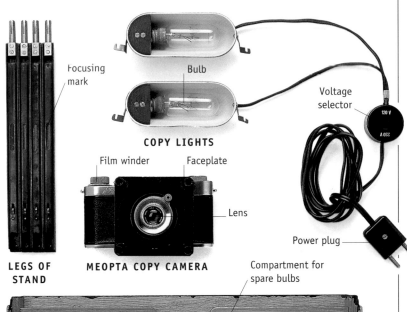

- Focusing mark
- Bulb
- Voltage selector
- **COPY LIGHTS**
- Film winder
- Faceplate
- Lens
- Power plug
- **LEGS OF STAND**
- **MEOPTA COPY CAMERA**
- Compartment for spare bulbs

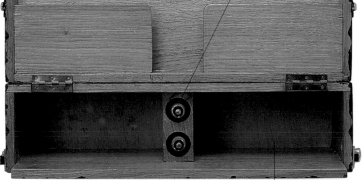

EMPTY CASE FOR CAMERA KIT
- Compartment for metal legs

CAMERA SET UP FOR USE

- Camera
- Cable release
- Faceplate
- Lens shroud
- Four-legged copy stand
- Voltage selector
- Copy light
- Focusing mark

Copy cameras II

Rollover camera

This KGB rollover or brush camera can copy up to 40 pages before it needs reloading. The camera is concealed in a fake notebook resembling a real one that the spy carries and uses regularly. To use the camera, the spy folds back the cover of the fake notebook to reveal a lens in the inner spine. Tiny wheels in the spine activate the camera mechanism and its built-in light source as the spine is rolled over a document.

REAL NOTEBOOK

ROLLOVER CAMERA DISGUISED AS NOTEBOOK

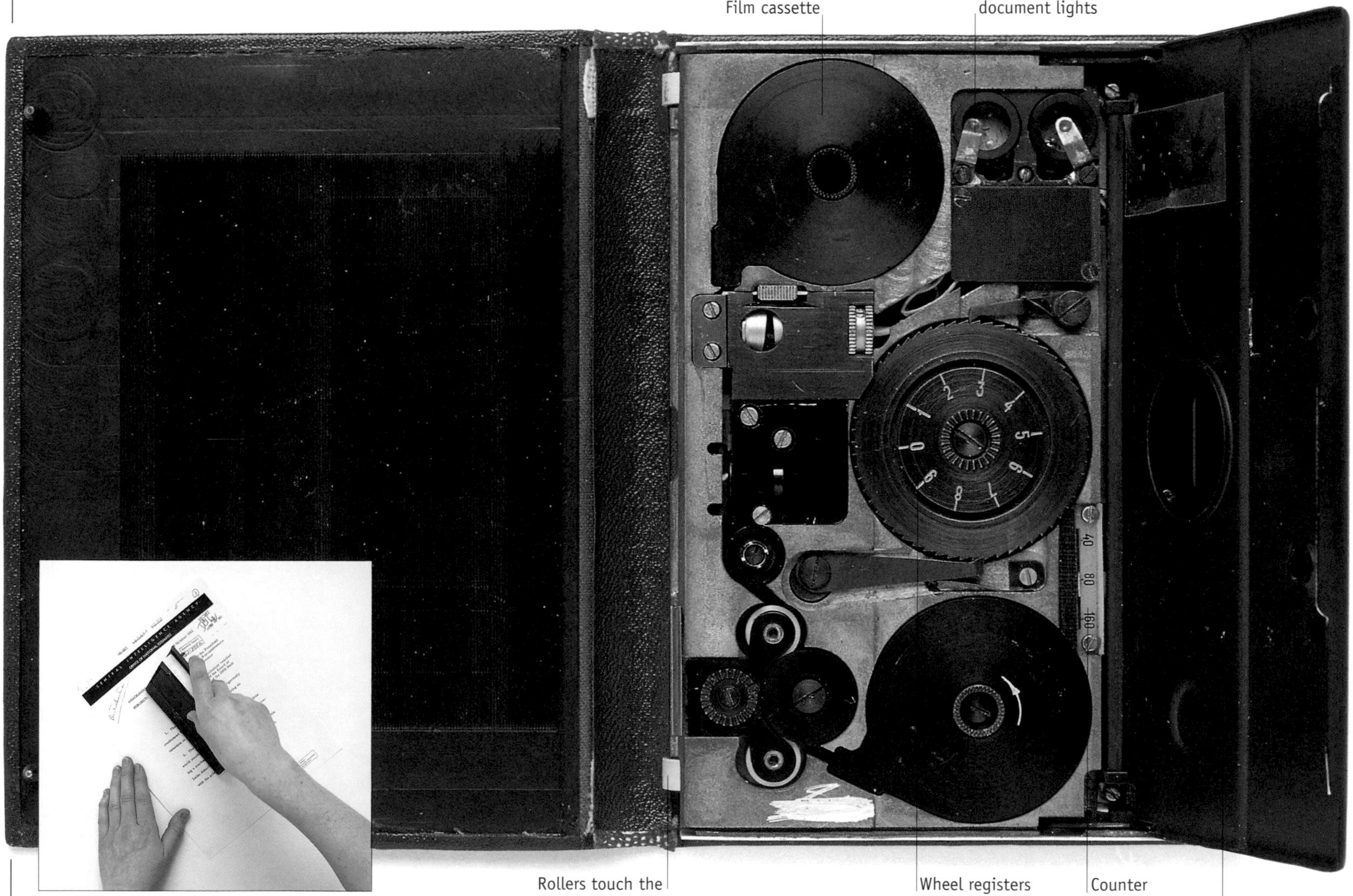

Film slitter
The slitter cuts standard 35mm film to the correct width for use in the cassette of the rollover camera.

35mm film

Handle is raised to allow film to be fed into the slitter

FILM SLITTER

Film cassette

Batteries for document lights

Rollover photography
The KGB camera being rolled over a document to copy it. The camera can cross the page in any direction.

Rollers touch the document

Wheel registers film position

Counter

Hinged cover

MECHANISM OF THE ROLLOVER CAMERA

Miniature Document Camera

Shown actual size, this small KGB camera was intended for use in facilities where strict security is maintained. It has no viewfinder and few external controls – just a shutter release and film advance. A film slitter cuts standard 35mm film down to a width of 9.5 mm for use in a Minox (see p. 88) cassette.

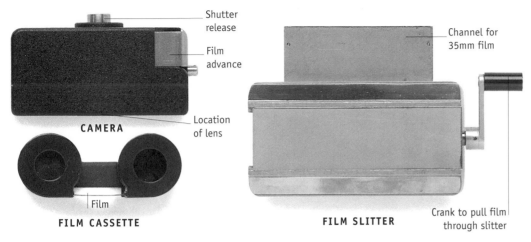

CAMERA

Shutter release

Film advance

Location of lens

Film

FILM CASSETTE

Channel for 35mm film

Crank to pull film through slitter

FILM SLITTER

Camera

Using the document camera
The camera has a fixed focus, so in order to take clear photographs it must be held as shown, at a specific distance from the document. A constant light should be directed on the document.

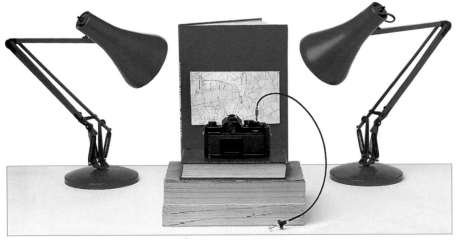

SIMPLE COPY SETUP

Improvised copy techniques

Agents are trained to improvise copy setups so that they can obtain good copies even in circumstances in which time or equipment are limited. Because they consist of ordinary office equipment, these setups do not attract suspicion when dismantled.

Simple copy technique
This technique was developed by Victor Ostrovsky (see p. 74) for Mossad. The document, taped to a book, is stood in front of the camera, which is stuck to another book with chewing gum. Desk lamps are used for illumination. A remote shutter release is used to avoid shaking the camera.

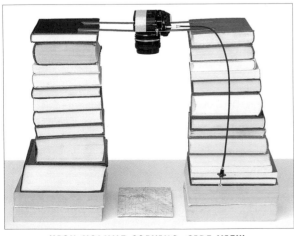

HIGH-VOLUME COPYING: SIDE VIEW

TOP VIEW

35mm camera taped between two rulers

Ruler

High-volume copying
Large quantities of documents can be copied quickly with this technique because once the equipment is set up, each document can be rapidly placed in the correct position and photographed. A standard 35mm camera is used, along with books, adhesive tape, rulers, and desk lamps. With practice, the best combination of exposure time, focus, and lighting can be established. The setup is then exactly reproduced for each copying session.

Copy cameras III

Film take-up knob · Eyepiece viewer · Frame reset lock · Frame reset button · Shutter release · Film-speed setting knob

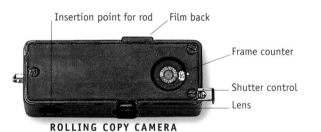

Take-up spool · Negative mask · Reduced area of exposure · Winding spool · Roller · Film back keeps film flat against exposure area

Modified Kodak Retina IIIS camera

The technical service of the HVA (see p. 56) modified this Kodak camera to take microphotographs of documents. The aperture setting and shutter speed were locked, and a smaller mask was inserted to produce ³⁄₁₀ x ½in (8 x 12 mm) microphotographs on high-resolution 35mm film. If found in a search, the camera would probably be overlooked.

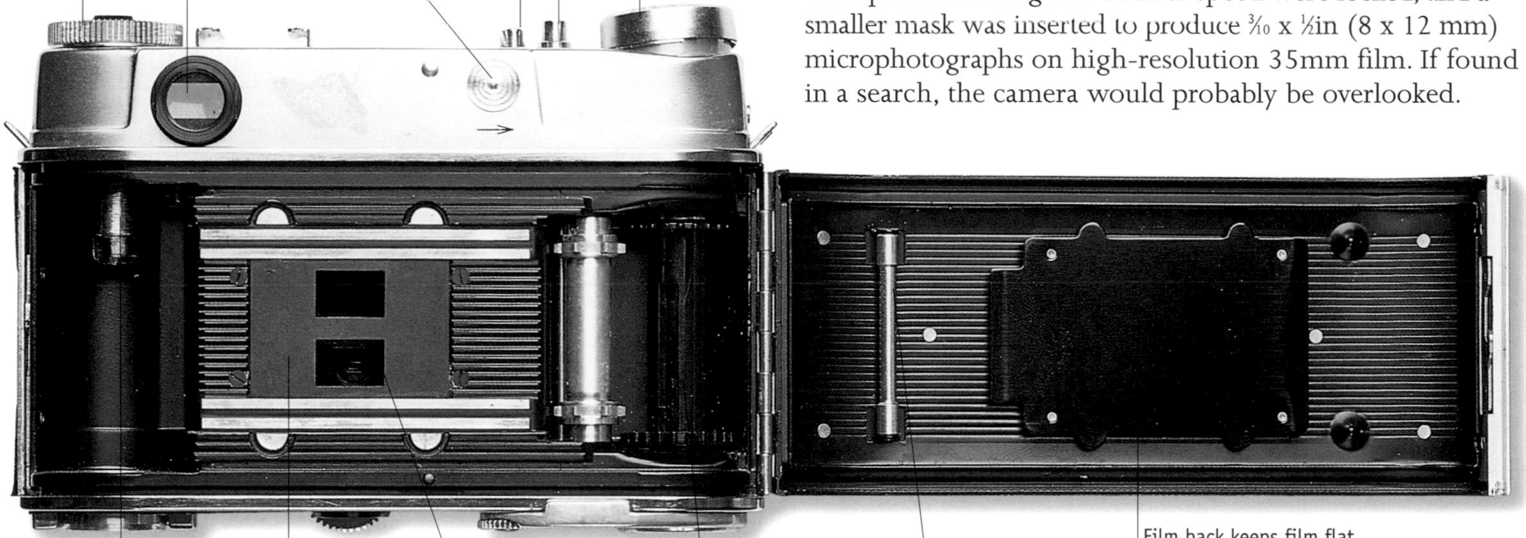

Granitnick-1 rolling copy camera

Masked in a cigarette box, this KGB camera, which was made in 1965, could photograph up to 40 pages of documents as it rolled across them. The small lens appeared when the lever was placed on the document.

Insertion point for rod · Film back · Frame counter · Shutter control · Lens

ROLLING COPY CAMERA

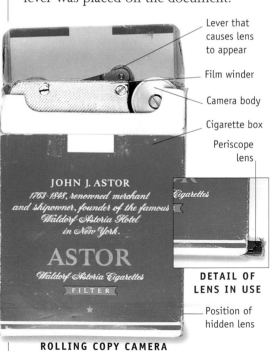

Lever that causes lens to appear · Film winder · Camera body · Cigarette box · Periscope lens

JOHN J. ASTOR
1763-1848, renowned merchant and shipowner, founder of the famous Waldorf-Astoria Hotel in New York.

ASTOR
Waldorf-Astoria Cigarettes
FILTER

DETAIL OF LENS IN USE

Position of hidden lens

ROLLING COPY CAMERA

Rolling camera prototype

In 1961, the KGB designed a prototype rolling camera with a Minox film cassette for the rapid photographing of a document. The rod positions the camera the correct distance above the paper, and a propeller inside the camera advances the film as the wheel moves across the document.

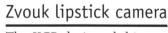

Wheel

ROD

Zvouk lipstick camera

The KGB designed this small lipstick camera in the 1970s, especially for female agents. The camera could photograph up to 30 documents using special 6mm film cassettes. The agent was also issued with an identical lipstick tube for daily use.

Top · Lipstick · Film cassette · Camera body · Lens

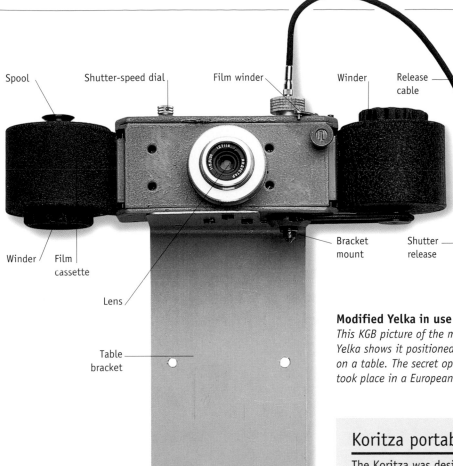

Spool
Shutter-speed dial
Film winder
Winder
Release cable

Winder
Film cassette

Lens

Table bracket

MODIFIED CAMERA

Bracket mount
Shutter release

Modified Yelka camera

The Illegals Directorate of the KGB had this Yelka copy camera modified for covert use in an airport hotel, using only ambient room light. The bracket allowed the camera to be mounted on a bedside table in order to photograph documents placed on the floor.

Modified Yelka in use
This KGB picture of the modified Yelka shows it positioned for use on a table. The secret operation took place in a European Hotel.

Zachiyt microfiche copier

The KGB produced the Zachiyt in the 1970s to covertly copy the increasing number of microfiches being used to store scientific, technical, and military information. The copier was disguised as a book and could make up to 35 copies without recharging.

Book cover
Main power switch
Release button

Mini – Prospectus (Mockba 1976 GAF (Nederland) B.V. microfiche
24 x

Hinged cover of camera
Microfiche
Lock of internal cover

Koritza portable document copy camera

The Koritza was designed by the KGB as a portable copy machine to photograph hundreds of documents onto 35mm film. The bottom of the copier could be removed and the camera used to photograph a map or image mounted on the wall. It was manually operated but required external power to operate its internal lights. An adaptor allowed it to be used inside a car.

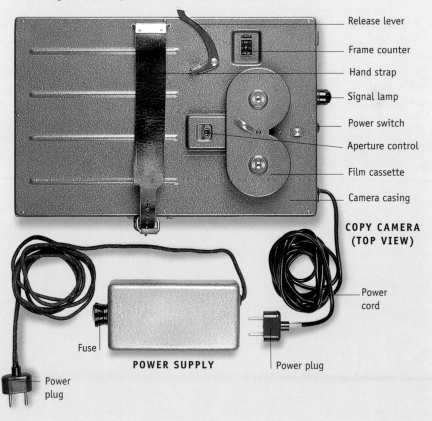

Release lever
Frame counter
Hand strap
Signal lamp
Power switch
Aperture control
Film cassette
Camera casing

COPY CAMERA (TOP VIEW)

Power cord

Fuse

POWER SUPPLY

Power plug

Power plug

SECRET OPERATIONS

Bugs and plugs
Items of electrical equipment, such as plugs, make good hiding places for listening devices and infrared receivers. They draw their power from the electrical socket and can work for years if not detected.

THE CENTRAL TASK of an intelligence agency is to obtain secret information, but this is only one of a range of secret operations that are vital to it. Others include communications, countersurveillance, sabotage, and escape and evasion (avoiding capture or recapture by the enemy). For all these activities, the large intelligence agencies train skilled personnel and develop special techniques and equipment. In the KGB, this used to be done by a Directorate known as OT (this stood for Technical Operations). The CIA counterpart is the Office of Technical Services. In Israel, Mossad employs technical experts known as *marats* for the same purpose.

WATCHING AND LISTENING

A major role for the technical experts in an intelligence agency is to provide the means of carrying out surveillance. Photographic and video cameras may be employed to monitor the activities of foreign agents. A number of notable spies have been caught as a result of visual surveillance operations. Audio surveillance, too, can yield much valuable intelligence. Specialists

Miniature monocular
This KGB monocular, held between the fingertips when used, is small enough to be stored inside a 35mm film canister.

are trained to place listening devices – known as bugs – in locations where secret conversations or meetings may take place. In certain circumstances the listening devices are linked by wire to a nearby listening post. Alternatively, the bug may be coupled with a transmitter, which sends the sound in the form of a radio signal. The signals are picked up by special receivers, some of which incorporate a recording device. Another branch of audio surveillance entails taking the listening device personally to where it is needed. Microphones and recording devices that can be hidden in an agent's clothing have been developed for this purpose.

Wire recording device
The KGB Mezon recording device is sufficiently compact to be hidden in the clothing and activated by a control switch in the pocket. The device uses thin wire instead of tape to store its recordings.

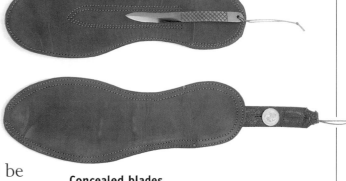

Concealed blades
Special concealments were devised for escape aids. Here, leather inner soles provide hiding places for a blade and five gold coins.

GAINING ENTRY

In order to plant a listening device or gain access to secret material, it may be necessary to make a surreptitious entry. The value of whatever intelligence is gained will be reduced if the targets suspect a breach of security. The first step in carrying out a surreptitious entry is reconnaissance. One or more visits must be made to the target location. Using specialized equipment, it is even possible to see under doors and through keyholes. A key will be needed, and the best way is to "borrow" a key that can be copied and then returned. If this cannot be done, a lock will have to be picked, and this again is a specialized skill.

Lockpick and tension wrenches
The type of lock found in the target location will determine which of the many different tools are selected for use.

WARTIME OPERATIONS

In wartime, personnel sent to operate behind enemy lines are equipped and trained to escape from, or evade capture by, the enemy. During World War II, many concealments were devised for escape aids, such as the maps and compasses that were issued to aircrew flying missions over enemy territory.

World War II also led to increased development of tools and techniques for sabotage behind enemy lines. Many forms of explosive device were produced. Some were disguised as coal or animal droppings. Some had delay devices, such as pencil fuses, facilitating controlled detonation. Enemy ships in harbor were attacked using special small boats and canoes, and limpet mines were attached magnetically to the hulls. Sabotage is not merely profitable in terms of the destruction it causes, but also due to the large numbers of troops the enemy is forced to divert to guard transportation, communications, and industrial installations.

Pencil fuses
These devices were used by saboteurs during World War II to delay the detonation of explosives. Delays gave the saboteurs enough time to escape in safety (see p. 119).

Visual surveillance I

VISUAL SURVEILLANCE is the art of watching without being detected. Intelligence agencies train and employ special teams to perform this role, using such equipment as handheld optical devices (including night vision equipment) and film and video cameras. Cameras may be set up for long-term surveillance, or miniaturized for concealment on the spy's person. In American and British agencies, visual surveillance experts are called watchers; their talents are employed in internal security and counterintelligence operations. In the Soviet Union, the KGB designated a whole directorate (the seventh) for the role of surveillance.

SPY PROFILE Oleg Penkovsky

An officer in Soviet military intelligence, Oleg Penkovsky (1919–63) was active as a mole at the height of the Cold War. During 1961 and 1962 he passed information to the CIA and MI6 (see p. 201) about the military capabilities and the intentions of the Soviet Union. Eventually, the Soviets arrested Penkovsky, probably as a result of visual and photographic surveillance carried out by the KGB. He was executed after a public trial.

Photographic evidence
In this KGB surveillance photograph, Penkovsky, working as a mole for the West in Moscow, enters a building used as a dead drop site (see p. 160).

Remote shutter release

Adaptor plug for car cigarette lighter socket

Auto Camera Mark 3

This fixed surveillance camera was produced in Britain during the 1950s and is such an effective surveillance tool that it is still used today. The large film chambers hold enough 35mm film to take up to 250 pictures before reloading. It may be powered by a 12-volt power pack or through a car's cigarette lighter during mobile surveillance.

Surveillance binoculars

Made in France in the 19th century, this pair of binoculars has an angled mirror inside the instrument's right hand part. This enabled the user to pretend to look straight ahead, while covertly looking to the right. The left side gave a normal view.

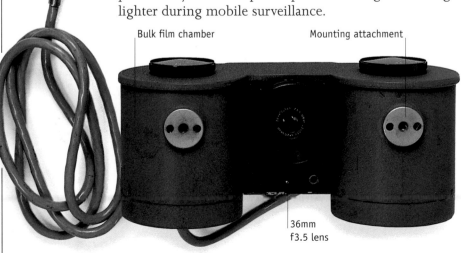

Bulk film chamber

Mounting attachment

36mm f3.5 lens

Side viewing port

Right angle view through side port

Normal view

Folding monocular

Members of the KGB used this folding monocular for secret visual surveillance. The monocular was jointed so that it could be unfolded (as shown here) and held in the fist for surreptitious surveillance without attracting attention.

Objective lens

Joint to fold monocular

Eyepiece

Miniature monocular

Shown here at its actual size, this monocular was so small that its KGB users were able to conceal it in an empty 35mm film container. The monocular had a magnification of 2.5 times. The finger ring enabled the spy to hold the instrument, when it was not in use, in one hand while not appearing to be concealing anything.

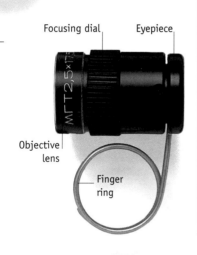

Focusing dial

Eyepiece

Objective lens

Finger ring

KGB Border Guards

The Border Guards of the Soviet Union formed a separate directorate within the KGB. This was a fully equipped military force, with its own artillery, armored fighting vehicles, and patrol boats. The force comprised 300,000 to 400,000 personnel at its peak. It fulfilled the dual role of keeping foreign intruders out of the Soviet Union and preventing any unauthorized exits. To help them with these duties, the Border Guards were issued with specialized visual surveillance equipment, such as the passive PN-1A night vision device (shown below left).

BORDER GUARD'S MEDAL (REVERSE)

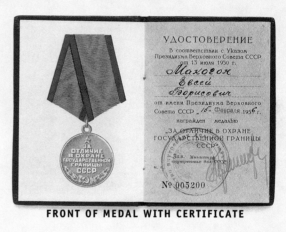

FRONT OF MEDAL WITH CERTIFICATE

Passive PN-1A night vision device

Modern passive night vision devices amplify existing light, such as starlight, so that the user can see in almost total darkness. This handheld device works almost silently, and it is extremely difficult for anyone to detect it being used.

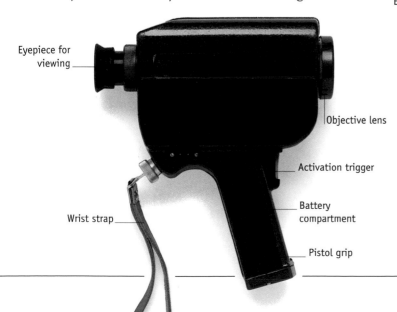

Eyepiece for viewing

Objective lens

Activation trigger

Wrist strap

Battery compartment

Pistol grip

Fiberscope

Derived from medical equipment, the fiberscope receives images through 7,500 strands of fiber-optic cable. It is used to conduct surveillance beneath a door, or through a small hole drilled in a wall.

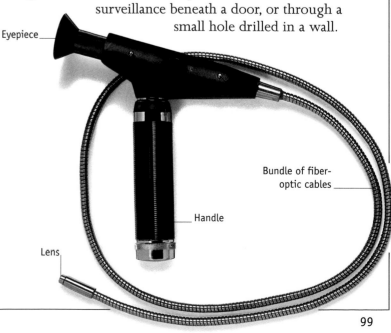

Eyepiece

Bundle of fiber-optic cables

Handle

Lens

Visual surveillance II

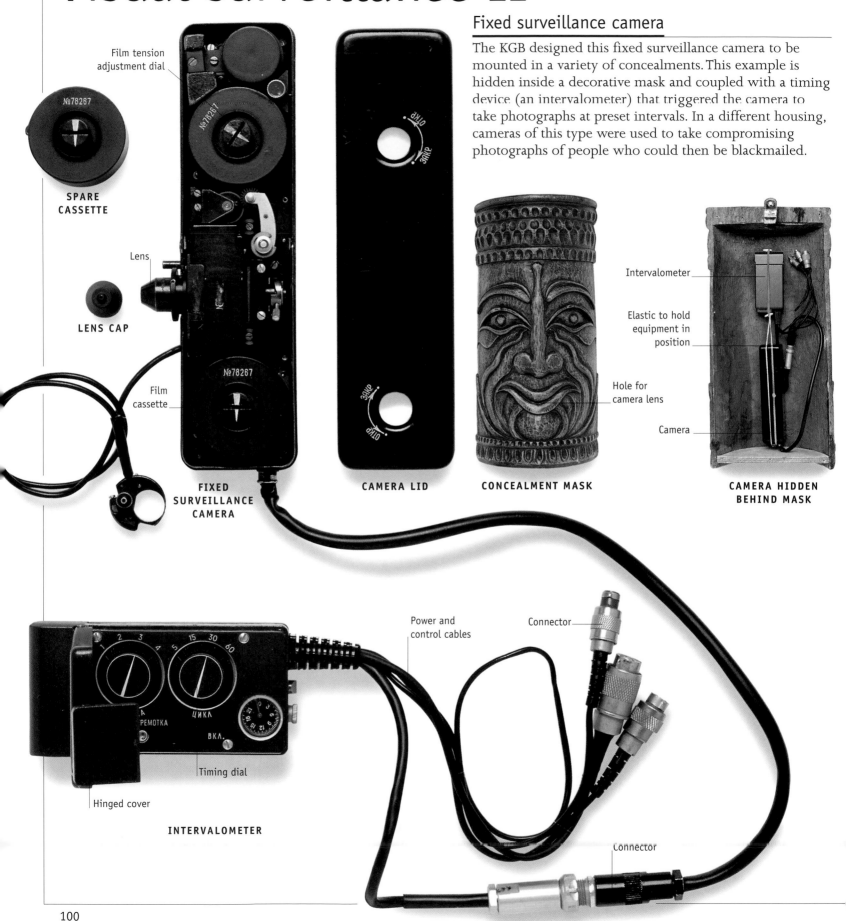

SPARE CASSETTE

Film tension adjustment dial

№78267

LENS CAP

Lens

Film cassette

№78267

FIXED SURVEILLANCE CAMERA

CAMERA LID

Fixed surveillance camera

The KGB designed this fixed surveillance camera to be mounted in a variety of concealments. This example is hidden inside a decorative mask and coupled with a timing device (an intervalometer) that triggered the camera to take photographs at preset intervals. In a different housing, cameras of this type were used to take compromising photographs of people who could then be blackmailed.

CONCEALMENT MASK

Hole for camera lens

CAMERA HIDDEN BEHIND MASK

Intervalometer

Elastic to hold equipment in position

Camera

Power and control cables

Connector

INTERVALOMETER

Timing dial

Hinged cover

Connector

Buttonhole movie camera

This device was used by the KGB during the 1960s and 1970s. It was the movie equivalent of the KGB's F21 camera (see p. 82), and like the F21 it filmed through a false button, which opened to reveal a lens. It used a film cassette that was mounted on the camera at right angles to the lens. The user turned the camera on and off with a switch hidden in a pocket. A battery pack, concealed in another pocket, powered the camera.

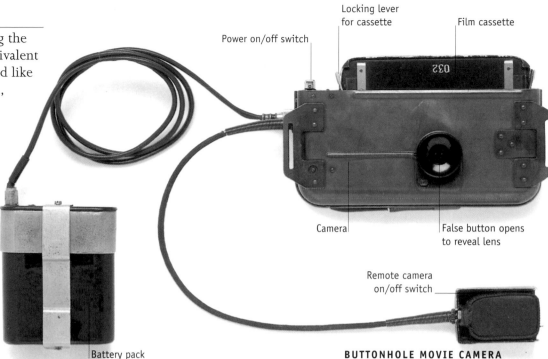

Power on/off switch
Locking lever for cassette
Film cassette
032
Camera
False button opens to reveal lens
Remote camera on/off switch

SPARE FILM CASSETTE

Battery pack

BUTTONHOLE MOVIE CAMERA

PC-87XP video surveillance camera

The world's smallest color CCD (charge-coupled device) surveillance camera is ⅞ in x 1 in (22 x 26 mm) and has a field of view of 45 degrees.

Lens

Circuit board (outer case has been removed from camera)

Microvideo surveillance cameras

The tiny PC-72 pinhole camera has a low-light ability that allows it to produce black-and-white images in the dark. The PC-53XP is the world's smallest color pinhole surveillance camera.

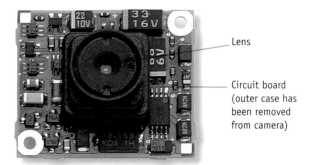

Pinhole lens

Pinhole lens

PC-72 PINHOLE CAMERA (ACTUAL SIZE)

PC-53XP PINHOLE CAMERA (ACTUAL SIZE)

Glasses surveillance system

For close-contact surveillance operations, these modified glasses conceal in the bridge a CCD (charge-coupled device) camera, with a pinhole opening for the lens. Images are transmitted through cables to a processing unit and a microvideo recorder hidden in the operator's clothing.

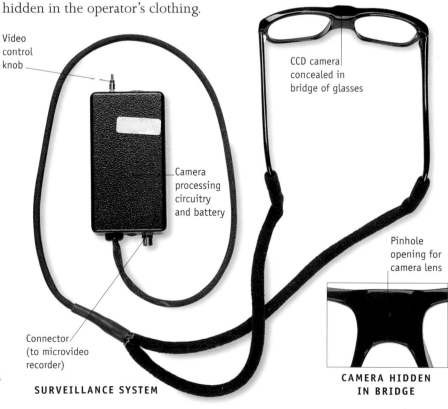

Video control knob

CCD camera concealed in bridge of glasses

Camera processing circuitry and battery

Pinhole opening for camera lens

Connector (to microvideo recorder)

SURVEILLANCE SYSTEM

CAMERA HIDDEN IN BRIDGE

Listening devices I

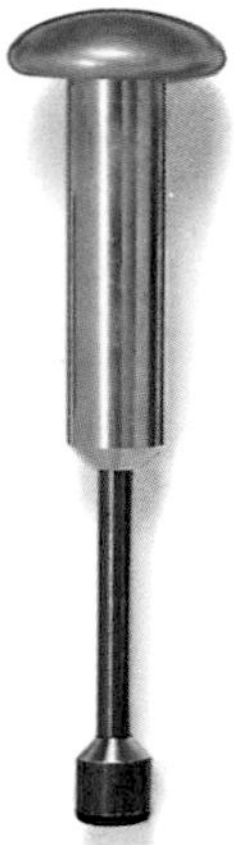

INTELLIGENCE AGENCIES make great efforts to develop devices that will enable them listen to their enemy's conversations. Tiny eavesdropping microphones are coupled with miniature amplifiers, transmitters, or tape recorders, while other devices intercept signals from telephone wires. Once created, the equipment must be planted. Specialized equipment, such as the fine-wire kit or the silent hammer, is available for installing microphone wires in walls. A transmitted signal from a listening device should be strong enough to be received at a listening post, but weak enough to make it difficult to locate using ordinary antibugging devices. Now listening devices exist that can store signals digitally and transmit them to a listening post at a predetermined time.

SILENT HAMMER

Miniaturized listening equipment

Many types of miniaturized equipment have been made for spying purposes: a bugged mouthpiece, ready for insertion in a public telephone; a multipurpose bug, small enough to hide almost anywhere; and a through-the-wall device, with a plastic tube that would not be discovered by metal detectors.

BUGGED MOUTHPIECE FOR PUBLIC TELEPHONE

Antenna

Microphone

Power cord

GENERAL PURPOSE MINIATURE OUTFIT

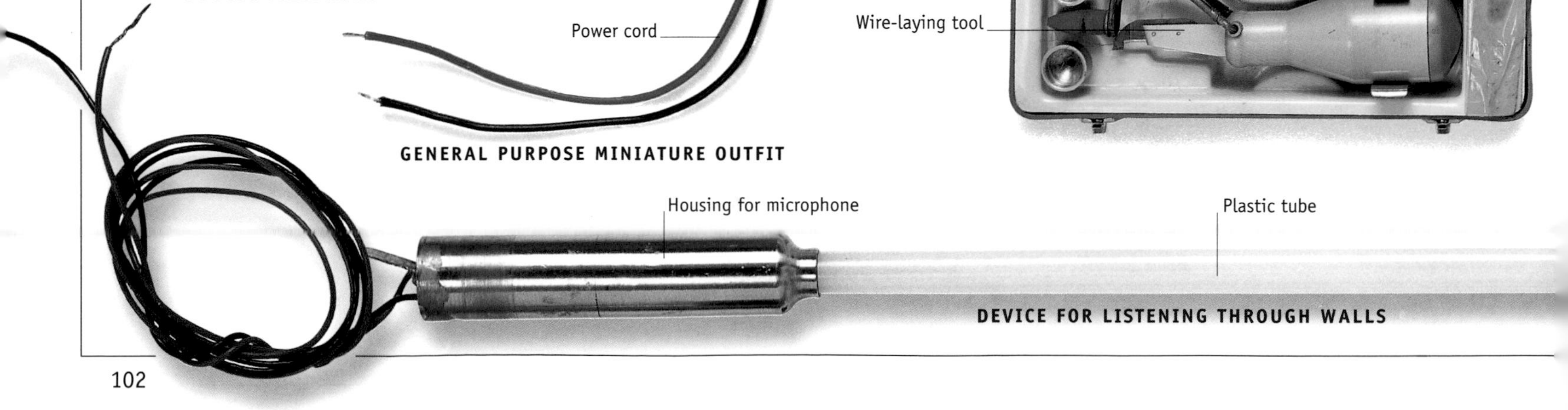

Fine-wire kit

To hide the wires when installing a bug, American technicians developed this wire-laying tool and its accessories. The tool is capable of forcing fine wires or cables into soft building materials or cracks. A monitoring circuit warns if the circuit is broken during installation.

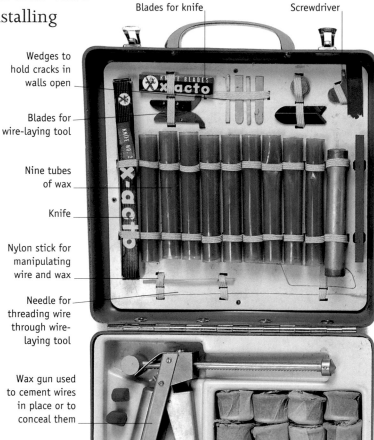

Blades for knife

Screwdriver

Wedges to hold cracks in walls open

Blades for wire-laying tool

Nine tubes of wax

Knife

Nylon stick for manipulating wire and wax

Needle for threading wire through wire-laying tool

Wax gun used to cement wires in place or to conceal them

Thirteen spools of very fine wire cable

Wire-laying tool

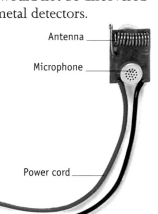

Housing for microphone

Plastic tube

DEVICE FOR LISTENING THROUGH WALLS

Pen and book devices

During the decades after World War II, an officer who wanted to record a meeting surreptitiously might be equipped with a listening device disguised as a pen. Another ingenious device fitted into the spine of a book, which could be placed in a room without causing suspicion. These were typical bugs of the 1960s – today's devices make use of digital technology and are much smaller.

Induction telephone tap

This device can be clamped onto any single-line external telephone cable and connected either to a transmitter or tape recorder. Both sides of the conversation can be received clearly. With no physical connection to the wire inside the telephone cable, the tap is difficult to detect.

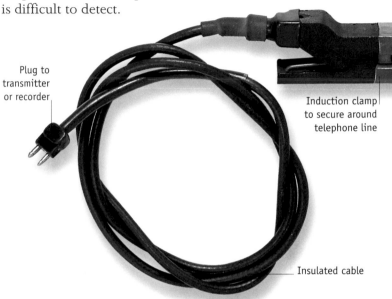

Plug to transmitter or recorder

Induction clamp to secure around telephone line

Insulated cable

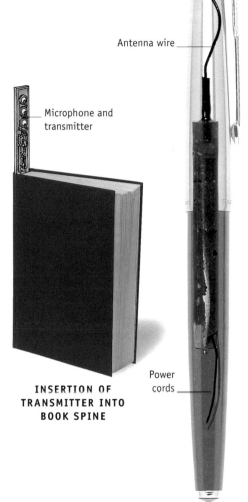

Antenna wire

Microphone and transmitter

INSERTION OF TRANSMITTER INTO BOOK SPINE

Power cords

MICROPHONE AND TRANSMITTER FOR BOOK SPINE

MICROPHONE AND TRANSMITTER CONCEALED IN PEN

Sound travels along tube to the microphone

Peter Wright

Peter Wright (1916–1995) was the British Security Service's first technical officer. He joined the Security Service (MI5) in 1955, having done scientific work throughout World War II. The early years of his career were spent inventing specialized listening devices for various operations. Wright also attempted to work out how the Soviet listening devices that were found in the buildings of the Western nations worked. The Thing (see p. 104) was a Soviet listening device found in the Great Seal of the United States embassy in Moscow. Wright was the first Westerner to understand fully how it worked. Having shown an aptitude for all aspects of counterintelligence work, Wright moved to D Branch, which was responsible for counterespionage, particularly Soviet activities in Britain. He eventually went on to become an Assistant Director of MI5.

MI5's chief scientist
Despite having no formal scientific education, Peter Wright was a brilliant innovator, constantly trying to find scientific solutions to MI5's problems.

Listening devices II

Small microphone

This compact, hard-wired microphone was designed and produced in the late 1980s by the OTS, the technical service of the Stasi (see p. 73). The microphone has a built-in preamplifier for greater sensitivity and is capable of picking up conversations over a large area.

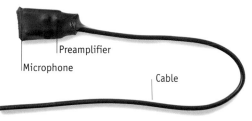

Preamplifier

Microphone

Cable

Pinhole drill kit

This KGB kit (codenamed Karn) was used for drilling pinhole openings in a wall for the installation of a hidden microphone. The technician drilled into the wall from another room, using progressively smaller bits.

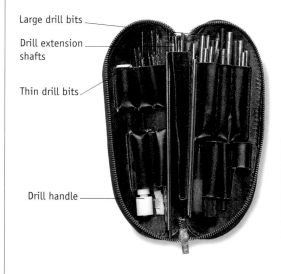

Large drill bits

Drill extension shafts

Thin drill bits

Drill handle

The "Thing"

In the early 1950s, a Soviet listening device was found in the US embassy in Moscow. It consisted of a cylindrical metal object that had been hidden inside the wooden carving of the Great Seal of the United States – the emblem on the wall over the ambassador's desk – which had been presented to him by the Soviets. The Great Seal features a bald eagle, beneath whose beak the Soviets had drilled holes to allow sound to reach the device.

Western experts were baffled as to how the device, which came to be known as the "Thing" (see below), worked, as it had neither batteries nor electrical circuits. Peter Wright (see p. 103) of Britain's MI5 (see

FRONT OF THE GREAT SEAL

p. 196) eventually discovered how it worked. MI5 then produced a copy of the device (codenamed SATYR) for use by both British and US intelligence.

The device came to world prominence when displayed at the United Nations by the US ambassador in May 1960.

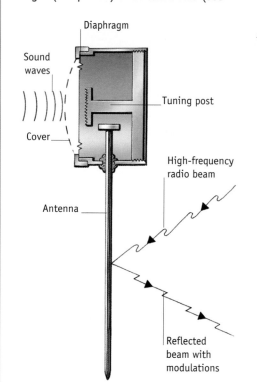

Diaphragm

Sound waves

Tuning post

Cover

High-frequency radio beam

Antenna

Reflected beam with modulations

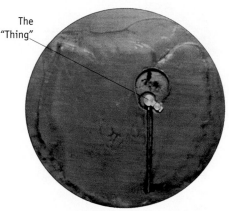

The "Thing"

BACK OF THE GREAT SEAL

How the "Thing" worked

A radio beam was aimed at the antenna from a source outside the building. A sound that struck the diaphragm caused variations in the amount of space (and the capacitance) between it and the tuning post plate. These variations altered the charge on the antenna, creating modulations in the reflected radio beam. These were picked up and interpreted by the receiver.

Belt-buckle microphone

Concealed in a belt buckle, this small microphone picks up the sound of conversation through a tiny hole. The device can be linked to either a transmitter or to a tape recorder, also hidden beneath the clothing of the wearer.

Microphone

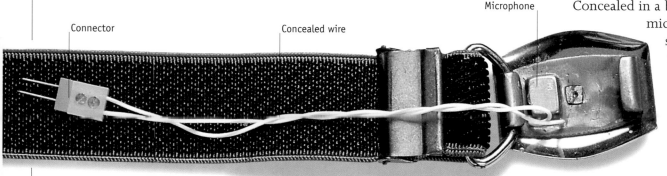

Connector

Concealed wire

Modified furniture components

Bugs can be hidden in fake furniture parts, which are then substituted for the original piece. Inside the components shown here, microphones and transmitters have been installed.

One is part of a desk, modified by Czech technicians. The other is a brace that can be adapted for any wooden furniture; it was used by an American audio-surveillance team.

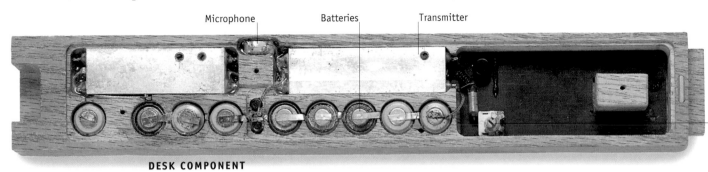

Microphone · Batteries · Transmitter

Tuning post to adjust frequency

DESK COMPONENT

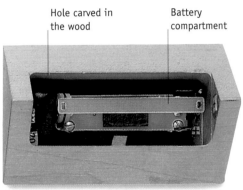

Hole carved in the wood · Battery compartment

MULTIPURPOSE WOODEN BRACE

Adaptor listening device

This microphone-and-transmitter set concealed in a British adaptor allows unlimited transmitting time without concern for battery drain, because its power is taken directly from the socket. A distinct disadvantage of this device is that the transmitter is permanently powered, which would enable a trained counterintelligence "sweep team" to detect it easily.

Transmitter

INTERIOR OF ADAPTOR

FRONT OF ADAPTOR

Turner detective dictograph outfit

This battery-driven device, used in World War I, provided the operator with a concealable transmitter, sound regulator, and earpiece for eavesdropping on suspects and conspirators up to 78 ft (24m) away. The dictograph was the first eavesdropping apparatus to be sold commercially, and its operators were warned not to use it for blackmailing and other illegitimate purposes.

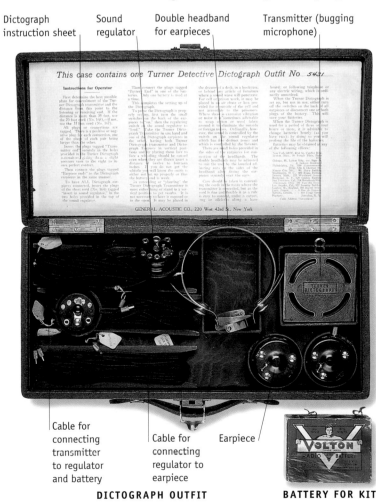

Dictograph instruction sheet · Sound regulator · Double headband for earpieces · Transmitter (bugging microphone)

Cable for connecting transmitter to regulator and battery · Cable for connecting regulator to earpiece · Earpiece

DICTOGRAPH OUTFIT

BATTERY FOR KIT

Listening devices III

Nagra SN recorder and pen

The Stasi (see p. 73) used this small reel-to-reel recorder for high-quality recordings. The recorder could be hidden in a person's clothing or concealed in a car or apartment. The agent was also supplied with two pens. One was functional and used on a daily basis so that colleagues became used to seeing it; the other looked identical but concealed a microphone. The agent would secretly switch the real pen for the microphone to record conversations.

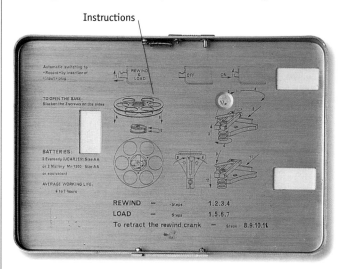

Instructions

LID WITH INSTRUCTIONS

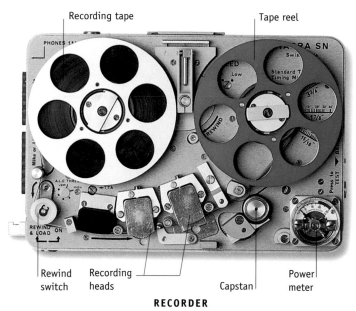

Recording tape · Tape reel

Rewind switch · Recording heads · Capstan · Power meter

RECORDER

MICROPHONE PEN

Drill bug in breeze block

This sophisticated eavesdropping device was planted inside the wall of a newly built Soviet embassy building. The remotely controlled apparatus incorporated a drill bit that bored a hole from the inside of the block toward the surface of the wall. At intervals, a microphone was inserted into the hole, also by remote control. When it could pick up sounds, the microphone was left in place. To avoid discovery, the listening device remained dormant when first built into the wall and was afterward activated by a radio signal.

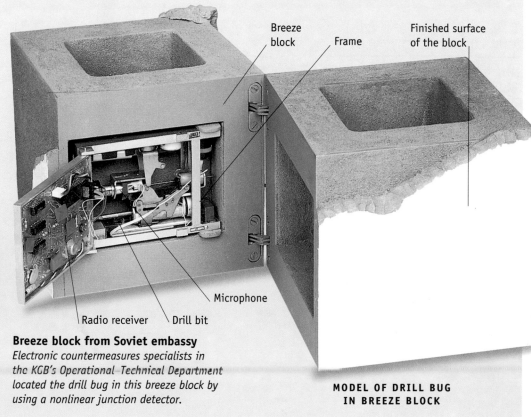

Breeze block · Frame · Finished surface of the block

Microphone

Radio receiver · Drill bit

Breeze block from Soviet embassy
Electronic countermeasures specialists in the KGB's Operational Technical Department located the drill bug in this breeze block by using a nonlinear junction detector.

MODEL OF DRILL BUG IN BREEZE BLOCK

Bug in a shoe

In the 1960s, the US ambassador working in Czechoslovakia ordered shoes from the United States that were shipped through regular mail. The Czech intelligence service (StB) intercepted the shoes and planted an eavesdropping system in the heel. The system was activated by the ambassador's valet when the ambassador attended secret meetings.

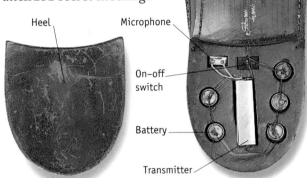

Heel

Microphone

On–off switch

Battery

Transmitter

Laser listening device

This laser device was connected to a series of microphones hidden in a part of a Soviet embassy building. Conversations were transmitted out on the laser's light beam to avoid detection.

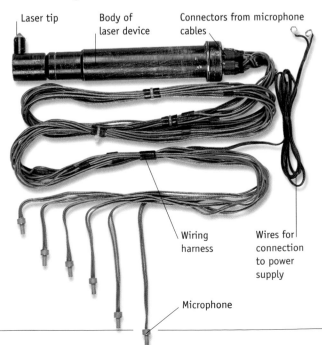

Laser tip

Body of laser device

Connectors from microphone cables

Wiring harness

Wires for connection to power supply

Microphone

Listening system

The remotely controlled or voice-actuated Z-5690 (microphone and transmitter) was hidden inside a piece of furniture. It transmitted a "masked" signal to the Lakmus receiver at a listening post located 492–984 ft (150–300 m) away.

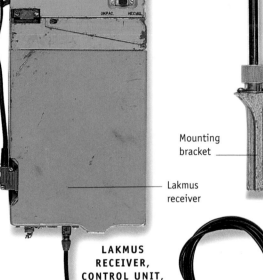

Antenna

Control unit

Mounting bracket

Lakmus receiver

LAKMUS RECEIVER, CONTROL UNIT, AND ANTENNA

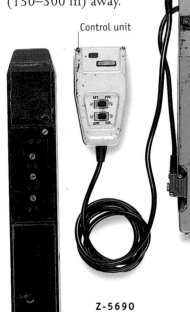

Z-5690 MICROPHONE AND TRANSMITTER

Rifle microphone

This highly directional US rifle microphone allowed a listening post monitor to pick up the conversations of a target while excluding other conversations and background noises. The microphone would be connected to a tape recorder and was commonly used to listen in on conversations of targets walking outdoors.

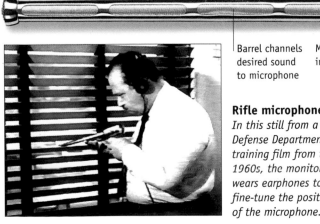

Barrel channels desired sound to microphone

Microphone in casing

Handgrip

Rifle microphone
In this still from a US Defense Department training film from the 1960s, the monitor wears earphones to fine-tune the position of the microphone.

Connector (for cable to tape recorder)

Receivers I

LISTENING IN ON AND RECORDING conversations is an important part of surveillance; its usual end product is a tape recording. Bugs (see p. 102 and p. 104) are hidden listening devices that either transmit a conversation to a listening post some distance away or are connected to a recording device. Shown here are two further categories of audio-surveillance gear. The first is the equipment used at the listening post: radio receivers, tape recorders, and other electronic hardware. The second consists of the devices carried on the person of a spy to record a conversation on the spot. These are mostly miniaturized microphones and tape recorders. The earpiece microphone shown above is a variation on this theme, designed for making recordings of telephone conversations.

EARPIECE MICROPHONE

Trigon and Peterson

Alexsandr Ogorodnik, codenamed Trigon, was a Soviet diplomatic service secretary who, in 1974, began to supply information to the CIA. In July 1977, the KGB arrested his CIA case officer in Moscow, Martha Peterson. She asked for a US embassy representative, who on arrival, as the KGB noted, wore two watches – one of them a disguised microphone. Peterson was expelled from the Soviet Union. Trigon, also arrested, committed suicide.

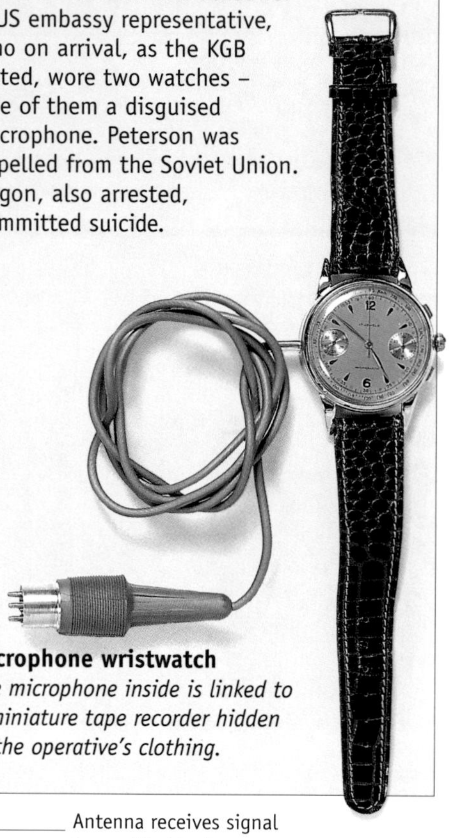

Microphone wristwatch
The microphone inside is linked to a miniature tape recorder hidden in the operative's clothing.

Listening post receiver

This is a portable American-made radio receiver, designed in the 1960s. Its function was to receive signals from bugs in a target location nearby. Its output was carried by cable, either to a tape recorder or to other types of monitoring equipment.

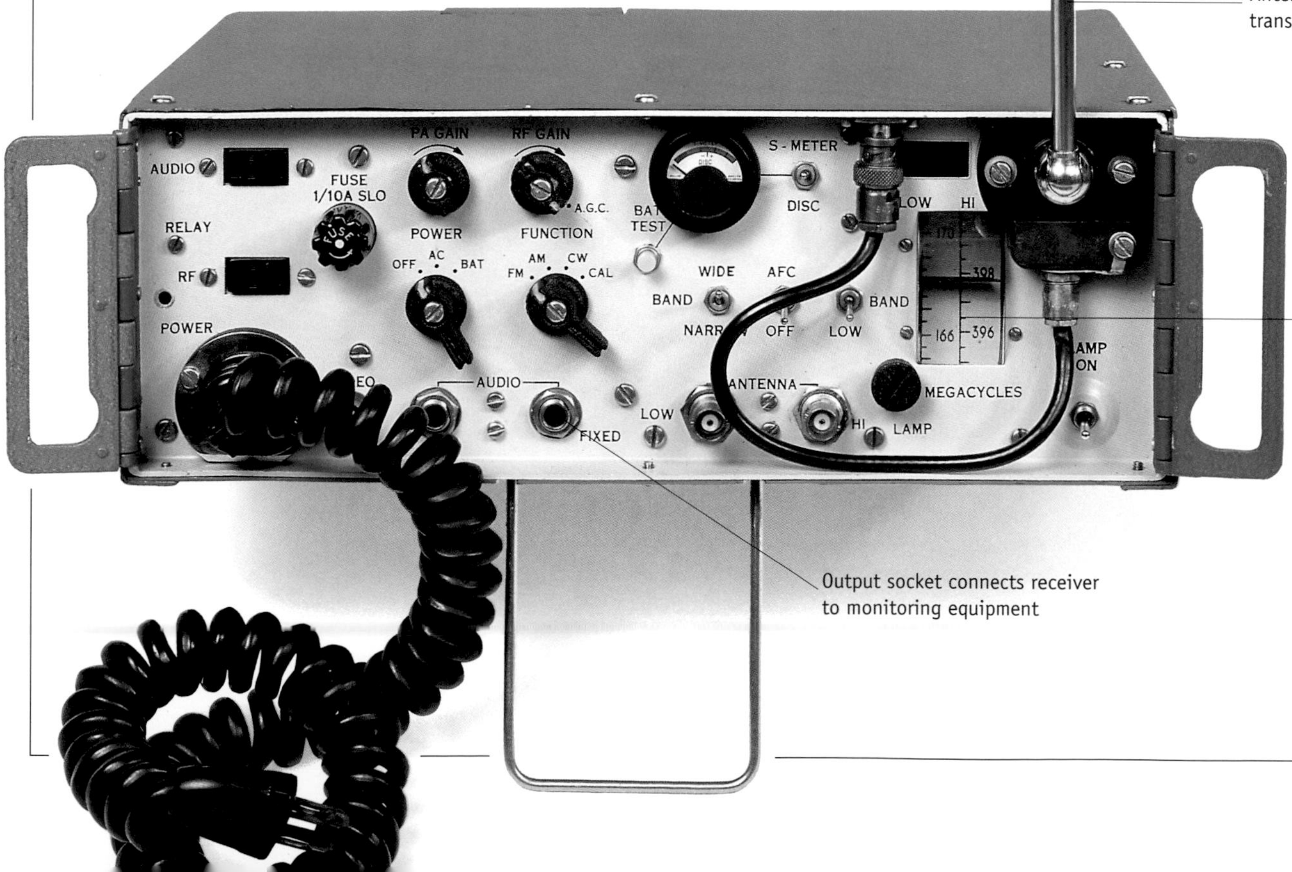

Antenna receives signal transmitted by bug

Band selector is adjusted to the frequency at which the bug transmits

Output socket connects receiver to monitoring equipment

Pen with microphone

The KGB had fountain pens made that contained small microphones, allowing spies to record conversations. The signal was passed to a small tape recorder or transmitter hidden in the spy's clothing. A selection of different styles of pens was available to match the different types of cover under which spies operated.

MICROPHONE IN POSITION

"Motel kit"

The contact microphone of this kit is firmly taped or glued to a wall or door and lets the user eavesdrop on a conversation in the next room. The microphone picks up sound waves and converts them into an electronic signal so that the conversation can be sent, via an amplifier that filters out some background noise, to a tape recorder or headphones.

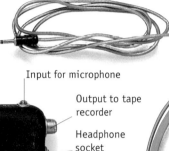

CONTACT MICROPHONE

Input for microphone

Output to tape recorder

Headphone socket

Sound filter

PHONES

NOTCH

GAIN

AMPLIFIER

Amplification control

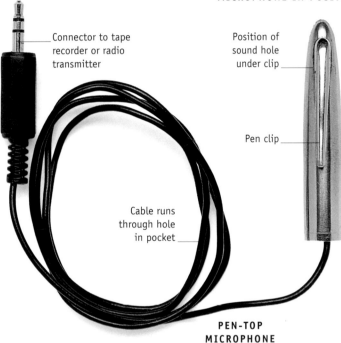

Connector to tape recorder or radio transmitter

Position of sound hole under clip

Pen clip

Cable runs through hole in pocket

PEN-TOP MICROPHONE

LEAD TO TAPE RECORDER

Earphones used for monitoring conversation

HEADPHONES

Kang Sheng and the Chinese secret service

During the 1920s, the fledgling Chinese Communist Party formed its own secret police force in imitation of the Soviet OGPU. The head of this organization (and its successor organization, the Social Affairs Department or SAD) was Kang Sheng (1898–1975). Kang lived the life of a gentleman scholar and calligrapher while holding secret police and Communist Party security posts for over 40 years. After the formation in 1949 of the communist government under Mao Zedong (Mao Tse-tung), Kang attained ever greater powers. He went on to reinforce his position by fostering the personality cult of Mao Zedong, and ensuring that Mao married Jian Qing, a former lover of Kang's. From his base in

Beijing, known as the Bamboo Garden, Kang monitored almost everything that happened in China. This included surveillance of the Communist Party itself. He used a wide variety of electronic eavesdropping devices to achieve this, and is even believed to have bugged the office of Mao Zedong himself.

In the 1970s, when Kang was growing weak with cancer, SAD began to extend its activities to other countries. The organization was able to earn hard currency by carrying out industrial espionage in foreign countries and helped enhance China's political influence by aiding such groups as the Shining Path in Peru and the PLO in the Middle East.

KANG SHENG

Receivers II

Mezon recording device

The Mezon, which dates from the 1970s, records sound on a wire 0.05 mm in diameter instead of a tape. The KGB issued accessories adapting it for a variety of operational situations. It could be controlled by a remote switch concealed in the pocket, and included an attachment for recording telephone conversations. Screw plugs ensure the accessories will not become unplugged while in use. A shoulder harness allows the Mezon to be worn under a jacket.

Pager with concealed recorder

A tiny tape recorder and microphone are concealed in this American-made fake pager from the 1990s. Worn on the user's belt, the machine is operated by an on/off switch at the bottom.

COMPLETE OUTFIT IN CASE

Microphone can be pinned beneath lapel to record conversations

Plug

MEZON MICROPHONE

Microphone plug

Credit-card-sized tape recorder

On/off switch

Casing of fake pager opens to enable cassette to be changed

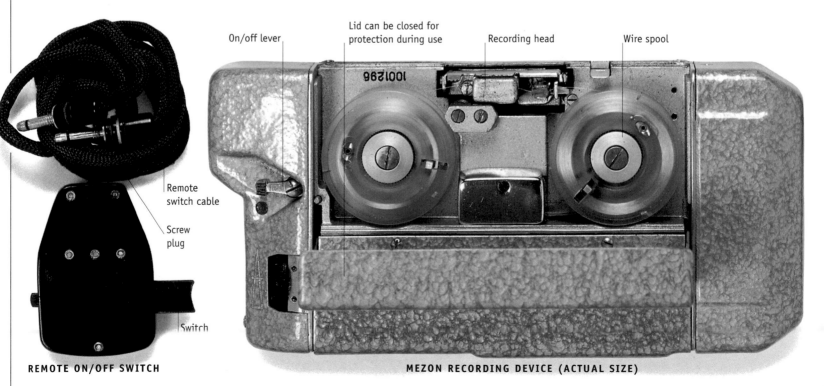

Remote switch cable

Screw plug

Switch

REMOTE ON/OFF SWITCH

On/off lever

Lid can be closed for protection during use

Recording head

Wire spool

1001296

MEZON RECORDING DEVICE (ACTUAL SIZE)

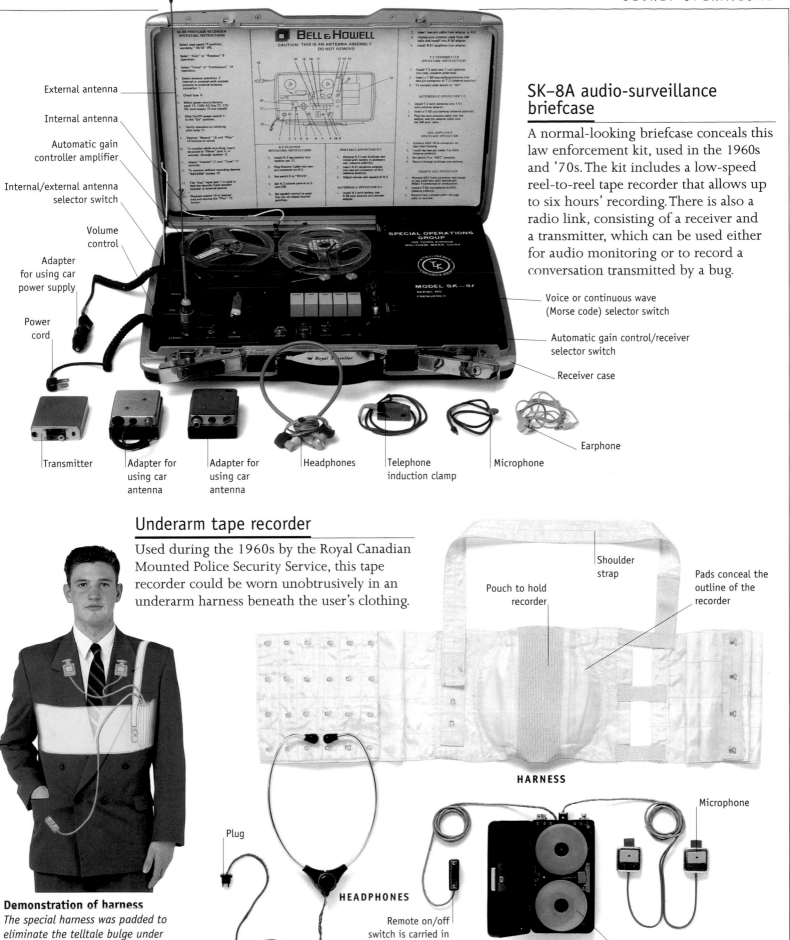

External antenna

Internal antenna

Automatic gain
controller amplifier

Internal/external antenna
selector switch

Volume
control

Adapter
for using car
power supply

Power
cord

Transmitter

Adapter for
using car
antenna

Adapter for
using car
antenna

Headphones

Telephone
induction clamp

Microphone

Earphone

SK–8A audio-surveillance briefcase

A normal-looking briefcase conceals this law enforcement kit, used in the 1960s and '70s. The kit includes a low-speed reel-to-reel tape recorder that allows up to six hours' recording. There is also a radio link, consisting of a receiver and a transmitter, which can be used either for audio monitoring or to record a conversation transmitted by a bug.

Voice or continuous wave
(Morse code) selector switch

Automatic gain control/receiver
selector switch

Receiver case

Underarm tape recorder

Used during the 1960s by the Royal Canadian Mounted Police Security Service, this tape recorder could be worn unobtrusively in an underarm harness beneath the user's clothing.

Shoulder
strap

Pads conceal the
outline of the
recorder

Pouch to hold
recorder

HARNESS

Microphone

Demonstration of harness
The special harness was padded to eliminate the telltale bulge under the arm made by the tape recorder.

Plug

HEADPHONES

Remote on/off
switch is carried in
jacket pocket

TAPE RECORDER

Tape reel

Surreptitious entry

INTELLIGENCE AGENCIES need personnel who can enter places secretly to gather intelligence. Such surreptitious entries require very careful planning, and are usually carried out by expert personnel using special equipment. Picking locks is avoided if possible, because it is difficult and unpredictable. It is better to steal a key and quickly duplicate it. If no key is available, it is possible to manufacture one with a special key-impression kit. Once burglar alarms have been neutralized, the final safeguard before entry is to ensure that the target location is unoccupied. One way to do this is to telephone: if anyone answers, the operation is canceled. Portable dialers used to be issued to entry specialists for making these calls.

Key-casting kit

It may be possible to steal a key temporarily, returning it to avoid detection. Its impression is instantly taken in clay and a quick copy made, using a low-melting-point metal alloy that melts in a candle flame. A permanent copy can be cut later.

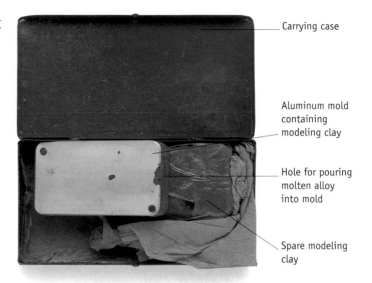

Carrying case

Aluminum mold containing modeling clay

Hole for pouring molten alloy into mold

Spare modeling clay

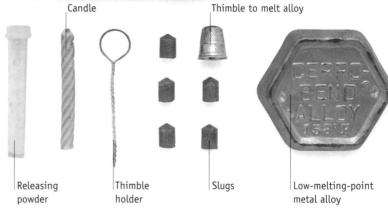

Candle

Thimble to melt alloy

Releasing powder

Thimble holder

Slugs

Low-melting-point metal alloy

Portable dialer

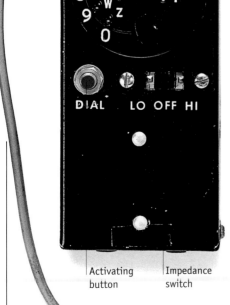

Plug

Rotary dial

Dialers of this type were used in the United States in the 1950s and 1960s. They were physically attached to the telephone line by means of a tapping device. This one has an impedance switch to adjust the resistance to that of the telephone circuit. Today, cellular telephones have made dialers obsolete.

DIAL   LO OFF HI

Activating button

Impedance switch

Plug for connection to tapping device

SPY PROFILE   G. Gordon Liddy

Formerly an FBI special agent and an attorney, G. Gordon Liddy (b.1930) was one of the central figures involved in the 1972 Watergate break-in. In the previous year he had taken part in the surreptitious entry at the home of the psychiatrist treating a prominent Vietnam War protester. Liddy used a Minox C camera and a measuring chain (see p. 88) to help identify the lock types and keyways at the apartment.

Key-pattern device

This device is used to copy keys of the old-fashioned type of locks known as warded locks. Thumbscrews hold the key in position while the feelers are adjusted to conform precisely to the pattern of the teeth. Once made, the pattern can be copied.

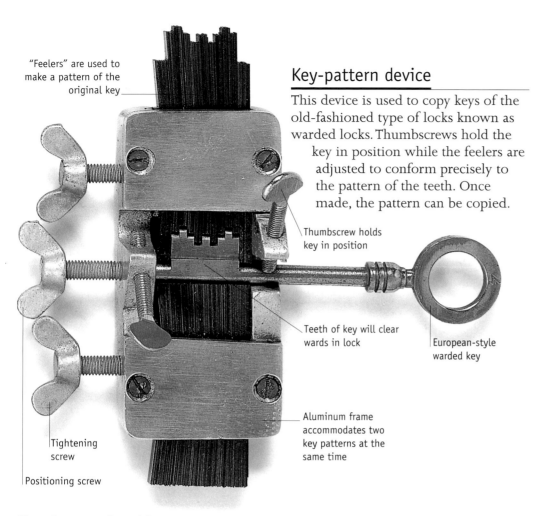

"Feelers" are used to make a pattern of the original key

Thumbscrew holds key in position

Teeth of key will clear wards in lock

European-style warded key

Tightening screw

Positioning screw

Aluminum frame accommodates two key patterns at the same time

Office of Technical Service

The Office of Technical Service (OTS) is the part of the CIA that specializes in technical operations. Among its members are experts in picking locks, surreptitious entry, clandestine photography, and audio surveillance. The OTS devises disguises, concealments, and dead drop containers, and is also responsible for secret writing and microdots. Today, the organization is part of the CIA's Deputy Directorate of Science and Technology.

EMBLEM OF THE OTS

Key-impression kit

This works for a variety of different types of keys. A specially prepared impression tool inserts a key blank into the lock and picks up marks from the mechanism. An expert can interpret these marks and hand-file the key.

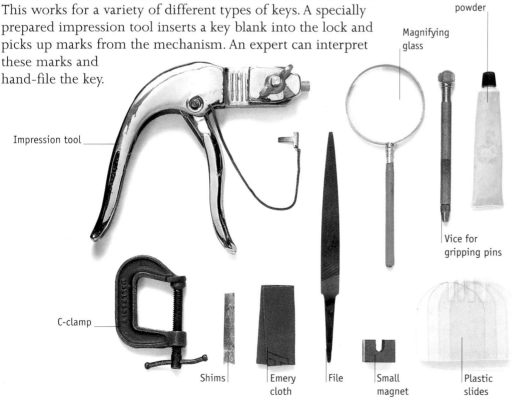

Impression tool

Magnifying glass

Graphite powder

Vice for gripping pins

C-clamp

Shims

Emery cloth

File

Small magnet

Plastic slides

Burglar alarm evasion kit

Old alarms used a wire-borne signal; if this was broken, the alarm was raised. With this kit, agents could intercept the signal, tamper with the wire, and prevent a break-in from being detected.

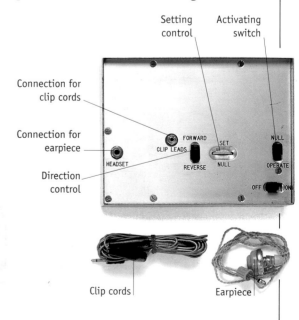

Setting control

Activating switch

Connection for clip cords

Connection for earpiece

Direction control

FORWARD

CLIP LEADS

HEADSET

REVERSE

SET

NULL

NULL

NULL

OPERATE

OFF   ON

Clip cords

Earpiece

Lockpicks

INTELLIGENCE SERVICES OFTEN NEED to pick locks to gain access to secret material. Lockpicking devices, and kits with small tools, are available for opening most types of lock used worldwide. To open a pin-tumbler lock, a pick tool and a tension wrench are inserted and manipulated to simulate the results that would be obtained by using the key. The spy may have to try several tools before the lock will open. For faster results, a lockpicking "gun" or electric lock-opening device may be used. Lockpicking is a specialized branch of intelligence work, but it uses the same tools as commercial locksmiths.

Tubular lockpick

This device opens the type of high-security locks that use a tubular key. The lockpick is inserted and adjusted within the

Pocket lockpicking kit

This assortment of picks and tension tools is small enough to slip into a pocket and can be used by an expert to open most pin-tumbler type locks – the most common type of lock, used all around the world.

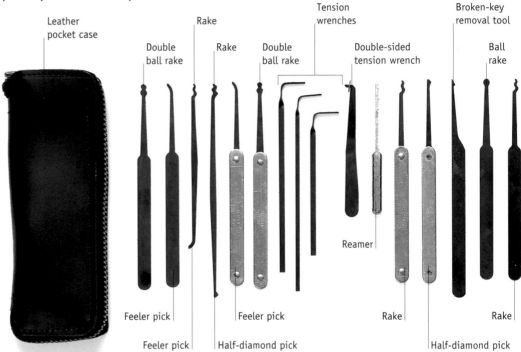

Leather pocket case

Rake

Double ball rake

Rake

Double ball rake

Tension wrenches

Double-sided tension wrench

Reamer

Broken-key removal tool

Ball rake

Feeler pick

Feeler pick

Rake

Rake

Feeler pick

Half-diamond pick

Half-diamond pick

The Watergate break-in

The 1972 Watergate break-in was part of an illegal plot in support of the reelection of US President Richard Nixon. The headquarters of Nixon's rival, the Democratic candidate George McGovern, were located in the Watergate office complex in Washington, DC. A White House aide, E. Howard Hunt, Jr., recruited a group of Cuban exiles to break into the building. In their first entry, the Cuban team photographed various documents and installed a number of listening devices.

A second entry was undertaken to gather more information and reposition one of the listening devices. But the burglars were inexperienced lockpickers and this entry was discovered by a night watchman – tape holding a door lock open had been left visible from the outside.

The police were called, and they arrested the Cubans. Later, the two men responsible for planning the operation, Hunt and G. Gordon Liddy (see p. 112), were also arrested, tried, and convicted. The Watergate scandal led to the resignation of President Nixon.

The Watergate burglars
The men recruited to carry out the burglary in the Watergate office complex were exiles from Fidel Castro's communist regime in Cuba.

E. Howard Hunt, Jr.
A former CIA officer, Hunt recruited the Watergate entry team using his contacts in the Cuban exile community.

Surreptitious entry kit

An entry specialist may not know what locks will be found once inside a target location. So a tool kit is needed that is capable of opening as many different types of locks as possible. The selection of tools will be influenced by the personal preferences and skills of the expert lock opener, also taking into account the types of lock likely to be found in the country of the operation.

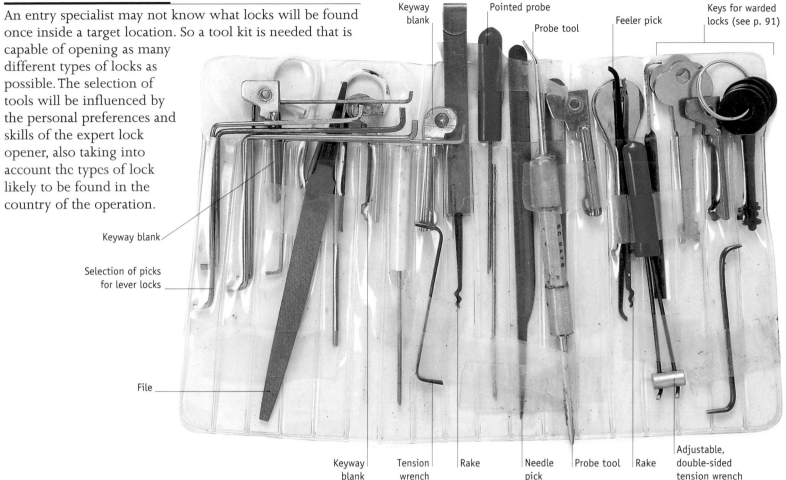

Keyway blank

Pointed probe

Probe tool

Feeler pick

Keys for warded locks (see p. 91)

Keyway blank

Selection of picks for lever locks

File

Keyway blank

Tension wrench

Rake

Needle pick

Probe tool

Rake

Adjustable, double-sided tension wrench

Lockpick gun

This device can quickly open most pin-tumbler locks. Squeezing the trigger causes the pick to strike the pins that work the lock mechanism. A tension wrench is used to turn the lock cylinder when the pins are properly aligned.

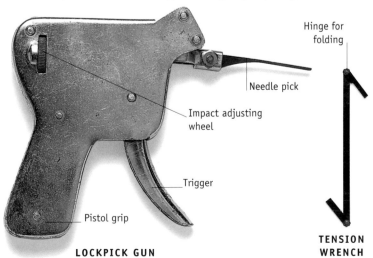

Hinge for folding

Needle pick

Impact adjusting wheel

Trigger

Pistol grip

LOCKPICK GUN

TENSION WRENCH

Electric lock-opening device

The user selects a pick, inserts one end in the device and the other in the lock, then switches the device on. This bounces the pins in the lock until they are aligned, so the lock opens. No additional tool is needed to turn the lock cylinder.

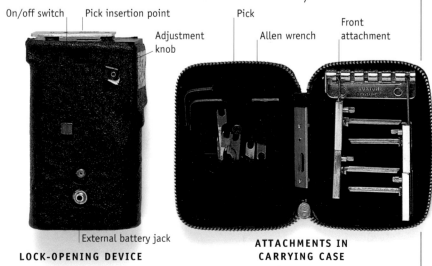

On/off switch

Pick insertion point

Adjustment knob

Pick

Allen wrench

Front attachment

External battery jack

LOCK-OPENING DEVICE

ATTACHMENTS IN CARRYING CASE

Escape and evasion

EVERYDAY ITEMS SUCH AS hairbrushes, pens, and coins made ideal concealments for World War II escape and evasion aids. These aids included small compasses, maps, and knife blades. They were developed to assist prisoners of war in escape attempts and to help spies and airmen operating in enemy territory to evade capture. The concealments hid these useful items, even if the enemy noticed the outer casing.

Hairbrush with secret compartment

This hairbrush concealed vital escape and evasion aids. To open it, a section of the brush was lifted by pulling on a specific row of bristles.

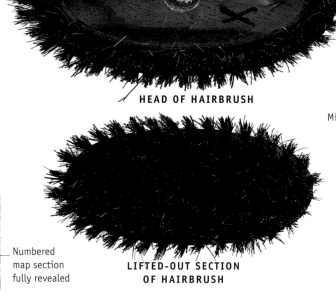

HEAD OF HAIRBRUSH

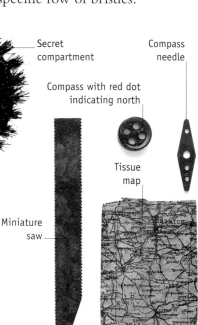

Secret compartment

Compass needle

Compass with red dot indicating north

Tissue map

Miniature saw

ITEMS CONTAINED IN HAIRBRUSH

LIFTED-OUT SECTION OF HAIRBRUSH

Playing cards with concealed map sections

The top layer of these cards was soaked off to reveal numbered map sections. The assembled sections formed a master from which escape maps were copied.

Card surface peeled back to reveal map

Numbered map section fully revealed

The man who was "Q"

Charles Fraser-Smith (1904-92) worked for British intelligence during World War II. His task was to supply the clandestine services with "Q" gadgets – named after Q-ships, the warships in World War I that had been disguised as ordinary merchant navy ships.

Many of his Q gadgets were concealments disguised as everyday objects. Others were items of equipment that had been miniaturized or adapted for concealment. Fraser-Smith employed over 300 companies, all of which were sworn to secrecy, to make his devices.

Charles Fraser-Smith
Fraser-Smith was the inspiration for the character "Q" in Ian Fleming's James Bond novels.

Pen with concealed map and compass

Secret chambers in this pen were secured with end caps attached by reverse threads. Any attempt to unscrew the caps in the normal (counterclockwise) direction merely tightened them.

Rolled-up map hidden inside barrel

Reverse-thread cap

Reverse-thread cap

Magnetized pen clip (standby compass)

Compass

Pipe with concealments

This pipe could be smoked without damaging the concealed items. The bowl had an asbestos lining inside which a map could be hidden without danger of catching fire.

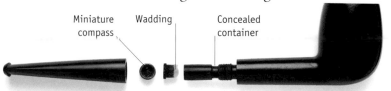

Miniature compass

Wadding

Concealed container

Escape from Colditz Castle

Colditz Castle, a historic fortress in eastern Germany, became a prison for high-risk Allied prisoners of war during World War II. Many of these had already escaped or tried to escape from German captivity, and by concentrating them at Colditz, the Germans unwittingly created what became known as the Colditz Escape Academy. A group of prisoners coordinated escape attempts and made, by hand, a range of items, such as clothes and forged documents, to supplement escape aids that were smuggled into Colditz from Britain. In January 1942, an escape by British Lieutenant Airey Neave and Dutch Lieutenant Toni Luteyn involved disguising themselves first as German officers and then as Dutch workers. On his return to England, Neave became an adviser to MI9, an office in British intelligence that was involved in helping prisoners of war to escape.

Airey Neave
After his Colditz escape, Neave became an adviser on escape aids in order to assist other prisoners.

Colditz Castle
Allied prisoners of war who had tried to escape from other camps were often brought to Colditz.

Hidden blades

Small blades were hidden in objects that were unlikely to be confiscated from prisoners. A coin with a hidden blade, mixed with other pocket change, might easily be overlooked by the enemy. Shoe-heel blades could be used by prisoners whose hands were tied to their feet and behind their back.

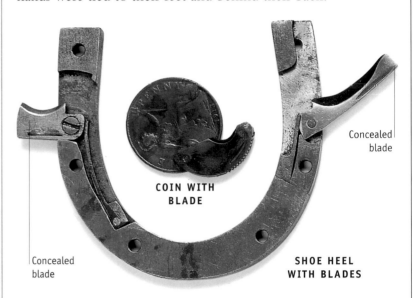

Concealed blade

COIN WITH BLADE

Concealed blade

Concealed blade

SHOE HEEL WITH BLADES

Rectal tool kit

Escape tools and ways of concealing them continued to be needed in the years after World War II. This CIA kit from the 1960s was designed for rectal concealment if a search was anticipated.

Plastic case for rectal concealment

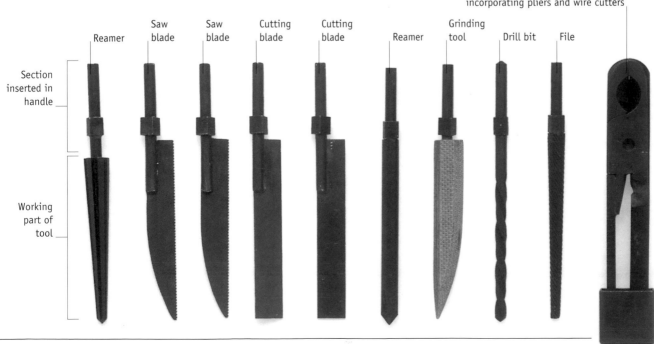

Section inserted in handle

Working part of tool

Reamer
Saw blade
Saw blade
Cutting blade
Cutting blade
Reamer
Grinding tool
Drill bit
File
Handle to which tools were attached, incorporating pliers and wire cutters

Sabotage I

ACTS OF SABOTAGE aim to disable part of an enemy's infrastructure. Sabotage operations are usually carried out for one of two reasons: to damage the economies of potentially hostile countries during peacetime, or to disrupt an enemy's industry and communications during wartime. Wartime attacks not only cause destruction, but also force the enemy to divert troops from the front line to guard vulnerable areas. During World War II, both the SOE (see p. 30) and the OSS (see p. 32) were engaged in sabotage in cooperation with resistance groups. These operations often entailed the use of specialized explosives and fuses, such as bombs disguised as pieces of coal.

Grenades

Unlike most grenades, which have time-delay fuses, these grenades explode on impact, making them effective against hard-to-hit moving targets. (The name "gammon" is a British word for ham.)

Secondary arming mechanism and fuse

Primary safety ring

Percussion fuse inside screw cap

BEANO GRENADE

Black cloth skirt

GAMMON GRENADE

Tree spigot mortar

This unusual device was meant for use against both vehicles and individuals. A trip wire set off the mortar, which hurled a shell filled with high explosives in the direction of the target. The shell exploded on impact.

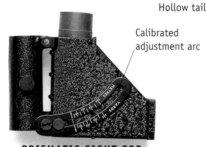

PRISMATIC SIGHT FOR SPIGOT MORTAR

Calibrated adjustment arc

RAIN SHIELD FOR SPIGOT MORTAR

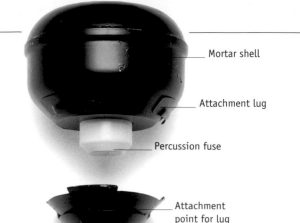

Mortar shell

Attachment lug

Percussion fuse

Attachment point for lug

Propellant container

Hollow tail

Firing pin

Spigot

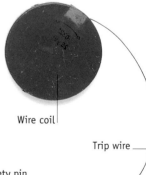

Mounting the spigot
The mortar was set up by screwing the spigot into a tree trunk, then pointing it in the direction the enemy was to approach from. The hollow tail was fitted over the spigot, and the shell was placed in a funnel at the the top of the hollow tail.

Wire coil

Trip wire

Clip to secure hollow tail

Safety pin

Mounting handle

Universal joint

Clamping plate

Mounting screw

MORTAR

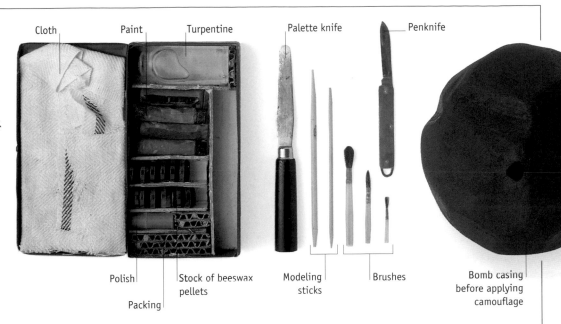

Cloth   Paint   Turpentine   Palette knife   Penknife

Polish   Stock of beeswax pellets   Modeling sticks   Brushes   Bomb casing before applying camouflage

Packing

Explosive coal kit

Kits for disguising explosives as pieces of coal were issued to some OSS sabotage teams during World War II. These kits contained all that was needed to make the outer case of the bomb resemble the type of coal used in the operational area. The case was filled with explosive and placed in an enemy coal dump – these were often inadequately guarded. The bomb would detonate when burned in a locomotive's furnace or a factory boiler.

Codename Pastorius

In 1942, eight German saboteurs were put ashore from two submarines on the American coast. Their mission was codenamed Pastorius. Four landed in Florida and four in Long Island, New York. The Coast Guard spotted the New York group and alerted the FBI, who searched the beach and found explosives and fuses. One saboteur, Georg Dasch, surrendered to the FBI. He provided information that resulted in the arrest of the others. Six of the saboteurs were sentenced to death and executed. Dasch and one other were given jail sentences and sent home after the war.

Georg Dasch
In order to save himself from execution, Dasch provided information that led to the arrest of his fellow saboteurs.

Pencil fuses

These World War II devices would detonate an explosive after a set time, giving a saboteur time to get away. The saboteur pulled off a safety strip and squeezed the appropriate point on the side of a copper crush tube, which broke an ampoule of acid inside. The acid corroded a wire to release a striker that struck a percussion cap and a detonator. Colored bands indicated the length of time delay for each fuse.

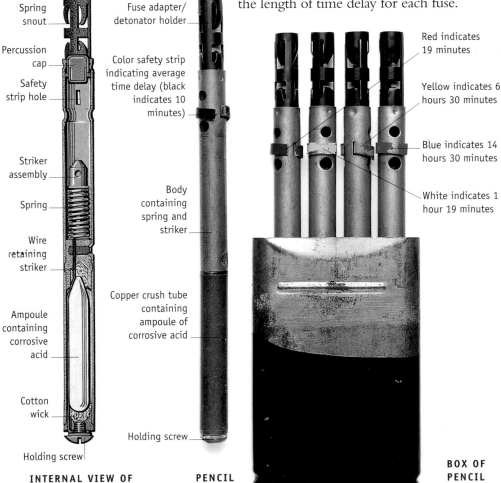

Spring snout
Percussion cap
Safety strip hole
Striker assembly
Spring
Wire retaining striker
Ampoule containing corrosive acid
Cotton wick
Holding screw

Fuse adapter/ detonator holder
Color safety strip indicating average time delay (black indicates 10 minutes)
Body containing spring and striker
Copper crush tube containing ampoule of corrosive acid
Holding screw

Red indicates 19 minutes
Yellow indicates 6 hours 30 minutes
Blue indicates 14 hours 30 minutes
White indicates 1 hour 19 minutes

INTERNAL VIEW OF A PENCIL FUSE

PENCIL FUSE

BOX OF PENCIL FUSES

Sabotage II

Guard dog tranquillizers

An agent can silence guard dogs by feeding them ground beef mixed with tranquillizer capsules. The animals are unharmed but may sleep for several hours. The typical dose for an average-sized dog is four capsules, but more may be necessary for particularly ferocious animals. When the agent has finished, a dose of antidote can be given to speed the dog's recovery.

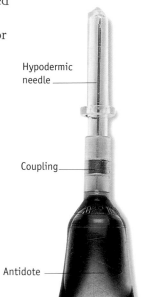

Hypodermic needle

Coupling

Antidote

SINGLE DOSE OF ANTIDOTE

TRANQUILLIZER CAPSULES

Operation Mongoose

In 1961, Attorney General Robert Kennedy and the Whitehouse directed the CIA to eliminate Cuban leader Fidel Castro and his government. The plan was code-named Operation Mongoose. Despite Kennedy's personal involvement at all levels, the plan did not result in Castro's overthrow. Faced with the Cuban missile crisis in October 1962, Kennedy instructed that the operations against Cuba be stopped in the fear that the Soviets might use them as an excuse to justify installing nuclear weapons in Cuba.

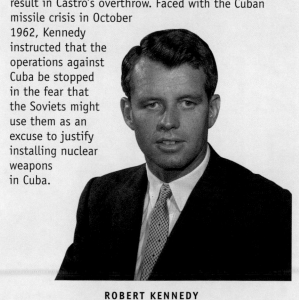

ROBERT KENNEDY

Sabotage booklet

The CIA produced pictorial sabotage booklets, to eliminate the language barrier. The pages below show how to assemble and plant a fog signal, a device used to set off a charge of high explosives for the demolition of trains. The device is activated by the wheels of the train passing over it.

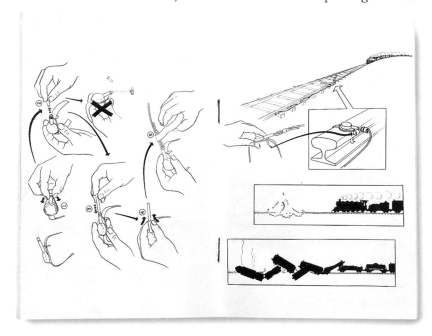

Thirty-day clockwork

This waterproof 30-day clockwork incorporates a time-delay mechanism that can be used to detonate various types of explosive. The clockwork could be set to delay the explosion for any period between 1 hour and 30 days.

Time lock is kept on after setting until activation is desired

Activating screw

Time adjustment sets desired time-delay in days and hours

Hours read-out

Days read-out

TIME-DELAY MECHANISM

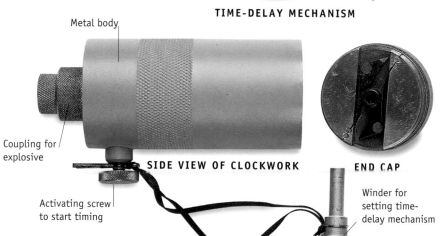

Metal body

Coupling for explosive

SIDE VIEW OF CLOCKWORK

END CAP

Activating screw to start timing

Winder for setting time-delay mechanism

Hand-emplaced expendable jammer

The expendable jammer is designed to deny an enemy the use of radio communication equipment. It transmits within a broad range of frequencies for a preset period of time within an operational area. At the end of the period, the jammer self-destructs so that the enemy will not be able to use the radio if found.

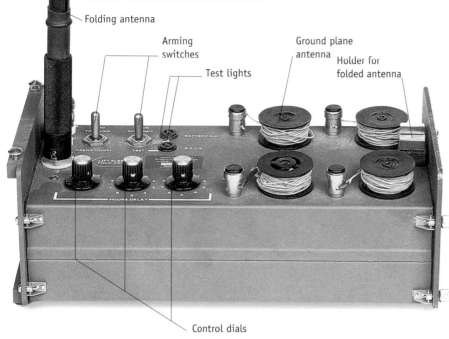

Folding antenna

Arming switches

Test lights

Ground plane antenna

Holder for folded antenna

Control dials

Shaped charge

Capable of punching a hole through 7–10 in (18–25 cm) of steel, this plastic demolition charge contains 4 oz (100 g) of the explosive RDX. The charge is used to pierce shafts, bearings, gear boxes, and other vital parts of machinery. This type of charge is used to disable rather than destroy machines.

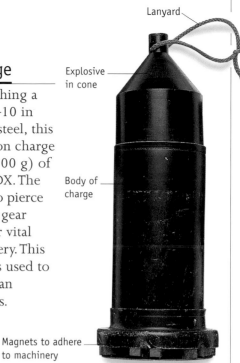

Lanyard

Explosive in cone

Body of charge

Magnets to adhere to machinery

Antidisturbance mine

This highly sensitive antidisturbance mine will, when properly loaded and activated, explode if moved in any direction or vibrated. It has a timing device that detonates it after 10–13 minutes and cannot be deactivated once the timer has started. The mine is waterproof up to a depth of 20 ft (6 m).

Safety ring

Metal body

Locking screw

Boat mine

Despite its resemblance to an aerial bomb, this buoyant boat mine, made by the CIA, has a hydrodynamic shape that allows it always to turn itself in the direction of the oncoming water current. In use, the boat mine is moored beneath the surface in a river, channel, or harbor, where it "waits" as its sensors count passing metal targets. After a preset number of targets have been detected, the mine explodes.

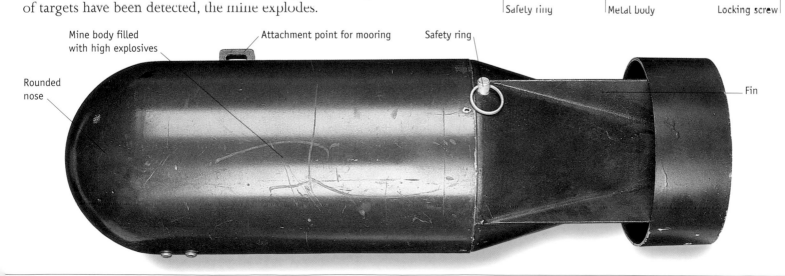

Mine body filled with high explosives

Attachment point for mooring

Safety ring

Rounded nose

Fin

Amphibious sabotage

THE CHIEF GOALS of amphibious sabotage are to destroy enemy ships and attack coastal defenses. Raiding parties, well trained and equipped with special craft, secretly enter enemy harbors and other waters to undertake perilous operations. During World War II, a number of innovations in tactics and equipment contributed to the effectiveness of amphibious raids. Canoes and submersible craft, such as the Sleeping Beauty, were developed for use in enemy harbors. And new types of explosive devices, such as limpet mines, were invented for use under water.

Acetone time-delay fuse

Limpet mines were attached magnetically to the hulls of ships. Many had acetone fuses that would detonate the mines after an interval indicated by the color of an acetone ampoule. The color represented the concentration of the acetone, which ate through a celluloid disk, releasing a firing pin and detonating the mine. The fuse was set manually by twisting an actuating screw, which crushed the ampoule and released the acetone.

Operation Frankton

During World War II, the Allied navies tried to blockade German-held France. However, German ships continued to call at the French harbors. In 1942, a party of British Royal Marines attacked German vessels in the French harbor of Bordeaux. The raiders were taken by submarine to a river estuary nearby, and then set off by canoe to the target. Only two of the five canoes reached Bordeaux. During the night the raiders attached sixteen limpet mines to six German ships, sinking four and damaging the other two ships. Only two of the 10 saboteurs survived and returned safely to Britain.

Royal Marine saboteurs
Major H. G. "Blondie" Hasler (in front) and Corporal W. E. Sparks were the only survivors of the successful raid on Bordeaux harbor.

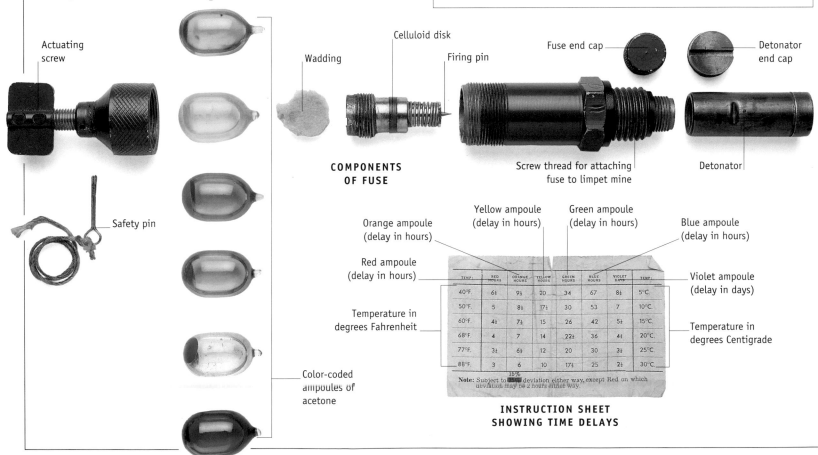

Actuating screw

Wadding

Celluloid disk

Firing pin

Fuse end cap

Detonator end cap

Safety pin

COMPONENTS OF FUSE

Screw thread for attaching fuse to limpet mine

Detonator

Color-coded ampoules of acetone

Orange ampoule (delay in hours)

Yellow ampoule (delay in hours)

Green ampoule (delay in hours)

Blue ampoule (delay in hours)

Red ampoule (delay in hours)

Violet ampoule (delay in days)

Temperature in degrees Fahrenheit

Temperature in degrees Centigrade

TEMP.	RED HOURS	ORANGE HOURS	YELLOW HOURS	GREEN HOURS	BLUE HOURS	VIOLET DAYS	TEMP.
40°F.	6½	9½	20	34	67	8½	5°C.
50°F.	5	8½	17½	30	53	7	10°C.
60°F.	4½	7½	15	26	42	5½	15°C.
68°F.	4	7	14	22½	36	4½	20°C.
77°F.	3½	6½	12	20	30	3½	25°C.
88°F.	3	6	10	17½	25	2½	30°C.

Note: Subject to 15% deviation either way, except Red on which deviation may be 2 hours either way.

INSTRUCTION SHEET SHOWING TIME DELAYS

Limpet mine and placing rod

A limpet mine was a waterproof bomb designed to sink or damage ships. The mine was positioned by means of an extendible placing rod, and held by magnets to the ship's steel hull. An acetone time-delay fuse was used to detonate the mine. The limpet mine could blow a hole of up to 25 sq ft (2.3 sq m) in a ship's hull.

Placing a limpet mine
Saboteurs had to approach the target ship silently, usually in a small boat. They attached the mine carefully, using an extendible placing rod 5 ft (1.5 m) below the waterline.

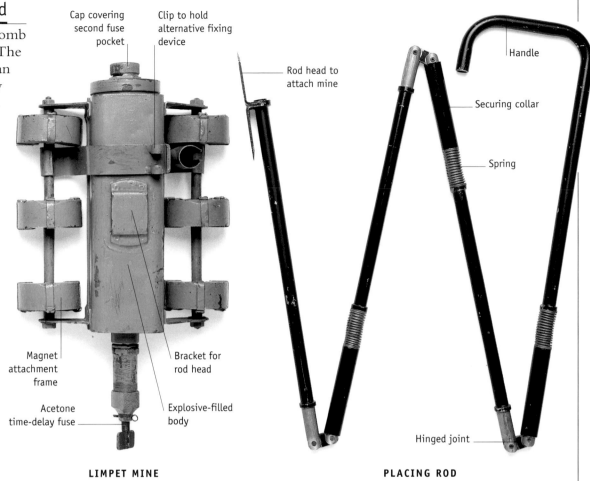

Cap covering second fuse pocket

Clip to hold alternative fixing device

Rod head to attach mine

Handle

Securing collar

Spring

Magnet attachment frame

Bracket for rod head

Acetone time-delay fuse

Explosive-filled body

Hinged joint

LIMPET MINE

PLACING ROD

Operation Rimau: the raid on Singapore Harbor

The Japanese took the island of Singapore from the British in 1942. Later that year, raiders belonging to the Allied Intelligence Bureau (a special operations force set up by Britain and its allies) launched an attack from Australia against Japanese ships in Singapore Harbor. The saboteurs entered the harbor in folding canoes and attached limpet mines to the ships. Seven ships, with a total tonnage of 45,200 tons (41,000 metric tonnes), were destroyed. A second raid was attempted in 1944, using a newly developed craft, the Sleeping Beauty. This electric-powered submersible canoe could either be operated fully under water or with the pilot's head above the surface. Raiders were about to launch these craft from a captured cargo ship when they were detected by water police. The operation was aborted. The saboteurs tried to escape, but all died fighting or were executed by the Japanese.

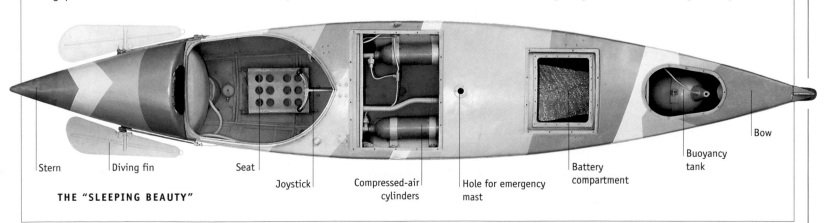

Stern

Diving fin

Seat

Joystick

Compressed-air cylinders

Hole for emergency mast

Battery compartment

Buoyancy tank

Bow

THE "SLEEPING BEAUTY"

COUNTER-INTELLIGENCE

"No Spies"
Members of FBI counterintelligence units adopted this unofficial lapel pin representing their commitment to keeping America free of spies. The pin was not worn operationally.

C OUNTERINTELLIGENCE IS INTENDED to penetrate hostile intelligence agencies and to prevent the passage of sensitive information to the enemy. A great deal of counterintelligence work targets enemy agents when they communicate with their handlers. Counterintelligence services employ highly trained agents, often skilled in using technologically advanced equipment – although they also need to have good judgment and intuition to contend with suspected enemy spies. Because of the numerous layers of deception involved, counterintelligence has been called a "wilderness of mirrors."

DETECTORS

Many devices have been developed for detecting hostile agents in the act of espionage. The use of clandestine radios by spies has led to the use of sophisticated radio direction-finding equipment by counterintelligence personnel. Other techniques are employed to track the movements of suspected agents. For example, powders that are invisible unless viewed with special equipment have been used by the KGB and FBI to reveal the footprints or fingerprints of spies. Detection equipment, such as cameras with telephoto lenses, is also used.

MI5 emblem
The internal counterintelligence service in Britain is known as MI5. It achieved an amazing record of apprehending German spies during World War II.

ANTIBUGGING DEVICES

Intelligence agencies frequently use listening devices, otherwise known as bugs, to eavesdrop on sensitive conversations. In response to this, the counterintelligence services have developed special electronic equipment and techniques for detecting bugs. Use of these has to be backed up by physical searches of the site

"Death to spies"
This slogan, abbreviated to SMERSH as seen in this set of credentials, was the name of the Soviet military counterintelligence service (see p. 202).

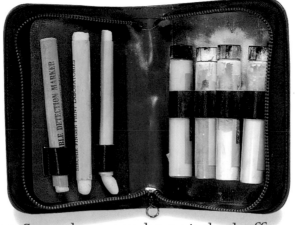

Invisible detection powders
To set a trap for an intruding spy, counterintelligence personnel put down invisible powders. After contact with human skin, these powders become visible under ultraviolet light.

being investigated for bugs. Audio countersurveillance devices work by picking up signals as the bugs transmit them. Such devices need to overcome certain difficulties that are commonly presented by bugs. Some bugs can be switched off remotely to avoid detection. Others hide themselves by transmitting on a frequency very close to that of a powerful radio station ("snuggling").

COUNTERSURVEILLANCE

The goal of countersurveillance is to provide safe conditions for friendly agents by deceiving or otherwise frustrating hostile surveillance. This craft is especially important for agents who are engaged in risky activities such as visiting a dead drop or meeting their case officers. It is carried out by teams of specially trained personnel, who maintain contact with one another by hidden radios. To avoid arousing any suspicion, these personnel may need to be in disguise.

LETTER INTERCEPTION

Spies can of course use the ordinary mail to send their messages. They may write in code, use secret writing, or incorporate microdots in their letters. The sheer volume of the mail is their best protection against discovery. Counterintelligence officers who do intervene in the mail service (which may not be possible without a warrant) may hope to find some spies' letters by concentrating on the addresses of suspects. Letters are opened by "flaps and seals" experts, so named because in the past their work had to do with envelope flaps and wax seals. There are now special tools and materials that open correspondence without alerting the recipient to the fact that the mail has been examined.

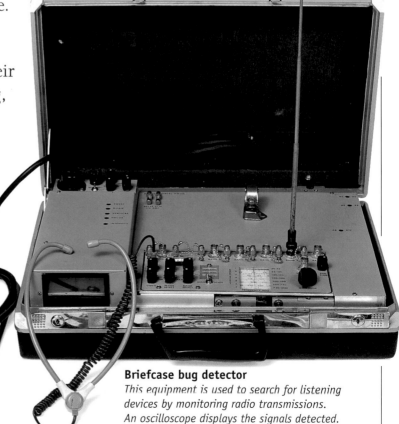

Briefcase bug detector
This equipment is used to search for listening devices by monitoring radio transmissions. An oscilloscope displays the signals detected.

Detectors

THE COUNTERINTELLIGENCE TOOLS that are used to monitor and trap spies are often referred to as detectors. Detectors are frequently electronic or photographic. But sometimes more subtle techniques are used, like the invisible spy dust laid down by the KGB to track the movements of CIA officers in Moscow. Various intelligence agencies, the KGB among them, have set up surveillance cameras with telephoto lenses to monitor movements of personnel at foreign embassies in the hope of detecting intelligence activities. Electronic detectors include the many devices used for detecting clandestine radios, such as radios used in a system referred to as radio direction finding (RDF). Elements of the Schulze-Boysen spy ring in Germany in World War II (see p. 38) and the Israeli spy Elie Cohen in Syria were caught using RDF.

Detection chemicals

The presence of a possible spy may be revealed by detection chemical kits. The chemicals that are used are invisible when dusted onto objects such as doorknobs, documents, or pieces of furniture. They react when touched by human skin and become visible, in ultraviolet light, on the hands or other body parts of anyone who has been in contact with them.

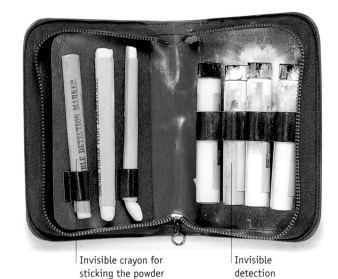

Invisible crayon for sticking the powder to a surface

Invisible detection powder

Elie Cohen

In 1962, Egyptian-born Elie Cohen (1924–65) began spying for Israel in Syria, posing as a wealthy Syrian businessman. He infiltrated Syrian society and used the contacts he made to gather intelligence. Cohen passed information about the Syrian armed forces by radio to Israel, but his frequent and predictable transmission schedule led to his detection by RDF equipment. He was tried and publicly hanged in 1965.

Photo-sniper

This 35mm surveillance camera is capable of taking high-definition pictures over long distances. It was used by counterintelligence teams of the KGB's Second Chief Directorate and by KGB Border Guards. The shoulder stock mounting for the camera allows it to be held steady without using a cumbersome and conspicuous tripod.

Rubber lens hood

300mm telephoto lens

Catch securing lens to shoulder stock

Focusing ring

GREEN FILTER

YELLOW FILTER

James J. Angleton

James J. Angleton (1917–87), a wartime OSS (see p. 32) officer, became the chief of the CIA's Counterintelligence Staff in 1954. During the 1960s, convinced by KGB defector Anatoli Golitsyn that a spy had penetrated the CIA, Angleton set up an investigation that disrupted the Agency and led to the rejection of several potential KGB defectors to the West. As a result of this affair and his role in an illegal "mail cover" operation, he resigned in 1974.

SCR-504 direction-finding suitcase radio

This set was used by American intelligence during and after World War II to locate clandestine radio transmitters. The suitcase allows it to be carried without attracting attention.

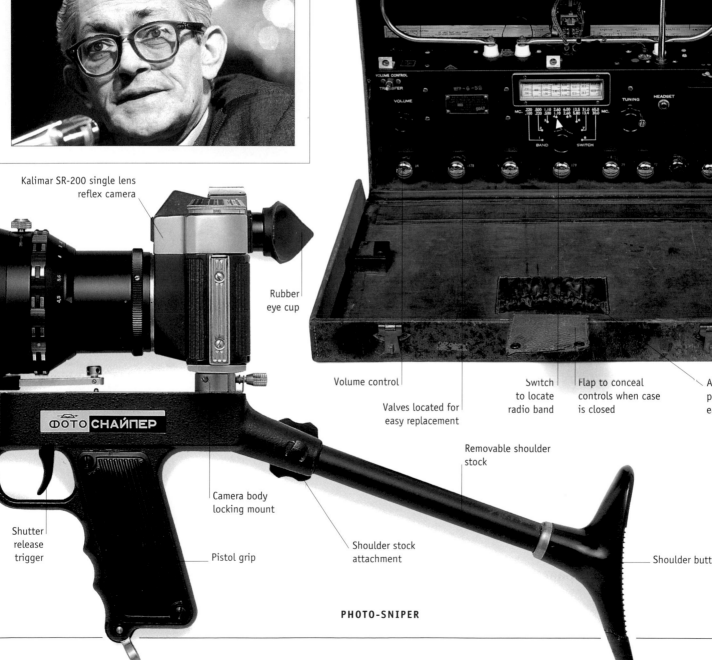

Telescopic antenna

Information on repairs

Loop antenna

Earpiece

Remote operating controls

Kalimar SR-200 single lens reflex camera

Rubber eye cup

Camera body locking mount

Shutter release trigger

Pistol grip

Shoulder stock attachment

Volume control

Valves located for easy replacement

Switch to locate radio band

Flap to conceal controls when case is closed

Accessory pocket for earpiece

Removable shoulder stock

Shoulder butt

ФОТО СНАЙПЕР

PHOTO-SNIPER

Antibugging devices

AN ANTIBUGGING DEVICE normally consists of a radio receiver, linked up with other electronic equipment, that is used to detect hidden transmitters. Equipped with an antibugging device, an audio-counterintelligence expert will "sweep" a room or any other site for bugs (see p. 102). This action is not enough on its own. The site must also be inspected by hand and eye, to spot bugs that are not transmitting. Afterward, the site must be guarded to prevent intruders from planting new bugs.

Portable detection kit

Included in this antibugging kit is an oscilloscope – an instrument that can display a radio signal as an image on a screen. This helps pinpoint secret transmissions, which often have a distinct appearance when displayed on the oscilloscope. Sometimes the signal from a bug may be masked by a powerful radio signal, which makes the bug difficult to locate.

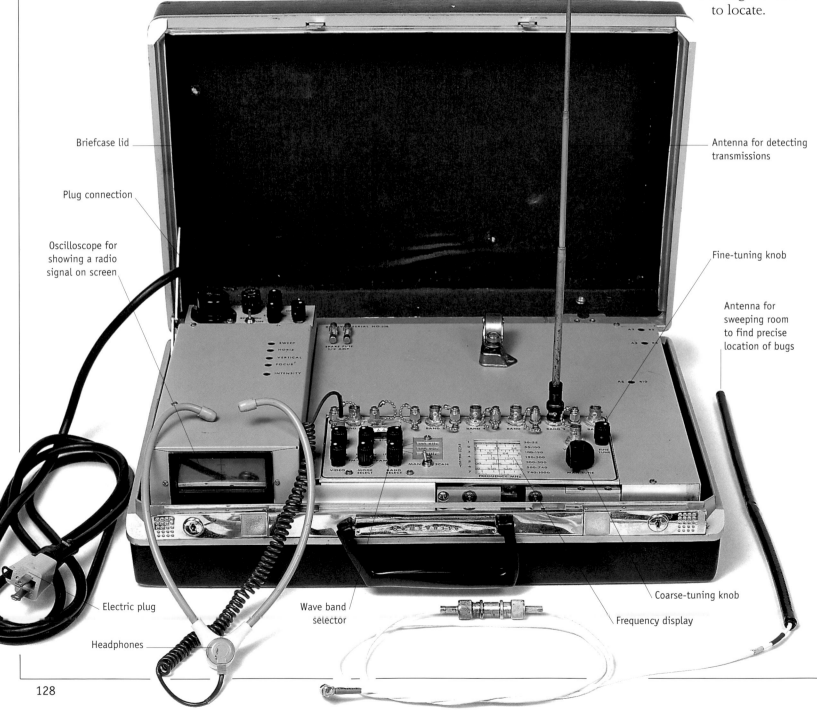

Briefcase lid

Plug connection

Oscilloscope for showing a radio signal on screen

Antenna for detecting transmissions

Fine-tuning knob

Antenna for sweeping room to find precise location of bugs

Electric plug

Wave band selector

Coarse-tuning knob

Frequency display

Headphones

Sound detect kit

American intelligence agents used the Sound Detect kit during the 1950s and 1960s. It included microphones, probes, and other devices for detecting bugs. Used in conjunction with the amplifier, it could help find most types of listening devices. Some of the components, such as the microphones, could also be used as listening devices themselves.

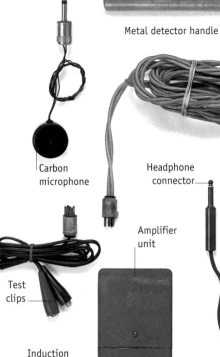

Metal detector handle

Metal detector unit

Contact microphone

Carbon microphone

Headphone connector

Amplifier unit

Power plug

Test clips

Radio frequency probe for detecting radio transmissions in the power line

Induction coil

Headphones

Transformer

Microphone

The Scan-lock

The Scan-Lock is a radio receiver that automatically locks on to the strongest radio signal. If an illegal transmitter is detected, the search wand can locate it. The Scan-Lock can also be set up outside a room where an important meeting is taking place, guarding constantly against remote-controlled bugs.

Antenna

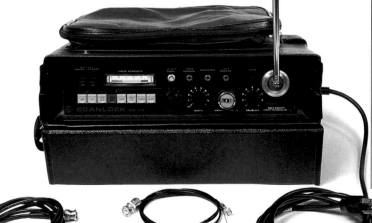

Heinz Felfe (b.1918) was a member of the World War II Nazi SD (see p. 34). In 1950 he was recruited as a Soviet spy and infiltrated the West German Foreign Intelligence Service, the BND. Felfe compromised West German intelligence operations for 11 years. With his inside knowledge he was able to warn Soviet audio technicians of the movements of BND sweepers, so the Soviets had time to remove or switch off their bugs.

Search wand

Extension cord

Power cord

Countersurveillance

SPIES RECEIVE SPECIAL TRAINING in countersurveillance, the object of which is to detect hostile surveillance, for instance of personnel, meetings, safe houses, or dead drops. The discovery of hostile surveillance is sufficient cause to cancel a meeting, bypass a safe house, or abort the planned servicing of a dead drop. Specialized technology exists that can help the countersurveillance team, including video and radio monitoring of likely threats. Team members may have to use disguises to avoid being recognized. The resources available to countersurveillance teams are likely to vary according to circumstances. Obviously, it is easier to mount such operations in a friendly country than in a hostile one.

Radio wristwatch

This watch was used by the KGB in the 1980s, both for surveillance and countersurveillance operations. It received prearranged signals, which it displayed on a screen. Its receiver was worn on the body, with a vibrator to indicate when a signal came in. The watch was used to control the movements of a spy. If the controllers became aware of hostile surveillance, they could send an emergency code ordering the mission to be aborted.

Surveillance radio

This body-worn radio was in use by the KGB in the 1960s. It was worn hidden under the clothing. A microphone and small speaker were concealed under the lapels, either of the coat or of a jacket underneath. A pocket buzzer warned of incoming messages. The user could surreptitiously communicate with other team members, or with a coordinating base station.

Microphone (worn behind lapel)

Speaker (worn behind lapel)

Microphone

Speaker

Transmitter

Cable to power supply (worn at the small of the back)

Power supply

Transmitter (worn at waist)

Buzzer (carried in pocket)

Antenna wires (hung in sleeves or pants legs)

Safety pin holds wire to clothing

Transmit/receive switch (carried in pocket)

Radio in position
This picture incorporates an imaginary X-ray view of the equipment in the position in which it would be worn. Bands of stretchy material around the waist hold the transmitter and power supply in place.

Antenna wire

Safety pin

Intelligence disguise kit

To avoid being recognized when carrying out countersurveillance, team members may have to alter their appearance, perhaps more than once. These changes may be as simple as changing the color of coat being worn, or adding or removing a hat. This 1960s kit contains materials for a wide range of disguises. As well as items for altering the appearance of the face and hair, it includes the more unusual device of a false heel to put in an agent's shoe. This overcomes the problem of an individual being recognized by his or her gait.

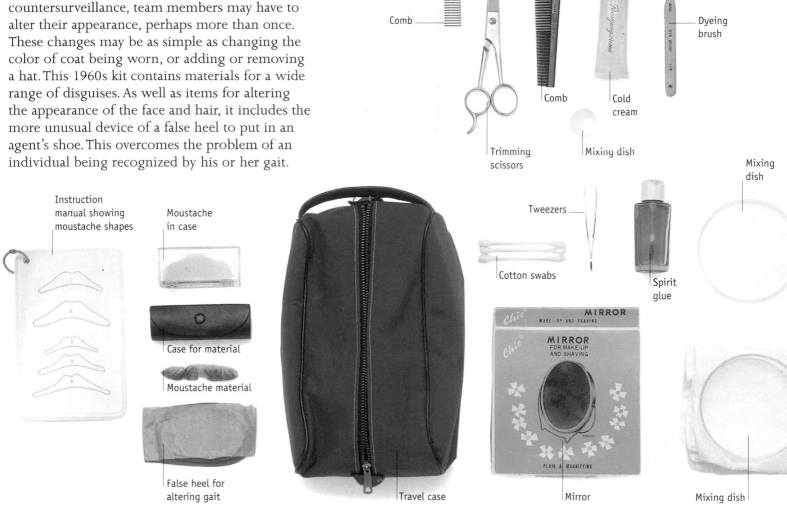

Comb

Comb

Cold cream

Dyeing brush

Trimming scissors

Mixing dish

Mixing dish

Instruction manual showing moustache shapes

Moustache in case

Tweezers

Spirit glue

Cotton swabs

Case for material

Moustache material

Travel case

MIRROR
MAKE-UP AND SHAVING

Chic MIRROR FOR MAKE-UP AND SHAVING

PLAIN & MAGNIFYING

Mirror

Mixing dish

False heel for altering gait

Facial disguise by artificial aging

Artificial aging is an effective and widely applicable method of disguise, since it does not rely too heavily on disguising the bone structure of the face. Makeup is used to accentuate existing wrinkles and creases. Care is needed to avoid an artificial appearance and to ensure that the hands and throat match the face. The stages in using makeup to simulate aging are shown on the right. In each picture, makeup is on the subject's right (our left) side only.

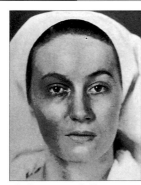

Skeleton modeling
Makeup can disguise the bone structure of the face to a small extent.

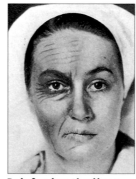

Reinforcing the lines
Existing facial lines are emphasized by applying dark makeup.

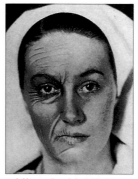

Adding the highlights
Areas of the face that stand out naturally are artificially lightened.

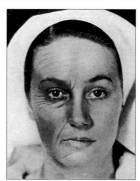

Blending
The balance of lines and highlights is adjusted to give a natural appearance.

Letter interception

WHEN SPIES SEND letters through the mail system they risk interception by enemy counterintelligence. The volume of regular mail makes it impossible for counterintelligence services to search it all, but they may search letters to and from suspect groups, individuals, or addresses. In Western countries, this cannot be done without first obtaining a warrant. Special techniques have been developed to take a letter out of an envelope without damaging it. There are also specialized technical terms: secret opening of mail is known as "flaps and seals" work. Three of the most common techniques are known as "steam openings," "dry openings" (using a separation of the glue), and "wet openings" (using water).

Flaps and seals tool roll

This American set of six tools may be used for surreptitious opening of most kinds of envelope. The tools are either used alone, or in conjunction with steam, water, or another solvent.

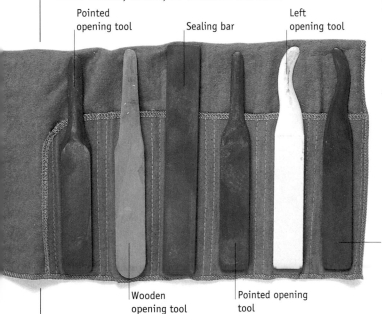

Pointed opening tool

Sealing bar

Left opening tool

Wooden opening tool

Pointed opening tool

Right opening tool

Letter extraction devices

Special devices were used in World War II to take letters from their envelopes without opening the seals. One such device was inserted into the unsealed gap at the top of an envelope flap. The letter was then wound around the device. The thin writing paper of the time made this method particularly effective. The device on the far right was used by the OSS (see p. 32); the other device was used at a postal interception station in Britain.

Willis George
The OSS surreptitious entry expert Willis George, inventor of the device shown on the far right, demonstrates the technique of removing a letter from its envelope with his device.

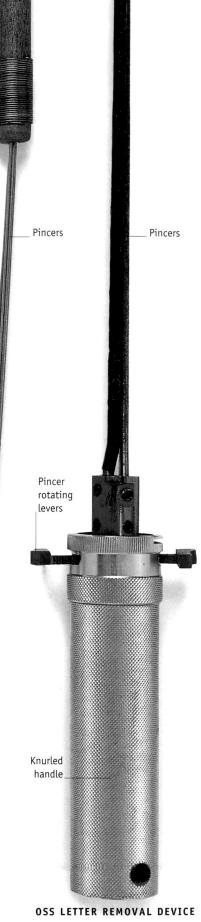

Pincers

Pincers

Pincer rotating levers

Knurled handle

End cap

BRITISH LETTER REMOVAL DEVICE

OSS LETTER REMOVAL DEVICE

Flaps and seals briefcase

This American flaps and seals kit from the 1960s was designed to be hidden in a briefcase. The kit contains everything needed for opening envelopes and other packages, as well as for lifting wax seals. There are special tools and containers of distilled water, glue, and chemicals. The base of the briefcase contains a heat table that can be used, in conjunction with damp sheets of blotting paper, to unstick the glue of an envelope.

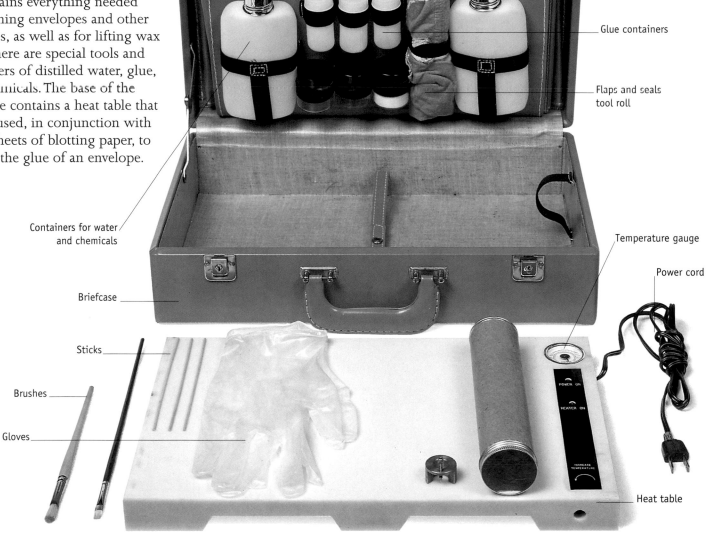

Blotting paper

Glue containers

Flaps and seals tool roll

Containers for water and chemicals

Briefcase

Temperature gauge

Power cord

Sticks

Brushes

Gloves

Heat table

Stamps for the French resistance

During World War II, French resistance groups (see p. 31) were engaged in secret operations against the occupying German army. These groups often used the mail to communicate when arranging meetings.

The Germans had a practice of luring patriotic Frenchmen to false resistance meetings, using forged letters. If a French resistance sympathizer received such a fake letter and, believing it to be genuine, turned up for a meeting, the Germans would arrest him. If, however, he gave the letter to the Germans to avoid being accused of complicity, he risked betraying the resistance if the letter should prove to be genuine after all.

To resolve this problem, British intelligence made fake French stamps that differed from genuine ones in a tiny detail known only to the resistance. Any "resistance" letters that did not bear this special stamp were assumed to be traps. The Germans never discovered the secret of the stamps.

GENUINE STAMP

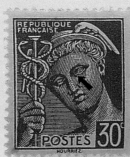

FAKE STAMP (ARROW SHOWS DIFFERENCE)

CLANDESTINE COMMUNICATIONS

Walnut concealment
Rolled-up sheets from a KGB one-time pad are hidden in an empty walnut shell. When used properly, the one-time pad system of coding messages is virtually impossible to crack.

IN ORDER TO OPERATE SUCCESSFULLY, it is essential for spies to have secret methods of communicating with their controllers. These clandestine communications must provide a safe and reliable form of contact between spy and spymaster, while remaining secure from interception by the enemy. Methods used for clandestine communication are extremely varied – they range from radio transmissions to secret writing and photographic methods. Common to all of these methods is the care taken to protect them from detection. Radios are made as small as possible, and secret messages are enciphered, or put into code, before transmission. Additionally, radio messages may be speeded up and transmitted in short bursts that are less likely to

Stamp concealment
A secret message has been written on the back of this postage stamp, mailed from Nuremberg in West Germany.

be detected. Information may be photographed and reduced to microdots. Special inks are employed to write invisible messages. Concealments have been developed to disguise or hide clandestine messages and the equipment used to produce them.

CLANDESTINE RADIOS

First conceived during the 1920s, special radios for communications were used extensively in World War II. They were often packaged inside suitcases when issued to personnel operating in enemy-occupied Europe, so that they could be carried without suspicion. Technological advances permitted the progressive miniaturization of radios during the war. Development continued after World War II with the introduction of transistors to replace bulky

Agent's radio
The compact Delco 5300 radio was used by CIA agents during the 1960s in Cuba. It could easily transmit messages from that country to the United States.

valves. Spy radios most often use Morse code, since this can be transmitted and received more clearly over long distances than voice signals. It is also easier to encrypt Morse code messages than to scramble voice messages. Burst transmissions were introduced at the end of World War II and continued to be important in the Cold War. The technique lessens a radio's transmitting time, decreasing the likelihood of it being located by radio direction finding (RDF).

CIPHER DEVICES

During the early 20th century, a number of electromechanical cipher machines were invented; these produced ciphers so complex that they were thought to be unbreakable. However, during World War II they were broken, both by human mathematical genius and by the use of the world's first electronic computer. One form of cipher that remains virtually unbreakable, even by modern computers, is the one-time pad system.

Kryha cipher device
Invented in 1924, the Kryha device employed a spring-driven alphabetic rotor to turn messages into code (encipher them). The device was used by the German diplomatic corps in World War II.

Ring with concealment
This British ring from World War II could conceal microdots or microfilm.

CONCEALMENTS

Concealments – objects designed to hide messages – are frequently used, and may resemble everyday objects, such as keys or pens. Discovery of a secret message by the enemy can often give away information about the source of the message, so some concealments are booby-trapped and explode if they are not opened in the correct way, destroying the contents. Information is also often sent in ways that assist in its concealment. Special inks can produce secret writing, which is invisible until it has been treated with the correct chemical reagent. Photographic negatives, greatly reduced in size, can convey information in the form of microdots, which are easy to hide and very difficult to find. To avoid the dangers of personal meetings, spies deliver or collect material at prearranged hiding places, known as dead drops. Some ingenious and convincing concealments have been devised to make dead drop containers blend in imperceptibly with their surroundings.

Modified objects
Technicians can modify everyday objects to make hiding places for such information as the dates and times of secret radio transmissions.

Suitcase radios I

THE CONCEPT OF CONCEALING and transporting radios in suitcases was first developed in the late 1930s by the French and German intelligence services. Quickly adopted by other nations, these suitcase radios were extensively used during World War II. Early examples were bulky and inefficient, but technological advances permitted a reduction in size, while performance was improved. Messages were transmitted in Morse code, which could be received over greater ranges than voice transmissions. Care had to be taken to ensure that the suitcases did not look out of place in the country in which they were to be used. In the United States, for example, the OSS (see p. 32) packaged some of its radios in suitcases obtained from European refugees arriving in New York. In the years following World War II, clandestine radios were small enough to be concealed in attaché cases.

Type B Mk II radio

The most widely used SOE suitcase radio of World War II was the Type B Mk II. It was developed by John Brown in 1942, and was originally designed to operate at a range of up to 500 miles (800 km). In practice it could manage twice that distance in good conditions.

Civilian suitcase

Power supply

Morse key

Spare parts box

Power plug

• • • • • • TECHNICAL DATA

Dimensions	18½ × 13½ × 6 in (47 × 34 × 15 cm)
Weight	32¾ lb (14.9 kg)
Range	up to 500 miles (800 km)
Power supply	97–250 V AC from house; 6 V DC from car battery
Power output	average 20 W
Transmitter	3.0 to 16.0 MHz in three bands
Receiver	4-tube superheterodyne receiving voice, tone, and Morse; 3.1 to 15.5 MHz in three bands

Battery clips

Frequency coils

Frequency tuning knob

Headphones

Spare tube

Transmitting
In a still taken from a film about the SOE, operative Jacqueline Nearne can be seen transmitting with a suitcase radio.

SPY PROFILE Jacqueline Nearne

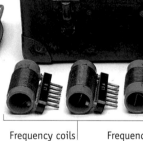

The SOE (see p. 30) recruited Jacqueline Nearne (1916–82) from the First Aid Nursing Yeomanry (FANY). She was taught how to make Morse code transmissions with a suitcase radio. In 1943 Nearne was sent to France to act as a courier. There she formed the link between several SOE groups covering a large area around Paris. The British later awarded Nearne the MBE (Member of the Order of the British Empire) for her work.

Type A Mk III radio

John Brown worked with the Marconi Company in 1943 to produce the Type A Mk III radio, which was smaller and lighter than any previous model. It was created by reducing the size of some components of the Type B Mk II radio. Because it was so light, the Mk III was an instant success with SOE operatives. Almost 20 lb (9 kg) lighter than the Type B Mk II, it had the same transmission range of about 500 miles (800 km).

John Brown: suitcase radio inventor

In 1941, John Brown (1917–93), a signals officer in the British Army, was posted to a secret research station where his task was to design specialized radios for the SOE (see p. 30). He invented the "biscuit tin" radio (see p. 140) and the Type B Mk II suitcase radio. These were both widely used during World War II, but it was Brown's Type A Mk III suitcase radio, which contained miniaturized components obtained from the United States, that became the lightest, smallest SOE suitcase radio of the war.

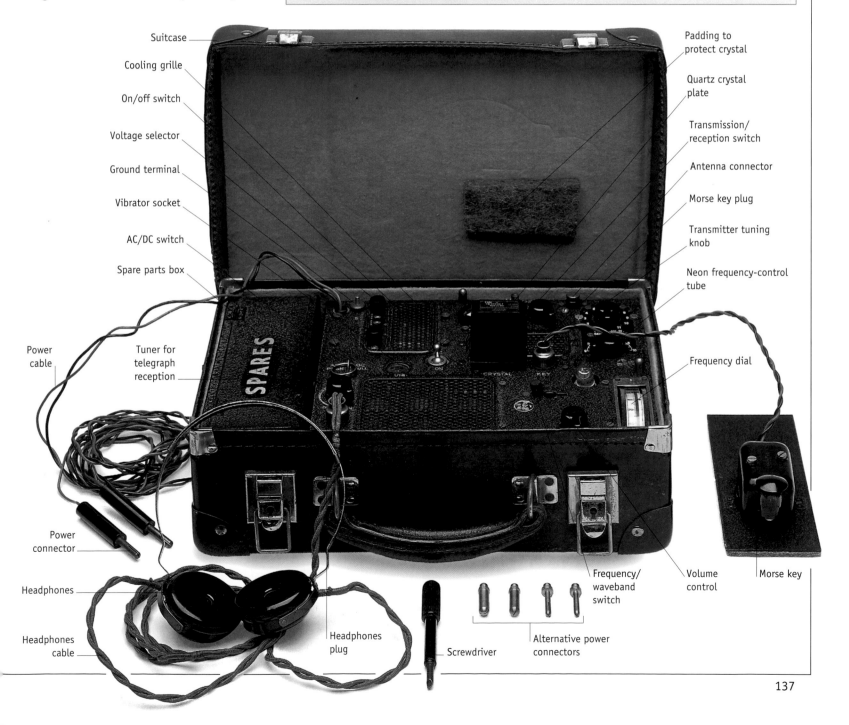

Suitcase

Cooling grille

On/off switch

Voltage selector

Ground terminal

Vibrator socket

AC/DC switch

Spare parts box

Power cable

Tuner for telegraph reception

Power connector

Headphones

Headphones cable

Headphones plug

Screwdriver

Alternative power connectors

Frequency/ waveband switch

Volume control

Morse key

Padding to protect crystal

Quartz crystal plate

Transmission/ reception switch

Antenna connector

Morse key plug

Transmitter tuning knob

Neon frequency-control tube

Frequency dial

SPARES

Suitcase radios II

SSTR-1 radio

This transceiver was the standard radio for the OSS (see p. 32). The transmitter, receiver, and power supply were packed in separate boxes for concealment. Often hidden in civilian suitcases for disguise, the radio was packed in the case illustrated here for some operations.

● ● ● ● ● ● **TECHNICAL DATA**	
Dimensions	4 × 9½ × 3½ in (10 × 24 × 9 cm)
Weight	20–45 lb (9–20 kg)
Range	300–1,000 miles (480–1,600 km)
Power supply	110/220 V AC; 6 V DC; generator
Power output	8–15 W
Transmitter	3.0 to 14.0 MHz in three bands
Receiver	5-tube superheterodyne receiving voice, tone, and Morse

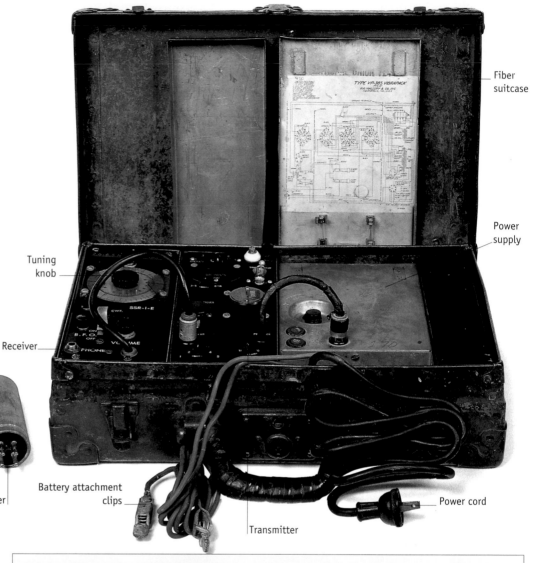

Fiber suitcase

Power supply

Tuning knob

Receiver

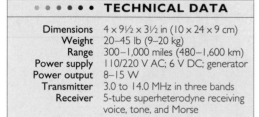

Crystals

Rectifier

Battery attachment clips

Transmitter

Power cord

Suitcase receiver

This compact 1920s radio was used in World War II by the French intelligence service, which clandestinely monitored German radio traffic for the British.

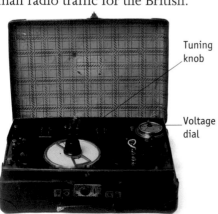

Tuning knob

Voltage dial

SOE radio security

During World War II, personnel who used suitcase radios transmitted their messages to receiving stations set up for the purpose. The SOE (see p. 30) established its stations (known as home stations) at various sites around Britain, with staff recruited from the First Aid Nursing Yeomanry (FANY).

To avoid the need for messages to be repeated, all transmissions were recorded – the longer an agent spent transmitting, the greater the danger of capture by the Germans, who had radio direction finding vehicles for hunting clandestine radios.

In the SOE home stations, a system known as fingerprinting was employed to recognize the distinctive Morse signature of each SOE sender. The system also made it possible to detect bogus transmissions made by the Germans on captured radios.

Inside an SOE home station
FANY radio operators at an SOE home station in Britain during World War II listen on sensitive receivers for coded messages that are sent from operatives in occupied Europe.

Attaché case radio

In the 1950s, radios were developed to fit into the standard attaché cases carried by business people. This radio could transmit for about 300 miles (480 km) using a short indoor antenna. With a longer outdoor antenna, the radio had a range of about 3,000 miles (4,800 km) for shortwave Morse code messages. This radio was used in Miami during the 1960s to communicate with agents involved in covert operations against the Castro regime in Cuba (see p. 169).

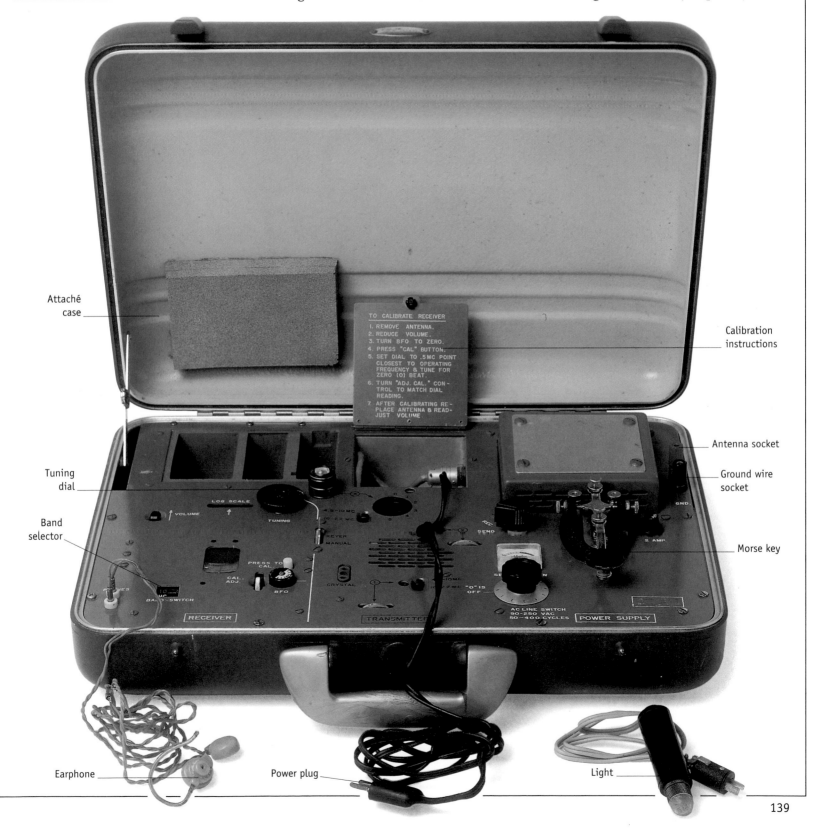

Attaché case

Calibration instructions

TO CALIBRATE RECEIVER
1. REMOVE ANTENNA.
2. REDUCE VOLUME.
3. TURN BFO TO ZERO.
4. PRESS "CAL" BUTTON.
5. SET DIAL TO .5MC POINT CLOSEST TO OPERATING FREQUENCY & TUNE FOR ZERO (0) BEAT.
6. TURN "ADJ. CAL." CONTROL TO MATCH DIAL READING.
7. AFTER CALIBRATING REPLACE ANTENNA & READJUST VOLUME.

Antenna socket

Ground wire socket

Tuning dial

Band selector

Morse key

RECEIVER

TRANSMITTER

POWER SUPPLY

Earphone

Power plug

Light

139

Agents' radios

AGENTS OFTEN USE SPECIAL RADIOS to communicate rapidly with their home bases. Radios may be used when it is important for an agent to communicate with a controller, or when it is necessary to send an intelligence report without delay. As well as being powerful enough to transmit over long distances, agents' radios must be small enough to carry and conceal with ease. World War II agents' radios often comprised two or three major component elements (known as modules), as this made them more portable. With advances in technology since the war, agents' radios have become considerably smaller and can now transmit to satellites.

Agents' radio

This type of Soviet equipment was used in the 1950s and early 1960s. Such radios were issued to KGB agents in western Europe and eastern Asia. They could both transmit and receive, and were used to send long-range signals in Morse code to receiving stations in the Soviet bloc. The example shown below was found in Japan in the late 1950s.

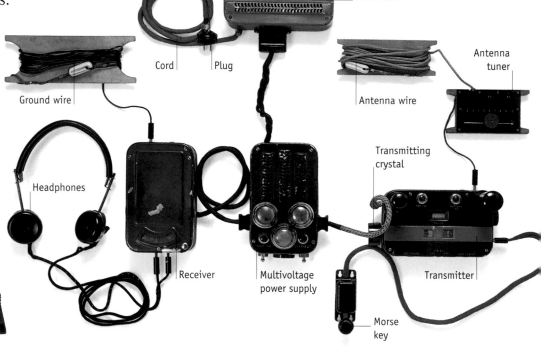

Line filter

Cord Plug

Ground wire

Headphones

Receiver

Multivoltage power supply

Morse key

Antenna tuner

Antenna wire

Transmitting crystal

Transmitter

Se-100/11 agents' radio

This powerful electrically powered radio was used by German military intelligence (Abwehr) agents. Like most agents' radios of World War II, this outfit was divided into three modules: transmitter, receiver, and power supply. Modular construction made the set portable and easy to hide. It was also simple to assemble quickly.

Receiver   Power supply   Transmitter

Communicating with resistance groups

During World War II, resistance groups made use of radios to receive coded broadcasts from Britain. As well as war news, broadcasts from the BBC provided secret messages from the SOE (see p. 30). The German army, realizing how important radio communications could be for resistance groups, confiscated all shortwave radios in the countries they occupied. SOE radio expert John Brown (see p. 137) designed a special covert

radio set, called the Miniature Communication Receiver Mk 1 (MCR-1). This outfit was issued to resistance fighters concealed in cookie tins. Thousands of these portable sets were sent to France during the war for distribution to the SOE and resistance groups.

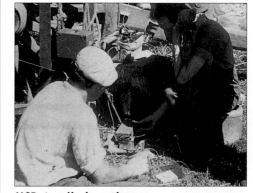

MCR-1 radio in action
SOE operatives in action use a "biscuit tin" radio to receive coded messages from base.

The MCR-1 "biscuit tin" radio
The main parts of the radio could be packed discreetly in cookie tins.

Delco 5300 radio

Used by CIA agents in the 1960s and 1970s, this small but powerful set had a number of advanced features for its time. It could send voice or Morse code transmissions. Messages were transmitted and received on separate frequencies to maintain secrecy. In an emergency, an agent could use a low voice for transmission by using the whisper switch, or even shut down the transmission instantly with the dead-man switch. A GRA-71 burst encoder (see p. 142) could be added to the radio.

• • • • • • **TECHNICAL DATA**	
Dimensions	10 × 5 × 4½ in (254 × 127 × 114 mm)
Weight	7½ lb (3.4 kg) with battery
Range	Antenna dependent
Power supply	Battery with 4, 12, and 28 volt taps
Power output	5 watts Morse, 1.5 watts voice
Transmitter	Morse/voice; 3 to 8 MHz in four channels
Receiver	Superheterodyne for voice, tone, and Morse; coverage same as transmitter

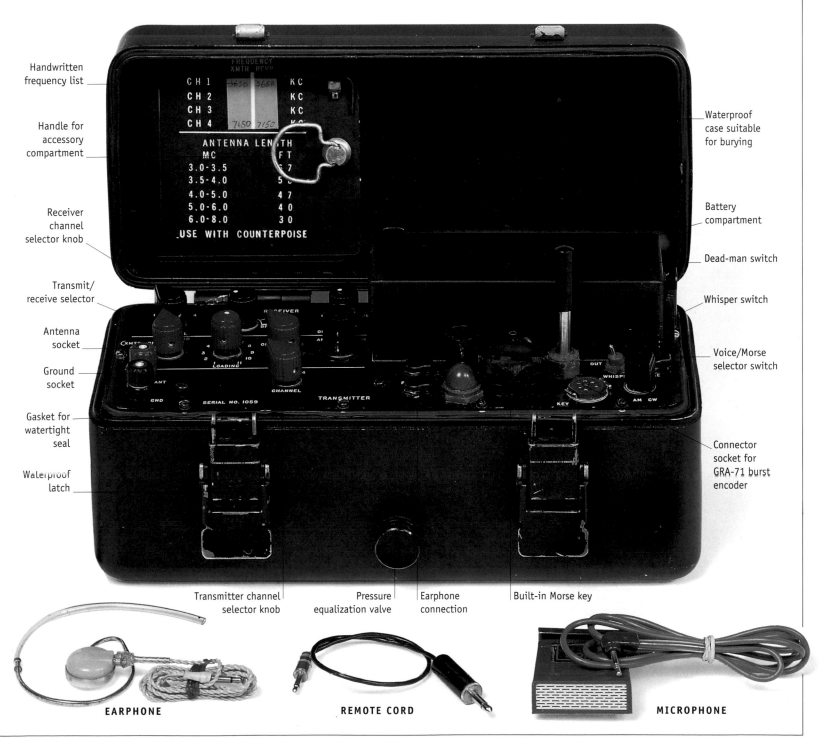

Handwritten frequency list

Handle for accessory compartment

Receiver channel selector knob

Transmit/ receive selector

Antenna socket

Ground socket

Gasket for watertight seal

Waterproof latch

Waterproof case suitable for burying

Battery compartment

Dead-man switch

Whisper switch

Voice/Morse selector switch

Connector socket for GRA-71 burst encoder

Transmitter channel selector knob

Pressure equalization valve

Earphone connection

Built-in Morse key

EARPHONE

REMOTE CORD

MICROPHONE

Specialized communications

FACE-TO-FACE MEETINGS ARE RISKY, so a variety of specialized devices have been developed to enable agents to communicate with their controllers. Those that facilitate contact within the same locality are known as short-range agent communications (SRAC) devices. For long-distance communications, messages are often sent in Morse code and compressed by means of a burst encoder, which reduces the chances of detection. Special radios are issued to "sleepers" – agents living unsuspected in their target country for years, while leading apparently normal lives. Sleepers tune in to prearranged radio frequencies at set times to listen for coded instructions from their controllers.

Radio with burst encoder

This equipment was used by the SAS (see p. 168). It consists of a transceiver coupled with a GRA-71 burst encoder, which compresses Morse code messages for transmission in a short burst. This reduces the chance of detection by radio direction-finding equipment.

KGB burst transmissions

The KGB provided its radio operators who were working abroad in the post-World War II period with specially designed equipment for sending messages back to the Soviet Union. Many of the radio sets given to the operators were coupled with equipment for preparing and sending burst transmissions. The equipment used to prepare the tapes, on which the secret messages were recorded in Morse code, had the advantage that it could also be loaded with standard 35mm photographic film, which was always readily available, as an alternative to audio tape.

CONVERTED 35mm FILM

Recorded message

CONVERTED AUDIO TAPE

Burst transmission tapes
Before transmission, the message was recorded in Morse code by punching a series of holes in 35mm film or audio tape.

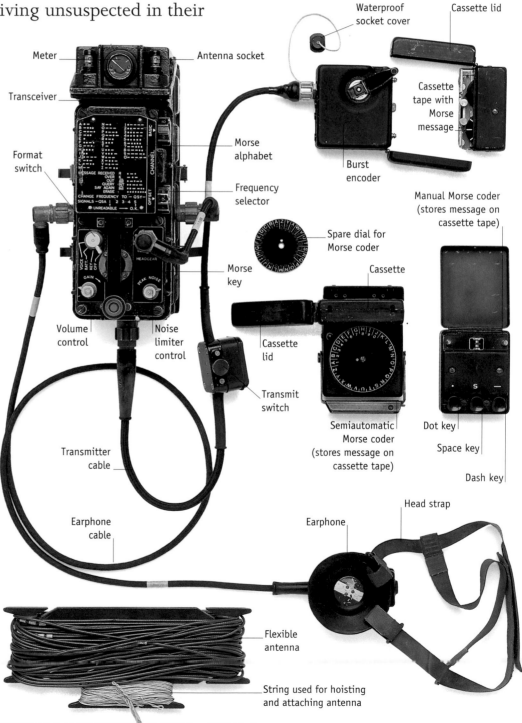

Meter

Antenna socket

Transceiver

Format switch

Morse alphabet

Frequency selector

Morse key

Volume control

Noise limiter control

Transmit switch

Cassette lid

Transmitter cable

Earphone cable

Waterproof socket cover

Cassette lid

Cassette tape with Morse message

Burst encoder

Manual Morse coder (stores message on cassette tape)

Spare dial for Morse coder

Cassette

Semiautomatic Morse coder (stores message on cassette tape)

Dot key

Space key

Dash key

Head strap

Earphone

Flexible antenna

String used for hoisting and attaching antenna

FE-10 agents' receiver

This small German receiver was issued to sleeper agents (see opposite) in the 1980s, complete with a signal plan. This stated the agent's call number and gave a transmission schedule and decoding instructions. The receiver was powered by a 9 volt rechargeable battery. Sleeper agents would use the receiver to monitor a variety of frequencies, inserting different crystals in the socket provided to receive signals on different frequencies.

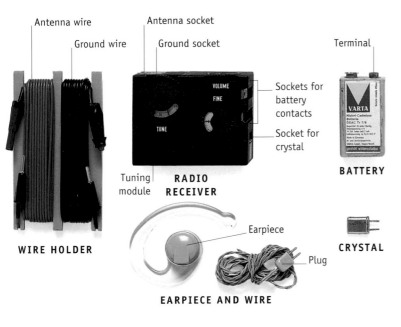

Antenna wire
Ground wire
WIRE HOLDER

Antenna socket
Ground socket
Sockets for battery contacts
Socket for crystal
Tuning module **RADIO RECEIVER**

Terminal
VARTA
BATTERY

Earpiece
Plug
EARPIECE AND WIRE

CRYSTAL

Hotel lamp transceiver

This is a mass-produced table lamp, suitable for use in hotel bedrooms, which was available on the American market in the 1960s. An American intelligence agency covertly modified a number of lamps for clandestine use, installing a radio receiver and transmitter (a transceiver) in the base. Such a lamp could be placed in the hotel bedroom of, for example, a Soviet double agent, enabling the agent to contact his or her controller in secret. Set up in a different way, the lamp transceiver could also be used as a listening device.

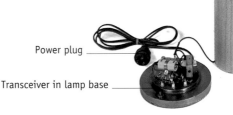

Power plug
Transceiver in lamp base

Infrared communication system

This German device from the 1960s transmits and receives voice messages over a 1.86-mile (3-km) range, using a beam of infrared light. The device can be used by day or night, but rain or fog reduce its performance. Unlike contemporary infrared systems for night vision, this system was (and still is) extremely difficult to detect or intercept.

Microphone
Talk button
Earpiece

Infrared transmitter
Infrared receiver

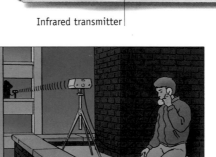

Infrared communication
This type of communication is particularly useful in an urban setting, allowing secure conversation between, for example, agent and case officer. A clear line of sight between the two is essential for the infrared beam to link the transceivers.

Cipher devices

CIPHER DEVICES are used to make messages unintelligible to all except the intended recipient. Essentially, they work by replacing the letters or numbers in a message with other letters or numbers. Early cipher devices used simple letter-for-letter substitution, in which a given letter is always enciphered as the same other letter. In the 1920s, French and American cryptographers (cipher experts) developed machines that used polyalphabetic substitution. In this more sophisticated method, a given letter may be substituted by a different one from a range of possible letters each time it occurs.

M-94 cipher device

The M-94, based on an 18th-century cipher device, worked by rotating the disks of letters around the cylinder. The M-94 cipher device was used by the US Army from 1922 until 1943, when it was replaced by the Converter M-209.

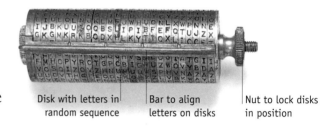

Disk with letters in random sequence | Bar to align letters on disks | Nut to lock disks in position

Kryha cipher machine

Designed in 1924, this machine employed polyalphabetic substitution. It was used in World War II by German diplomats, who were unaware that the cipher had been broken by the Americans.

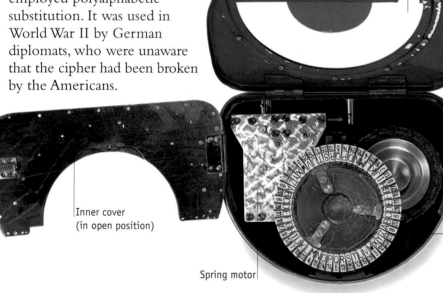

Reading aperture

Top cover (in open position)

Inner cover (in open position)

Concentric disks

Indicating disk

Spring motor

Bolton's patent cipher wheel

This device substituted one letter for another. It is typical of late 19th-century cipher devices and was based on the cipher disk of Leon Battista Alberti, a 15th-century Italian scholar and cryptographer.

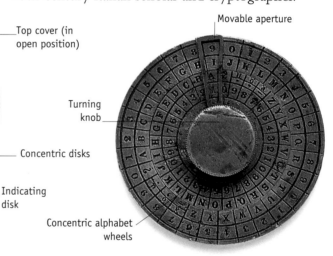

Movable aperture

Turning knob

Concentric alphabet wheels

The Hebern cipher machine

Edward Hebern (1869–1952) was a self-taught American inventor. From 1909 on he produced a series of electromechanical cipher machines with rotating disks. Hebern's machines were designed to send secret messages between businessmen who were anxious to prevent industrial espionage.

In 1915, Hebern introduced a system in which two typewriters were connected by wires to a rotor in the center. This concept was very advanced for its time, and was later used by the Japanese diplomatic service for its Red ciphers (see p. 36).

The US Navy evaluated this machine, but during testing, the cryptographer William Friedman (see p. 36) broke the cipher. Not deterred, Hebern developed the Mark II, or SIGABA, machine, which became the most secure American cipher system in use during World War II.

EDWARD HEBERN

1921 HEBERN CIPHER MACHINE

Converter M-209 cipher machine

The Converter M-209 cipher machine was designed by Boris Hagelin and was widely used by the US Army during World War II. It was a compact and portable machine that used a series of rotors to encipher and decipher secret military messages. Once a message was enciphered through the Converter M-209, it printed the text on paper tape in five-letter groups. The message was then transmitted by radio and deciphered. An enciphered M-209 message could be deciphered and printed on another M-209 machine.

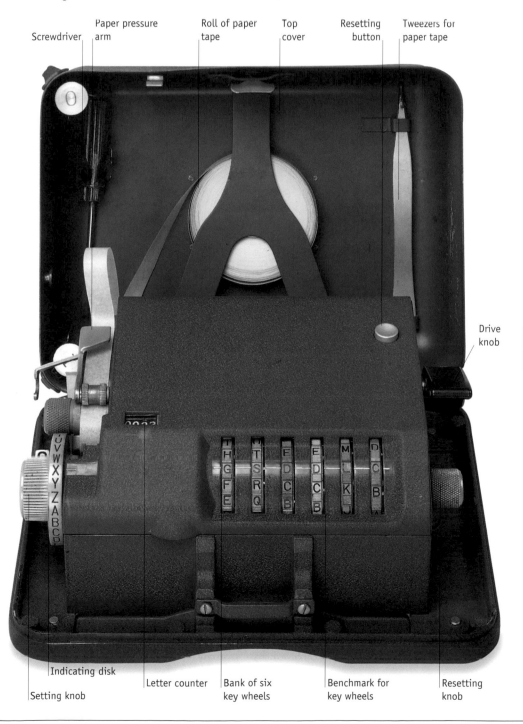

Screwdriver

Paper pressure arm

Roll of paper tape

Top cover

Resetting button

Tweezers for paper tape

Drive knob

Indicating disk

Setting knob

Letter counter

Bank of six key wheels

Benchmark for key wheels

Resetting knob

Boris Hagelin

In 1934, the Swedish cryptographer Boris Hagelin (1892–1983) designed a cipher machine for the French secret service. He developed this into the Converter M-209, which was used by the US Army. During World War II, more than 140,000 of these machines were produced.

CD 57 cipher machine

The CD 57 was designed by Hagelin for French secret police work. It was small enough to be carried in a pocket and had a thumb-operated lever, which left the other hand free to write the message.

Open cover with window

Key wheels

Thumb-operated lever

Alphabet disk

Enigma machine

GERMANY'S STRATEGY IN WORLD WAR II was to wage a war of total mobility on land, at sea, and in the air. This required the fastest and most secret communications possible, and the Enigma cipher machine, originally designed to protect the secrecy of business messages, was adopted for this purpose. Versions of the Enigma were developed for use in different German organizations, such as the armed forces, the security and intelligence services, and the diplomatic corps. German refinements to the Enigma increased the complexity of the cipher continually throughout the war. In 1943 the first computer in the world was needed to break it. The ability to break the Enigma cipher is seen by historians as a major contributory factor in the Allied victory in the war.

Japanese Enigma
A special version of the Enigma was made for use by Japan during World War II.

German soldiers using the Enigma
One soldier is typing a message, while another calls out the enciphered letters as they are illuminated. The enciphered letters are being copied down ready for transmission by radio.

Enigma cipher machine

Invented in 1923, this was a mechanized electric device for enciphering and deciphering messages. Each letter was enciphered separately through a series of plug connections and rotors.

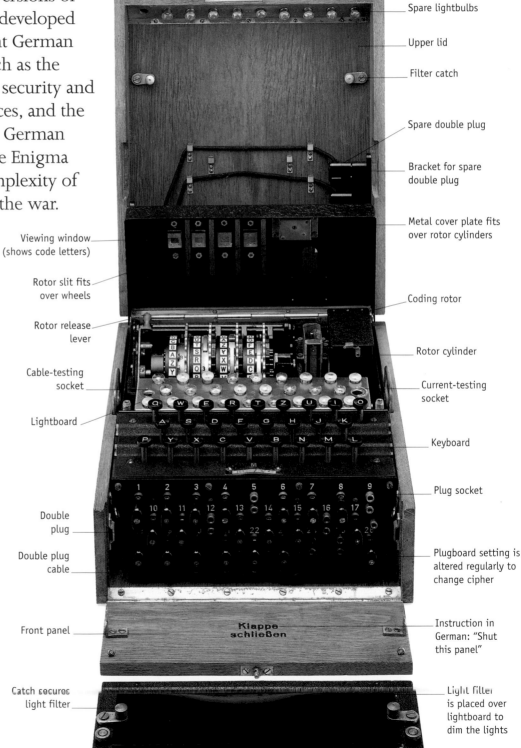

Spare lightbulbs

Upper lid

Filter catch

Spare double plug

Bracket for spare double plug

Metal cover plate fits over rotor cylinders

Coding rotor

Rotor cylinder

Current-testing socket

Keyboard

Plug socket

Plugboard setting is altered regularly to change cipher

Instruction in German: "Shut this panel"

Light filter is placed over lightboard to dim the lights

Viewing window (shows code letters)

Rotor slit fits over wheels

Rotor release lever

Cable-testing socket

Lightboard

Double plug

Double plug cable

Front panel

Catch secures light filter

Klappe schließen

Mechanism of the Enigma

The key to the security of the Enigma lay in the way the machine was set up. The order of the machine's alphabetical rotors, which were arranged on the rotor cylinder, and their internal wiring could be altered. The cipher was determined by the initial settings of these rotors. The plugs were inserted in the plugboard in any combination. All these variables – the key settings – were changed on a regular basis. Even if an enemy had a machine identical to the one used to create a message, he could not break the cipher without also learning the key settings used when the message was enciphered.

1 A lever is lifted to release the rotors. The rotors are removed and the internal wiring, known as the "ring setting," altered. The rotors are put back in the order specified in the current instructions.

2 A letter from each rotor shows through the windows of the cover. The rotors are turned until the letters are arranged as specified in the current instructions. These letters form the "ground setting."

3 Once the rotors are positioned correctly, the cover is shut over them. Then the connections on the plugboard are changed: they are manipulated to link pairs of letters specified by the operator's codebook.

4 The Enigma operator picks four random letters and enters them twice. The resulting eight-letter cipher is used as a message prefix. Before enciphering the message, the rotors are set to show the four random letters.

8 A reflecting disk at the end of the row of rotors reflects the signal back through the rotors.

ROTOR BOARD

7 A signal from 9 passes through the rotor cage and is altered each time it passes through a rotor.

LIGHTBOARD

5 The first letter of a message is typed on the keyboard. The letter H is used as an example to show the enciphering process.

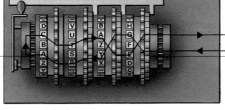

KEYBOARD

10 The signal goes to the lightboard. It lights A, which then becomes the first letter of the enciphered message. This procedure is repeated for each letter of the message.

9 The signal returns to the plugboard, in this example to 12. It is rerouted by a connection to 18.

PLUGBOARD

6 An electrical signal from H travels to 16 then 9 on the plugboard. At this stage, the letter is changed.

The Geheimschreiber

A more complex cipher device than the Enigma was the Geheimschreiber. It had either 10 or 12 rotors, which made enciphered messages extremely difficult to break. The Geheimschreiber was very large and was installed only in main communications centers, in Germany itself or in German-held territories.

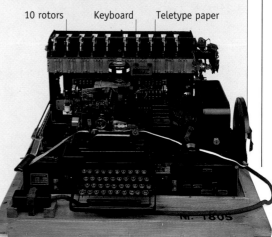

10 rotors   Keyboard   Teletype paper

GEHEIMSCHREIBER, SIEMENS MODEL (CODENAME STURGEON)

Ciphers and secret writing

SPIES OFTEN NEED TO WRITE messages that cannot be discovered or understood by the enemy. A written message can be encrypted by means of a cipher device (see p. 144) or with a cipher system such as a one-time pad, which, if properly used, is completely safe from code-breakers. (For the difference between a code and a cipher, see the glossary, p. 200.) Messages can also be hidden by means of secret writing, which is normally done by one of two methods: the wet system, in other words writing in invisible inks; and the transfer system, in which a piece of chemically impregnated paper, known as a carbon, transfers ink to a piece of normal paper when this is placed beneath it.

GERMAN WORLD WAR I INVISIBLE INK AND SPONGE

SPY PROFILE — Herbert Boeckenhaupt

Herbert Boeckenhaupt (b.1942) was a US Air Force radio communications specialist. As a young man, he volunteered to work for the Soviet Union for money. From 1962 until his arrest in 1966, Boeckenhaupt sent American military secrets to the KGB, often using secret writing. After his arrest, instructions concerning a dead drop, on 35mm film, and secret writing carbons were found in Boeckenhaupt's home.

Handkerchief with secret writing

Some invisible inks may be used on cloth as well as on paper. This handkerchief was prepared in West Germany in the 1960s. The message concerns a meeting that is about to take place and refers to information that will arrive from East Germany.

Section where a chemical has been applied to reveal message

Cipher sheets in walnut shell

Rolled up inside this walnut shell, which was found in the possession of a Soviet agent in former West Germany, are two cipher sheets from one-time pads.

Walnut shell

Cipher sheets

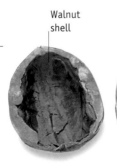

Madame de Victorica

US Military Intelligence intercepted a letter written in secret ink to a suspected German spy during World War I. The letter was traced back to Madame Marie de Victorica (1882–1920), who lived in New York. On her arrest in April 1918, she was found to own two silk scarves that were impregnated with water-soluble secret inks. She was indicted on spying charges but, as she offered to work for the government, she was not tried. She was a heroin addict, and the authorities supplied her with drugs to ensure her cooperation. Her drug control card is shown here.

DRUG CONTROL CARD

Sublatent photographic image

Section where a chemical has been applied to reveal message

Secret writing can be concealed by printing a photograph over it. The message is revealed by applying chemicals that remove only the top image. This photograph was used in the 1960s by the East German security service to cover a layer of secret writing, part of which has been revealed. Once a message has been concealed in this way it can be carried safely without fear of detection. Radio communication plans are often hidden in this way.

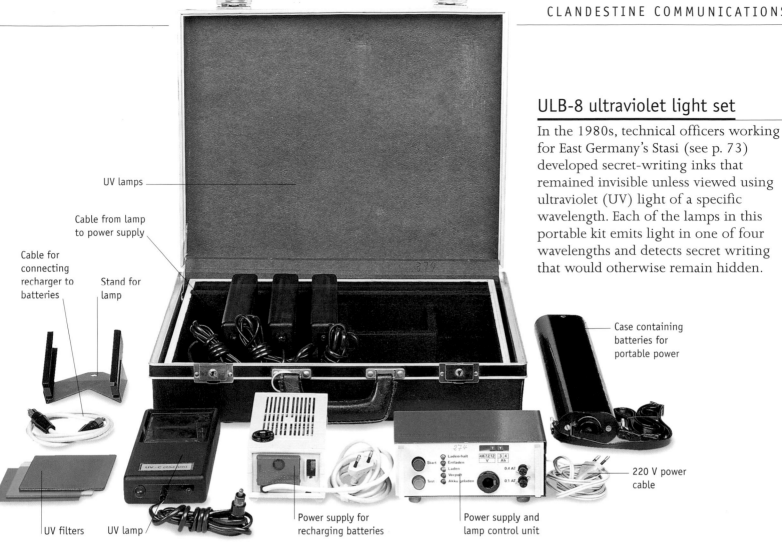

ULB-8 ultraviolet light set

In the 1980s, technical officers working for East Germany's Stasi (see p. 73) developed secret-writing inks that remained invisible unless viewed using ultraviolet (UV) light of a specific wavelength. Each of the lamps in this portable kit emits light in one of four wavelengths and detects secret writing that would otherwise remain hidden.

UV lamps

Cable from lamp to power supply

Cable for connecting recharger to batteries

Stand for lamp

Case containing batteries for portable power

UV filters

UV lamp

Power supply for recharging batteries

Power supply and lamp control unit

220 V power cable

One-time pads

The one-time pad system of enciphering was first used by the German diplomatic service during the 1920s. Both sender and recipient have an identical pad of cipher sheets, each of which is used to encipher single message and then destroyed. As the cipher is never repeated, it is theoretically unbreakable. However, if an opposing intelligence agency were to obtain a copy of one of the pads, the message might be compromised. In 1943, the system was adopted by the SOE (see p. 30). Pads, and the keys that were used for encoding and decoding, were printed on silk for its durability and ease of transportation.

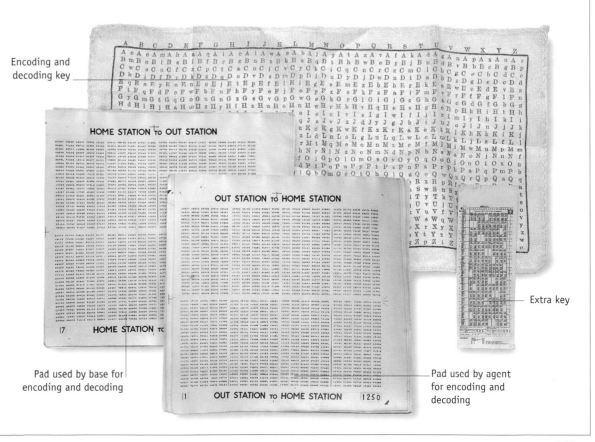

Encoding and decoding key

Pad used by base for encoding and decoding

Pad used by agent for encoding and decoding

Extra key

Microdots I

MICRODOTS ARE TINY PHOTOGRAPHS of messages, secret documents, or other images which are so small that they can be read only with a magnifying viewer. The camera and the method shown on these pages produce microdots as small as 1 mm in width; but cameras exist that can produce even smaller microdots. Historic accounts indicate that microphotography was used by spies and couriers during the Civil War in the 1860s. The KGB trained some of its agents, including its American spy Robert Thompson, to produce and conceal microdots. Methods of concealment include secret chambers in rings and coins, or a tiny piece of film that can be embedded in the edge of a postcard. Microdots are read with special viewers, and these, too, are often skillfully concealed.

Concealments

Microdots can be concealed in everyday objects or in special concealments. The German coin could conceal hundreds of microdots. The ring, designed during World War II, concealed either microdots or a compass. The slitter made incisions in the edges of postcards in which microdots could be hidden.

Reverse thread

Secret chamber

Secret chamber

RING

POSTCARD SLITTER

COIN

Microdot camera

The intelligence agencies of former Soviet bloc countries, such as East Germany, used this miniaturized microdot camera. Shown actual size and enlarged, this camera could be hidden easily. It was used to make the three microdots shown on the right, also actual size. The camera produces a finished microdot from the original photograph, without using an intermediate negative.

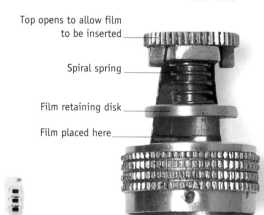

Top opens to allow film to be inserted

Spiral spring

Film retaining disk

Film placed here

PEN CAP

MICRODOT CAMERA (ACTUAL SIZE)

MICRODOTS (ACTUAL SIZE)

Microdot camera fits in hole made in ruler

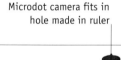

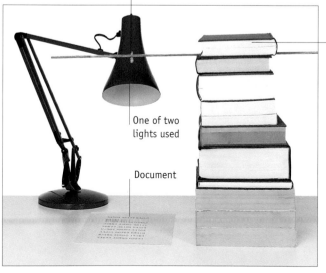

Books hold ruler at correct height

One of two lights used

Document

Using a microdot camera
The camera is attached to a ruler and positioned above the document to be photographed, using a stack of books. Each type of camera must be held securely at a specific distance from the document. Depending on the kind of film being used, the exposure time may be up to several minutes long.

Container for lens elements

MICRODOT CAMERA (ENLARGED)

Cap acts as a shutter for the long exposures used

SPY PROFILE Robert Glenn Thompson

In 1965, Robert Glenn Thompson (b.1925), a former member of the US Air Force Office of Special Investigations, was arrested and given a 30-year jail sentence for passing secrets to the KGB. He was trained by the KGB in Moscow in 1957, learning secret writing techniques, microphotography, and how to use a Minox camera. In 1978 Thompson was involved in a spy swap deal that allowed him to go to East Germany in exchange for an Israeli pilot.

Fountain pen viewer concealment

This East German microdot viewer is concealed within a 1950s fountain pen. A small ink sac could be installed, allowing the pen to work so that it would not arouse suspicion if examined. The pen would be used to transport the viewer between secure hiding places, or conceal it inside a desk.

Microdot readers

In order to read microdots, agents need high-powered magnifying devices. These can range from specially designed miniature viewers, small enough to be concealed in a cigarette, to commercially produced pocket microscopes. Agents operating in hostile countries prefer the most easily concealed types of readers.

Viewer small enough to fit in a cigarette

MICRODOT VIEWER **POCKET MICROSCOPE** **MINIATURE MICRODOT VIEWER**

FOUNTAIN-PEN NIB **MICRODOT VIEWER** **PEN BODY**

How to make a microdot

A microdot can be made with a high-quality 35mm camera by using a two-stage technique known as the British Method, which is shown here. Using high-contrast black-and-white film, a photograph of a document is taken so that the image of the document fills the whole frame of the film. The film is processed and the resulting negative is mounted in an opening cut in a piece of black cardboard. When lit from behind, the text on the negative shows up as white on black. This image is photographed from a distance of 4 ft 2 in (127 cm) – with a lens of focal length 50mm – to produce a black-on-white image that occupies a 1 mm length of the resulting negative. This tiny image is cut out to produce a microdot.

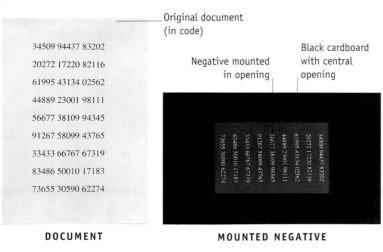

Original document (in code)

Negative mounted in opening

Black cardboard with central opening

DOCUMENT **MOUNTED NEGATIVE**

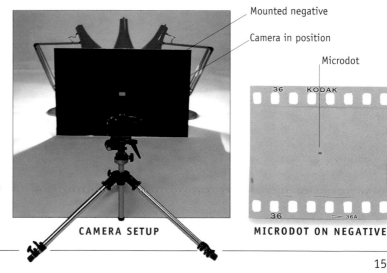

Mounted negative

Camera in position

Microdot

CAMERA SETUP **MICRODOT ON NEGATIVE**

Microdots II

Microdot system

This pocket-sized microdot system was made in the United States. It photographs the document, develops the image, dries the film, and allows the finished microdot to be punched out into the agent's hand. The camera's stainless-steel body allows developing chemicals to be poured directly into it, eliminating the need for other equipment. Its small size makes it easy to conceal.

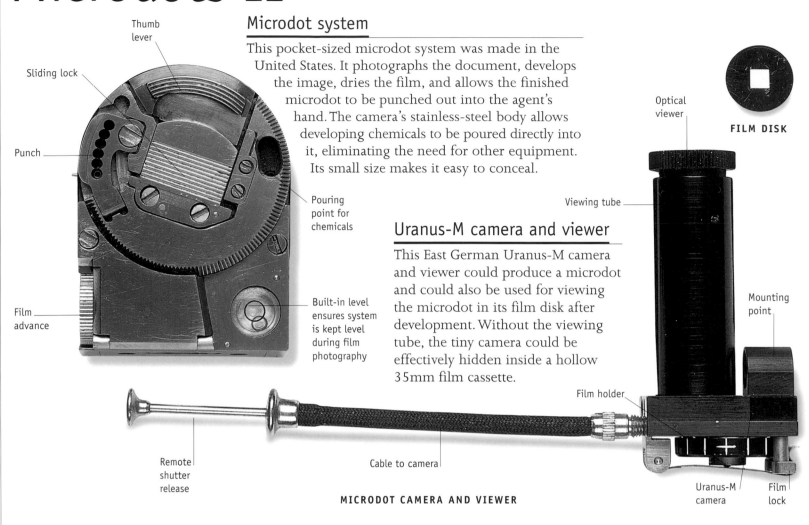

FILM DISK

Thumb lever

Sliding lock

Punch

Film advance

Pouring point for chemicals

Built-in level ensures system is kept level during film photography

Optical viewer

Viewing tube

Mounting point

Film holder

Remote shutter release

Cable to camera

Uranus-M camera

Film lock

MICRODOT CAMERA AND VIEWER

Uranus-M camera and viewer

This East German Uranus-M camera and viewer could produce a microdot and could also be used for viewing the microdot in its film disk after development. Without the viewing tube, the tiny camera could be effectively hidden inside a hollow 35mm film cassette.

Lucien Nikolai

Colonel Lucien Nikolai (1928–2000) joined the NKVD (predecessor of the KGB) in 1944 and was part of the graduating class of its first special Operational–Technical (OT) college in 1948. In the 1950s, Nicholai traveled throughout Europe providing secret tradecraft training to KGB "illegals" such as Rudolf Abel (see p. 196) and Konon Molody (see p. 50). In 1978, he was appointed head of the OT photographic department in the KGB's First Chief Directorate, where he pioneered special cameras and clandestine techniques for microdots and document copying.

Sliva microdot system

The KGB used the Sliva with a 100 W lightbulb, magnifying glass, and 35mm negative (of a document) to make microdots. The Zeiss lens of the Sliva focused the image from the negative onto a piece of cellophane, directly underneath the lens, that had been converted into high-resolution film using a collodion emulsion.

External shell

Zeiss lens

Mk IV microdot camera

This small camera is less than 1 in (25 mm) in diameter and produces 12 microdots onto a round film disk. Only the tiny lens protrudes from the flat surface of the camera, which could be disguised as a large coat button. The Mk IV is the only microdot camera officially acknowledged by the CIA.

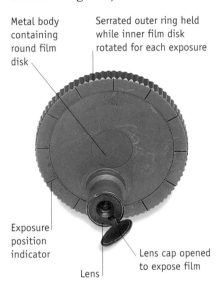

Metal body containing round film disk

Serrated outer ring held while inner film disk rotated for each exposure

Exposure position indicator

Lens cap opened to expose film

Lens

Bagulnik microcopy system

The Bagulnik microcopy system was developed by the KGB in the late 1960s. It was used by the Operative–Technical Department (OTU) for the quick production of microdots and other microphotographs from negatives. The system includes an image projector and a microscope table, which enables the operator to observe the image as it is being formed. To make a microphotograph, the negative's image is beamed onto a special photosensitive layer made from cellophane sensitized with a collodion emulsion.

● ● ● ● ● ● **TECHNICAL DATA**	
Date	Late 1960s
Lens	Zonnar f2 10 mm
Document size	1 × 1⅜ in (26 × 36 mm) film negative
Film type	Special photosensitive layers
Microdot size	1 × 1 mm or smaller
Voltage	127 or 220 volts
Copy lamp	30 or 75 Watts
Dimensions	16½ × 7⅞ × 10⅘ in (420 × 200 × 275 mm)
Weight	26½ lb (12 kg)

Uranus-2 microdot camera

In this East German device, a Zeiss lens has been attached to a standard Minox film cassette to create a small, easily concealable microdot camera. Separated from the cassette, the camera could be hidden inside a matchbox. Minox cassettes were used because they were readily available and reloadable with the high-resolution films necessary for producing microdots.

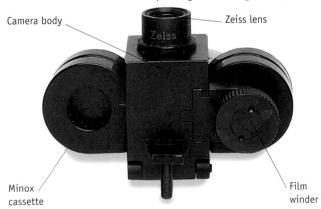

Camera body

Zeiss lens

Minox cassette

Film winder

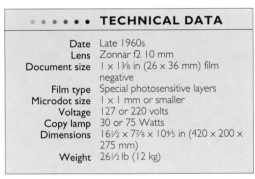

Lightbulb holder

Housing for lightbulb and cooling mechanism

Negative holder

Projector tube

Microscope eyepiece

Lens holder

Lens

Microscope table on which photosensitive cellophane is placed

Focusing adjustment

Concealments I

MANY INGENIOUS CONCEALMENTS have been devised to allow spies to hide information and equipment. They vary widely in size and format. The basic principle followed is to disguise or hide the item concerned so that it appears to be an innocent object that will not arouse suspicion. It is essential that the concealment used is in keeping with the lifestyle and circumstances of the agent equipped with it. Some concealments are made specifically for the purpose; others are converted from everyday objects. Some are booby-trapped, so that unauthorized attempts to open them will result in the destruction of their contents. Frequent use is made of reverse threads, which unscrew clockwise, rather than counterclockwise, as is usual.

Statuette concealment

This wooden carving of an elk covers a secret storage place for a subminiature camera. The elk can be lifted to reveal a compartment containing a Minox IIIS camera complete with a spare cassette of film. The statuette was found by the West German counterintelligence service (Bf V) in the apartment of an East German spy who had been operating in West Germany during the Cold-War period.

STATUETTE

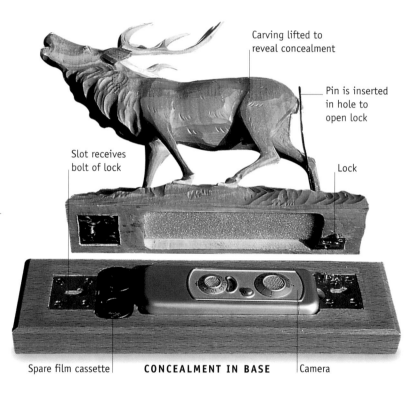

Carving lifted to reveal concealment

Pin is inserted in hole to open lock

Slot receives bolt of lock

Lock

Spare film cassette | **CONCEALMENT IN BASE** | Camera

Silver dollar concealment

Machined from two real 1978 coins for a Western intelligence service, this concealment was used to hide microfilm and one-time pads. It is opened by pressing on the eagle's wing tip.

Point that is pressed to open coin

Bottom half of hollow coin

Message to be concealed

Eye concealment

This German photograph dates from the period between the two World Wars. It illustrates the use of an artificial eye to conceal and transport a secret message.

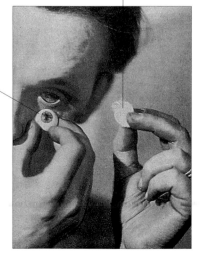

Artificial eye

SPY PROFILE | **Maria Knuth**

Polish intelligence recruited German Maria Knuth in 1948. She specialized in seduction as a means of recruiting agents to her side. Her first job was as a "letter box" for a spy ring in West Berlin. She was equipped with a number of concealment devices to hide microdots and sheets from one-time cipher pads. Later she attempted to recruit a member of West German counterintelligence (BfV), which led to her arrest in May 1952.

Brush concealment

Minox cameras were hidden in a variety of objects by the Soviet and East German intelligence services. The example shown here is concealed inside a gentleman's clothes brush. Services that issued such items had to ensure that they fitted in with the lifestyle adopted by their agent; otherwise, the concealment might arouse suspicion.

Slot for locking pin

Hole for inserting pin to open concealment

Minox IIIS camera

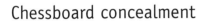

CLOTHES BRUSH CONCEALMENT

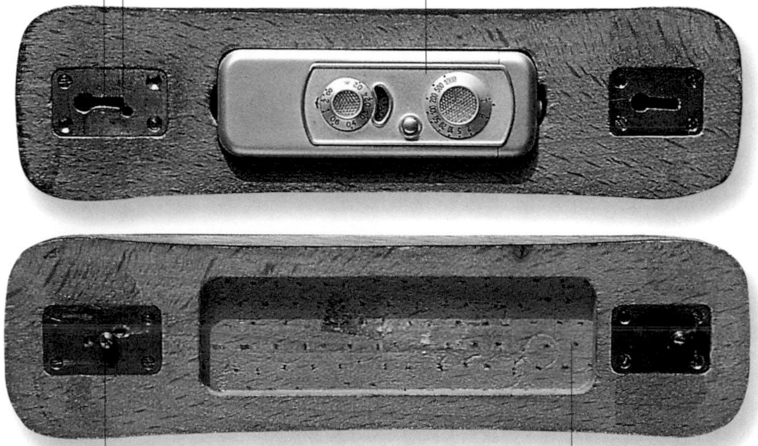

Locking pin keeps concealment shut

SECRET COMPARTMENT WITH CAMERA

Hollow to accommodate camera

Chessboard concealment

West German counterintelligence discovered this chessboard in an East German agent's possession. It has an internal cavity to conceal a microdot camera, accessories, and film. Such concealments were almost always "one-of-a-kind" items, designed in special workshops for specific missions.

Microdot camera (uses Minox film and cassette)

Hidden locking mechanism can be opened only with a paper clip

Manual winder to advance film in cassette

Socket for chess pieces (not part of the concealment)

Paper clip opens the concealment

Minox film cassette for microdot camera

PLAYING SURFACE

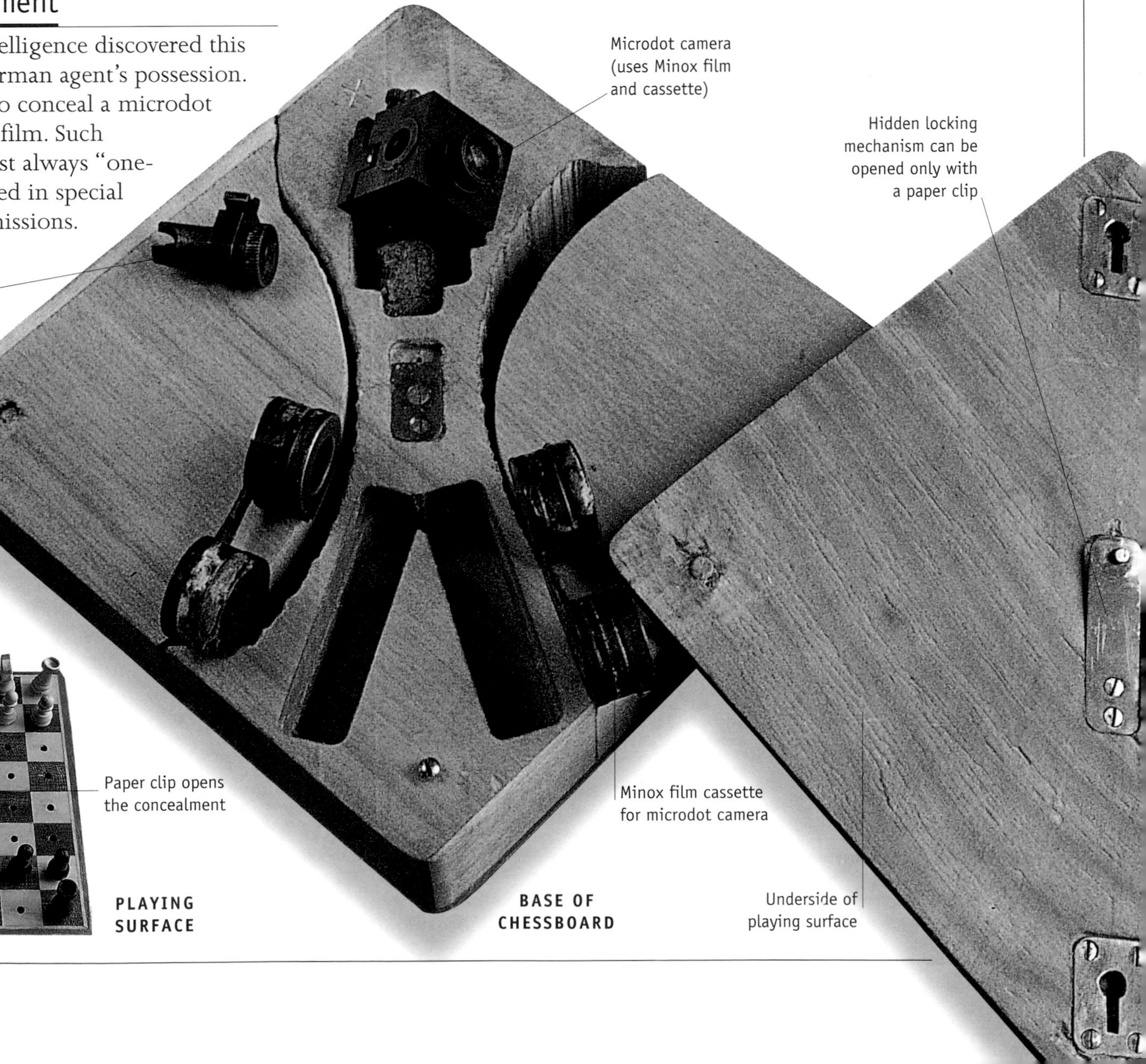

BASE OF CHESSBOARD

Underside of playing surface

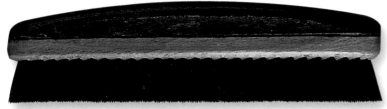

Concealments II

Button and stamp concealments

Even careful counterintelligence searches rarely reveal messages such as this inscription under a button, made during World War I, or the tiny message under a postage stamp, used in 1962.

Front of button

Message on back of stamp

Coded message on back

BUTTON

POSTAGE STAMP

Cigarette concealment

The Polish intelligence service made this metal cylinder so that spies and couriers could conceal tightly rolled "soft film" (film from which the celluloid has been removed to make the film extremely thin) in a cigarette.

Cigarette split open

Aluminum container

Soft film

Container lid

Battery casing concealment

This style of concealment was used by intelligence agencies in the countries of the former Soviet bloc. Inside the casing of a standard flashlight battery was a cavity in which film, money, and even microdot cameras and viewers could be hidden. Also in the casing was a much smaller real battery that gave the correct voltage so that the fake battery could actually be used. To open the fake battery casing, the base plate had to be unscrewed using a magnet.

INNER BATTERY

HOLLOW BATTERY CASING

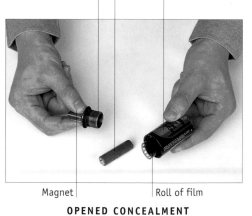

Base plate

Inner battery

Battery casing

Magnet

Roll of film

OPENED CONCEALMENT

Reverse thread

Base plate

Magnet

MAGNET AND BASE PLATE

Soap case concealment

The Czech intelligence service invented devices for couriers carrying film, such as this soap case. The devices destroy the evidence if opened incorrectly: here the film is wrapped around a flashbulb, which flashes and destroys the film if the case is not opened in the correct manner. To open the case safely, a magnet is placed beneath the case. The magnet pulls open a switch that deactivates the flash.

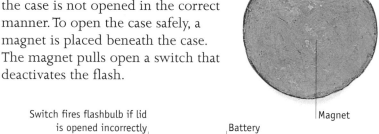

Magnet

Switch fires flashbulb if lid is opened incorrectly

Battery

Deactivating switch

Flashbulb

Lid

The artwork of Baden-Powell

Lord Baden-Powell (1857–1941) is best known as the founder of the Boy Scouts, but he was involved in intelligence-gathering during his early military career. One mission was to obtain details of enemy fortresses in the Balkans in 1890. Baden-Powell disguised himself as an entomologist and sketched butterflies in the area. The veins on the butterfly's wings contained a plan of the fortifications, while the spots on the veins denoted the size and position of guns. The drawing of the leaf was made to show trench lines.

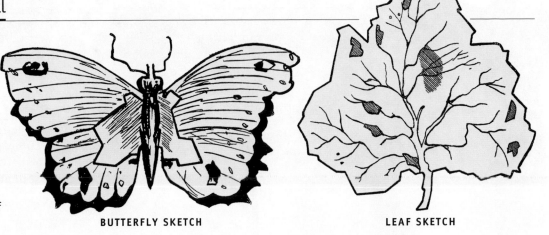

BUTTERFLY SKETCH

LEAF SKETCH

Shaving concealments

Everyday objects, such as these toiletry items, can be carried without attracting any suspicion. The handle of this French shaving brush has a cavity that opens only when the base is turned clockwise. The can holds and dispenses a small amount of shaving cream; the rest of the space in the can may be used for concealment.

Top of brush unscrews

Roll of film

SHAVING BRUSH

SHAVING CREAM CAN

Base of can

Hollow bolt

This hollow bolt was used as a dead drop (see p. 160) by Soviet agents operating in West Germany. The head of the bolt could be removed to reveal a cavity in which items could be concealed. Once the bolt was filled it could be screwed into the dead drop site, in this case a wooden railing on a bridge, ready for the arrival of an agent or handler.

Bolt in position

BOLT ON BRIDGE

Rolled-up message

HEAD OF BOLT

HOLLOW BOLT

DEAD DROP SITE ON BRIDGE

Concealments III

Iron concealment

A West German housewife used this modified iron as a concealment for one-time pads (see p. 149) and communication schedules. With her tradecraft items safely hidden, nothing else in the apartment linked her to the HVA (East German foreign intelligence service). Even when her apartment was later searched by the West German Criminal Police (BKA), the concealment was not discovered. The iron could not be operated when the concealment was filled.

Retainer clip
Body of iron

Attachment peg
False bottom of iron
Internal lock

IRON

FRAME OF CONCEALMENT

Plug

Lighter concealment

Popular Zippo-style cigarette lighters could be transformed into effective concealments. This KGB modified lighter functioned normally but also contained a hidden cavity built into the base for hiding microfilm.

Dampener
Vented hood
Thumb-wheel

LIGHTER WITH CAVITY

LIGHTER CASING

Body of lighter

Base opened to reveal concealment cavity

Rectal concealment

MI6 (the British foreign intelligence service) produced this small concealment to store microfilm. It was designed to be hidden in the rectum and came with its own condom.

Knurled surface

O-ring seal

Tube concealment

This tube appears unmodified and is pliable when squeezed. Inside is an inner shell that creates a waterproof concealment cavity, accessed by unscrewing the upper portion of the tube. The cavity is large enough to conceal a rolled-up false passport for a KGB agent to make an escape.

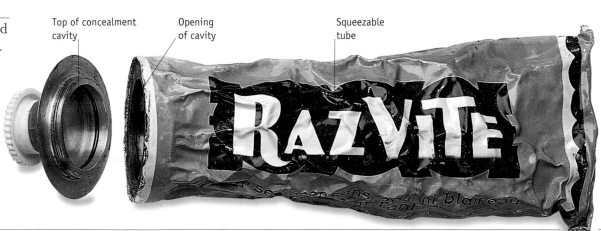

Top of concealment cavity

Opening of cavity

Squeezable tube

Spray
nozzle

laque
spéciale

eugène
INSTITUT

Composée d'éléments fixants
et adoucissants,
la laque spéciale
Eugène Institut
respecte et protège
les cheveux.
Elle convient donc
tout spécialement aux cheveux
de texture délicate.
Elle maintient la coiffure
en donnant aux cheveux
souplesse et brillance.
Elle disparaît
au premier brossage
et au shampooing.

Hole for
puncturing
condom

92°

eugène
INSTITUT

Paris
Made in France.

**AEROSOL
CAN**

Aerosol concealment

This can was used by KGB couriers to
transport undeveloped Minox film. Each
roll of exposed film was spooled onto an
outer ring, with each layer of film separated
by a layer of cotton ribbon. The rings fit
over an inner core containing an ammonia-
filled condom. If danger was detected, the
condom was punctured and the ammonia,
absorbed by the cotton, destroyed the film.

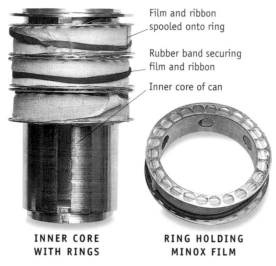

Film and ribbon
spooled onto ring

Rubber band securing
film and ribbon

Inner core of can

**INNER CORE
WITH RINGS**

**RING HOLDING
MINOX FILM**

Ashtray concealment for Minox camera

The HVA (see p. 56) designed this
ashtray to conceal a Minox IIIS camera.
The top unscrewed for quick access to
the camera but had to be turned the
"wrong" way because of its reverse
thread mechanism. The ashtray was
always left filled with cigarette ash,
making it unlikely to be searched.

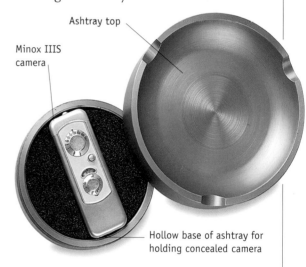

Ashtray top

Minox IIIS
camera

Hollow base of ashtray for
holding concealed camera

BASE OF CAN

Hollow construction nail

The KGB modified this construction
nail to create a small cavity for hiding
soft film (photographic emulsion that
has been separated from its thick plastic
backing). The fragile, thin film could
be easily rolled and hidden in the nail.

Shoe heel concealments

Shoe heels were used to create
concealment cavities for transporting
exposed, but undeveloped, film. The
woman's shoe (top) has a cylindrical
cavity in the heel large enough for
rolled-up one-time pads (see p. 149)
and microfilm. In the man's heel
(bottom), a metal reinforcement
prevents indentations in the heel that
might reveal the cavity, which was
used to hide Minox film. After the
introduction of metal detectors in
airports, heel concealments could
no longer be reinforced with metal.

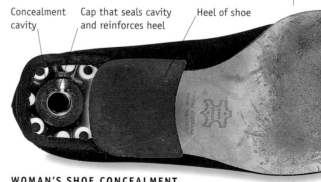

Concealment
cavity

Cap that seals cavity
and reinforces heel

Heel of shoe

WOMAN'S SHOE CONCEALMENT

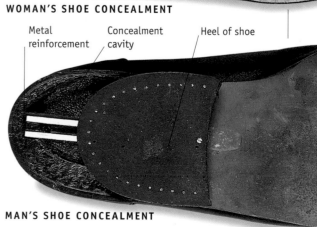

Metal
reinforcement

Concealment
cavity

Heel of shoe

MAN'S SHOE CONCEALMENT

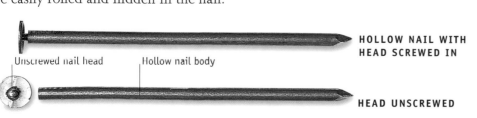

Unscrewed nail head

Hollow nail body

**HOLLOW NAIL WITH
HEAD SCREWED IN**

HEAD UNSCREWED

Dead drops I

A DEAD DROP IS A PREARRANGED location at which spies can leave information or from which they can collect instructions, cipher pads, microdot cameras, film, radio schedules, money, or any form of spying equipment. Items are usually placed in specially designed dead drop containers. Spies use dead drops because they are safer than personal meetings, which can jeopardize the safety of at least two links in a spy network. The sites used for dead drops must be inconspicuous, but easy for the agents to find. The procedure for making a dead drop involves a series of signals which the controller and the agent use to ensure that an enemy is not involved or watching.

Dead drop spikes

Shown full-size, these spikes are stuck in the ground; they are used to hold money, cipher pads, microdot cameras, and other items ready for collection at dead drop locations. One is designed to hold

Open lid

35mm film cassette

Spiked tip

DEAD DROP SPIKE FOR 35mm FILM CASSETTES

John Walker's final dead drop

On the evening of May 17, 1985, John Walker, an American spy for the KGB (see p. 54), drove to a dead drop site on a country road in Maryland, some 25 miles (40 km) northwest of Washington, DC. He was under surveillance by the FBI.

To signal to his KGB handler that he was in the area for the drop, Walker placed an empty soda can at the foot of a roadside utility pole. His secret documents were hidden inside a bag of garbage, and he placed this behind another utility pole.

The FBI, following Walker, saw him place the soda can and thought it might contain something of importance, so they removed it. The KGB officer, unable to find the can, terminated the procedure and returned safely to the Soviet embassy in Washington, where he was based.

The FBI retrieved the garbage bag, complete with the secret documents, and Walker was arrested later that night.

Annotated map

Instructions with place names in red

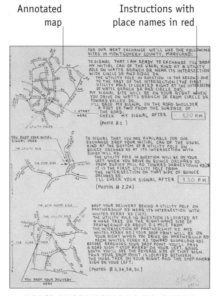

KGB'S INSTRUCTIONS TO GUIDE WALKER TO HIS DEAD DROP SITE

Garbage

Secret documents

CONTENTS OF WALKER'S DEAD DROP

Label for dead drop site

Utility pole

KGB PHOTOGRAPH OF THE DEAD DROP

Dead drop Emil

During the 1950s, Bruno Sniegowski spied for Poland in West Germany. The officers in charge of Sniegowski communicated with him using dead drops, one of which was codenamed Emil. A chalk mark at a prearranged place would inform Sniegowski that a message awaited him at Emil. The container used for dead drop Emil was a metal tube, which was hidden at the base of a wall, behind a brick.

SNIEGOWSKI AT DEAD DROP EMIL

Clam dead drop

A magnet holds this dead drop container to a metal object at the location of the drop. A dead drop location need not be in the ground — the clam container can be used in many places; for example, under an abandoned car or metal park bench.

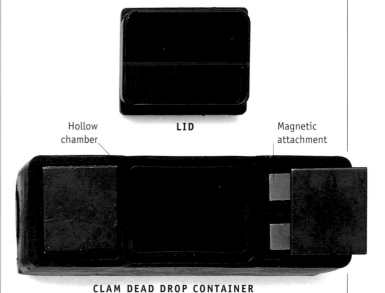

Hollow chamber **LID** Magnetic attachment

CLAM DEAD DROP CONTAINER

Waterproof dead drop

The weights in this waterproof pouch allow it to be be used to conceal material in a roadside ditch, or beneath marked rocks in a shallow stream.

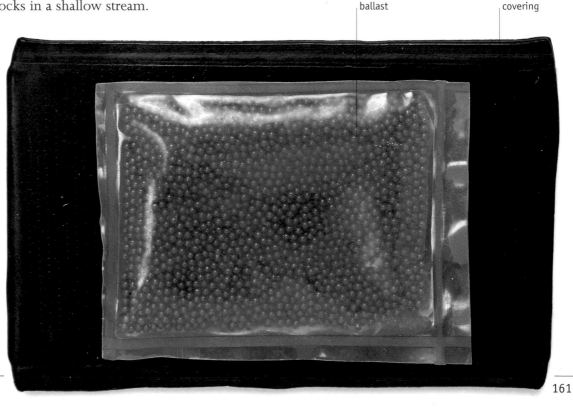

Lead shot for ballast

Plastic covering

DEAD DROP SPIKE

Dead drops II

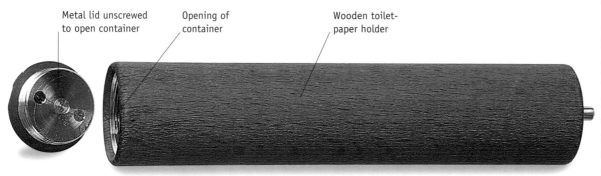

Metal lid unscrewed to open container

Opening of container

Wooden toilet-paper holder

Toilet-paper holder dead drop

The HVA (see p. 56) used this hollow toilet paper holder on trains that passed through East Germany from Western countries. The drop would be filled by an agent in the West and safely cleared by the HVA after the train crossed the border into East Germany.

Log dead drop

This wooden log was used in Australia during the 1950s for secret communications between a KGB officer and the Australian Security and Intelligence Organization (ASIO). The log appears to be an ordinary piece of cut firewood with a protruding bent nail. When the nail is removed, a spring-loaded wooden plug pops out to reveal a cylindrical, hermetically sealed metal container.

Dead-letter boxes

Britain's MI6 (see p. 201) used metal spikes as containers for passing film and messages. The spikes were often buried in grassy areas near the base of a lamppost or bench. Messages written on paper were rolled around a metal winder inserted into the hollow spike.

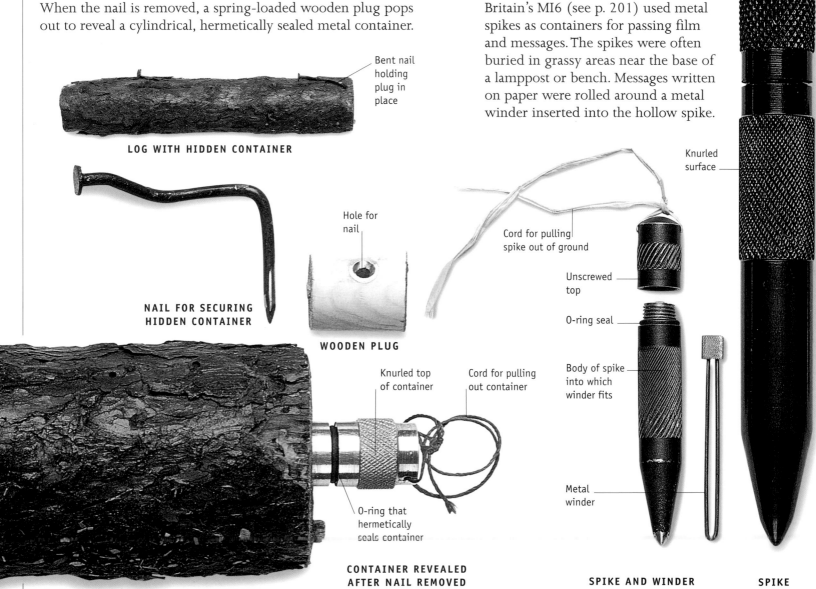

Bent nail holding plug in place

LOG WITH HIDDEN CONTAINER

Hole for nail

NAIL FOR SECURING HIDDEN CONTAINER

WOODEN PLUG

Removable top

Knurled surface

Cord for pulling spike out of ground

Unscrewed top

O-ring seal

Body of spike into which winder fits

Metal winder

Knurled top of container

Cord for pulling out container

O-ring that hermetically seals container

CONTAINER REVEALED AFTER NAIL REMOVED

SPIKE AND WINDER

SPIKE

Rock concealment

This fake rock was used as a concealment in a Soviet Military Intelligence (GRU) operation in the United States in the late 1970s. The rock's color and size were designed to blend in with naturally occurring rocks at the designated drop site.

Paper lining

Composite surface

Underwater document holder

When the East German government began to collapse in 1989, its foreign intelligence service (the HVA) worked to safeguard the identities of its agents still operating around the world. The HVA did this by caching sensitive computer printouts listing the real names of the agents (known elsewhere only by their codenames) in underwater holders.

Bolt for tightening lid

Waterproofing ring

Lid

Fiberglass tube

Metal cache

This titanium cylinder was used for long-term underground storage at a remote location. During the Cold War, the KGB secretly buried caches of spy equipment inside many Western European countries.

Titanium body

Grip for removing lid

Watertight lid

Cemetery spike

Agents who worked for the HVA (see p. 56) inside West Germany were provided with stainless-steel dead-drop spikes, which were often hidden in the ground in cemeteries. The large hollow spike provided ample room for documents, money, and even a rolled false passport for an escape.

Removable top

Hollow steel body

A perfect hiding place?
The cemetery setting provided many places to conceal a dead-drop spike and could also explain the presence of visitors at irregular times.

WEAPONS

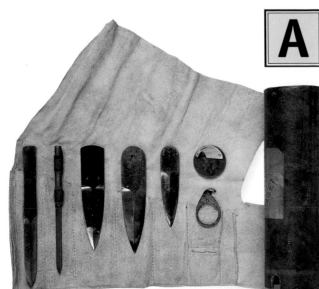

Concealed blades
During World War II, the British SOE developed a number of concealable edged weapons, as displayed in this knife roll.

A SPY WHOSE FUNCTION is purely to gather intelligence does not normally carry or own a weapon, since there is always a risk that an enemy counterintelligence force might discover the weapon, which would incriminate the spy. Intelligence agencies do, however, stock and even develop weapons for the use of personnel who carry out specialized roles: bodyguards, assassins, and other covert action personnel. In wartime, special forces operating behind enemy lines carry both conventional and specialized weapons.

SILENCED WEAPONS

Although the frequency of their use in espionage has been exaggerated by writers of spy fiction, silenced weapons do have a role in the work of intelligence agencies. Many were developed for special operations use during World War II. Because firearms can never be made completely silent or flashless, experiments were made with crossbows and with pistols adapted to fire darts.

CZ27 semiautomatic pistol with silencer
This Czech 7.65mm pistol from World War II was later used by West German intelligence.

Some of the silenced firearms employed in World War II, such as the Welrod (see p. 193) used by the SOE and the Hi-Standard pistol (see p. 171) of the OSS, remain part of the arsenals of major intelligence agencies.

In some cases, silenced weapons are issued for survival use – for example, for hunting if stranded in a remote area. In other cases, they may be issued as a defense against guard dogs, rather than for attacking human opponents.

CLOSE-COMBAT WEAPONS

Three-finger push dagger
This World War II British dagger had a three-fingered grip that allowed the blade to be thrust into a victim with tremendous force.

Specialized weapons made for fighting at close quarters are often carried in covert operations. A considerable degree of training is needed to use some types of close-combat weapons. The type of personnel who carry them are those ordered to attack individual targets by surprise, or those taking part in high-risk operations who may need a last-resort weapon for self defense. They range from traditional "brass knuckles" to specially designed weapons such as the World War II Peskett Device, which is a combined dagger, garrotte, and cosh.

The spring cosh is often the weapon of choice for subduing opponents. It may be used with lethal force, or merely to give a knockout blow. Other coshes are used as a means of forcing an enemy to surrender or to disclose information.

Knives are the classic close-combat weapons, and many different types have been developed for use in various situations. Small blades can be hidden under a jacket lapel for emergency use. However, the Fairbairn-Sykes fighting knife of World War II was designed for offensive use. It is so perfectly suited to its purpose that it continued in production and service into the 1990s.

Genrikh Yagoda
Yagoda (1891–1938) was head of the Soviet NKVD and set up a poison weapons workshop.

Assassination device
Hidden in a fake cigarette pack, this device fires acid that vaporizes into deadly cyanide gas in the victim's face, causing death within seconds.

CONCEALED WEAPONS

World War II saw the development of a number of concealed weapons. The main purpose of such weapons was to give an agent who had been detected some chance of escape. They included firing devices that could be worn on belts or carried up an agent's sleeve. Others were disguised as cigars, pipes, or pens. After the war, intelligence agencies continued to develop such weapons – a notable example being the 4.5mm caliber firing device issued by the KGB, which could be hidden in a variety of concealments, including a lipstick holder.

The KGB developed assassination weapons that could kill silently and in ways not detectable at autopsy; for example, by emitting poison gas or injecting poison pellets. These weapons have been disguised as canes or umbrellas, or concealed in newspapers.

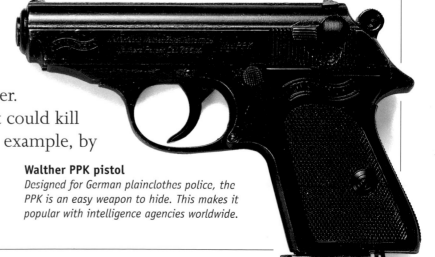

Walther PPK pistol
Designed for German plainclothes police, the PPK is an easy weapon to hide. This makes it popular with intelligence agencies worldwide.

Special issue weapons

INTELLIGENCE AGENCIES prefer to equip their personnel with weapons that can be bought commercially, provided the performance is up to operational requirements. Such weapons are cheaper than specially developed ones and, if discovered, less incriminating as they cannot be traced to the agency. The only noticeable difference might be that the agency's armorers may have fine-tuned the sights and trigger to improve performance. The term "special issue" refers to weapons obtained in this way, and to such weapons as the dear gun, manufactured for the CIA for issue to Vietnamese agents in the Vietnam war (1961–75). This cheap, single-shot gun was intended to enable an agent to kill an enemy soldier in order to capture his or her weapon.

CIA DEAR GUN

Royal Canadian Mounted Police

Until 1981, counterintelligence and security in Canada were the responsibility of the security service of the Royal Canadian Mounted Police (RCMP). An RCMP "Red Squad" was set up in the 1920s to stop the spread of communism. Canadian intelligence realized the extent of infiltration by Soviet spies in 1945, when a Soviet defector informed the Canadians of wide-ranging espionage operations in their country. In 1984, the Canadian Security Intelligence Service (CSIS) was set up to take over in this field from the RCMP. The Colt Bodyguard shown below is an example of the wide variety of weapons available to CSIS officers.

Crest of the RCMP
The members of the Royal Canadian Mounted Police are frequently known as Mounties.

Foresight

Hammer

Muzzle

Hammer shroud

Ejector rod

Cylinder

Colt emblem

Trigger guard

Trigger

Hand grip

•••••	**TECHNICAL DATA**
Maker	Colt Firearms
Frame	Detective Special
Caliber	.38 special
Length	4¾ in (121 mm)
Weight	19 oz (595 g) unloaded
Barrel length	2 in (54 mm)
Capacity	6-shot revolver
Ammunition	Variable

Colt .38 Bodyguard revolver

The Bodyguard was a modification of the famous Colt Detective Special. A shroud, added to the rear of the frame, prevented the hammer from snagging on clothing if the pistol was drawn from inside a pocket. The revolver was used by many security and intelligence services, including the RCMP.

Barrel

Ejector rod | Cylinder

Hammer

Hand grip

Trigger

Trigger guard

Colt .38 Commando revolver

This six-shot revolver was issued to OSS Sergeant C. W. Magill, who fought with the Greek resistance during World War II. It was one of a variety of pistol types used by the OSS (see p. 32) and was also supplied to American and Allied troops. The Commando was too large for covert operations that depended on concealment, but served well in resistance support operations.

Sergeant C. W. Magill
This World War II photograph shows Sergeant Magill at the age of 28, when he was serving with the OSS in Greece. His role was to work with Greek resistance units. The location here is the mountain village of Kastania.

The French secret service

Formerly known as the SDECE, the French secret service was reconstituted in 1981 and called the DGSE. French operatives have been involved in many high-profile operations, including attempts to assassinate and abduct foreign political leaders. They made several attempts to assassinate President Nasser of Egypt during the 1950s, despite the fact that he was being supported by the CIA.

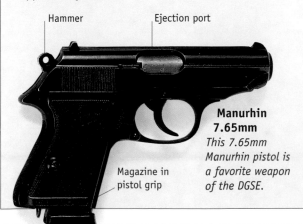

Hammer   Ejection port

Manurhin 7.65mm
This 7.65mm Manurhin pistol is a favorite weapon of the DGSE.

Magazine in pistol grip

Nagant 7.62mm secret police revolver

In the 1920s, a compact version of the standard Nagant service revolver was developed for the Soviet secret police. The 7.62mm Secret Police revolver was easily concealed. It was used until the 1940s, and armed the elite bodyguard unit that protected Stalin, the head of state, in Moscow.

Shortened barrel

Hammer

Trigger

Peter Deriaban
As a member of the KGB's elite Kremlin Guard Directorate, the defector Deriaban was issued with the Nagant.

Silenced weapons I

FIREARMS ARE NEVER totally silent, although they can be made quiet enough not to attract attention. A silencer eliminates most of the sound of the muzzle blast, but not the sound of the weapon's working parts. Ammunition that travels slower than the speed of sound is used, so avoiding the "crack" caused by supersonic bullets. Most silenced weapons were developed for assassinations or for special operations in armed conflicts. In peacetime, spies who are not on special assassination missions may carry silenced weapons for self-defense. The U-2 spy plane pilot Francis Gary Powers (see p. 52) was issued with the silenced Hi-Standard pistol for use as a hunting weapon in case his plane should be downed in remote enemy territory.

Mossad

The Institute for Intelligence and Special Operations, or Mossad, was formed in 1951 as Israel's external intelligence service. It is the equivalent of the United States' CIA or Britain's MI6, but employs far fewer personnel: only 30–35 Mossad case officers are active in the whole world. However, the organization often also draws on local Jewish volunteers, known as *sayanim* (see p. 197). Mossad is most active against hostile Arab states surrounding Israel and against Palestinian political organizations. One of its most prominent operations was the daring abduction of the Nazi war criminal Adolf Eichmann from Argentina in 1960 to stand trial in Israel for his crimes in World War II.

MOSSAD CREST

Beretta 7.65 mm pistol with silencer

Italian Beretta pistols are often used by Mossad. The small Beretta is easy to conceal and can be loaded with reduced-charge cartridges in order to increase the effectiveness of the silencer. This adaptation of a Beretta Model 70 was issued to members of Mossad's assassination teams (known as *kidon*).

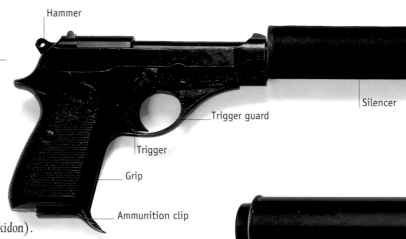

Hammer

Trigger guard

Trigger

Grip

Ammunition clip

Silencer

End cap

Silencer

Peter Mason

Former Defense Intelligence Staff Captain Peter Mason (b.1927) is one of the leading experts on special weapons and close-combat shooting. In 1946 he joined a British Special Air Service (SAS) "Hunter Team." Using captured enemy weapons, such as the Beretta used by the OVRA (see opposite), these three-man teams hunted down and secretly killed those guilty of murdering SAS or SOE members (see p. 30) during World War II.

SS Colonel Otto Skorzeny
Otto Skorzeny (1908–75) was the commander of Germany's Brandenburg commando detachment in World War II. He mounted a number of audacious operations, including the dramatic rescue of the Italian leader Mussolini from Italian resistance forces. Skorzeny often used a captured British silenced Sten submachine gun for his operations.

Silencers disguised as flashlights

These two silencers were disguised as flashlights so that they could be transported secretly without arousing any suspicion. Although the flashlights did not work, the disguise was effective when the flashlights were packed with other ordinary workshop tools. The parts added for disguise were easily removable, enabling the the silencers to be converted rapidly for their real purpose.

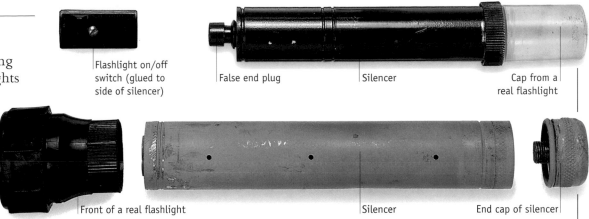

Flashlight on/off switch (glued to side of silencer)

False end plug

Silencer

Cap from a real flashlight

Front of a real flashlight

Silencer

End cap of silencer

Italian fascist secret police

Italy's Organizzazione di Vigilanza e Repressione dell'Antifascismo (OVRA) was formed in 1926 to suppress opposition to the Italian fascist government. During World War II, the OVRA operated against resistance groups in the French Alps and in the Balkans. The OVRA also recruited a number of double agents (see p. 9), who spied on the activities of Britain's SOE (see p. 30) in Italy. Some OVRA members remained loyal to the Italian fascist regime until the closing stages of the war. The pistol shown here was carried in 1945 by an OVRA team led by a German officer.

Endcap

Cutaway shows silencer baffles

OVRA crest

Hammer

Silencer

Trigger

Seven-round magazine

Silenced 9mm Beretta 1934 pistol
This is a silenced version of the standard Italian service pistol. A subsonic 9mm round made this pistol even more effective as a silenced weapon. The OVRA crest is painted on the silencer.

Foresight

Cocking handle

Rear sight

Magazine release catch

32-round magazine

Trigger guard

Trigger

Skeleton butt

Sten Mark II silenced submachine gun

The Sten gun was designed to be produced easily and cheaply in large numbers. It was durable and simple to use, with a lightweight, skeleton butt. Fully automatic fire would have damaged the silencer, so the Sten was usually used as a single-shot weapon. This silenced model was used by British commandos, but another version known as the Mark IIS was developed by the SOE (see p. 30).

Silenced weapons II

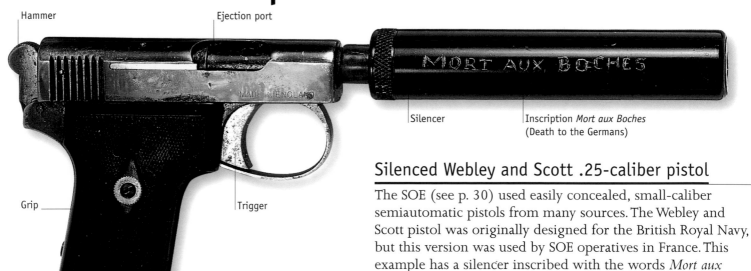

Hammer

Ejection port

Grip

Trigger

Ammunition clip

Silencer

Inscription *Mort aux Boches*
(Death to the Germans)

Silenced Webley and Scott .25-caliber pistol

The SOE (see p. 30) used easily concealed, small-caliber semiautomatic pistols from many sources. The Webley and Scott pistol was originally designed for the British Royal Navy, but this version was used by SOE operatives in France. This example has a silencer inscribed with the words *Mort aux Boches* (Death to the Germans).

Internal baffles to suppress noise

Silencer

Hammer

Sight (not usable with the silencer)

Barrel

Trigger

Soviet star emblem

Grip

Ammunition clip

Silenced Tokarev TT-33 7.62mm pistol

The Tokarev pistol replaced the Nagant (see p. 167) as the service pistol of Soviet intelligence agencies until the 1950s. A silenced model was used by counterintelligence officers of SMERSH (see p. 38). Special ammunition with a reduced propellant charge was used to keep bullets subsonic, thereby avoiding the crack that ordinary, supersonic bullets make as they go through the sound barrier. This Tokarev has been cross-sectioned by British intelligence to show its working parts.

Parker Hale silencer

Barrel

Attachment for optional sling

Home Guard Auxiliary Units

The Home Guard was a locally based army in Britain during World War II, composed of spare-time soldiers who also continued to work in their normal civilian jobs. The Auxiliary Units were an elite force drawn from its ranks. Units were trained to wage guerrilla warfare behind German lines in case of an invasion and were issued with secret stocks of weapons and explosives.

**AUXILIARY
UNIT BADGE**

Winchester Model 74 .22-caliber rifle

American Winchester 74 sporting rifles were purchased for the British Home Guard Auxiliary Units and modified by the addition of British-made accessories: a Parker Hale silencer and an Enfield telescopic sight. The rifles were intended for use against German soldiers and tracker dogs if the Germans invaded Britain — which never happened. However, during tests simulating the rough conditions of operating from underground shelters that would be likely in the event of an invasion, the rifles proved unsuitable for use because their sights were easily knocked out of alignment.

Colby's Jedburgh team

The World War II Jedburgh teams were made up of three men from SOE or OSS (see p. 30 and 32), and Free French units (see p. 31). Teams were sent to France in 1944 to coordinate resistance activities supporting the Allied invasion of France. OSS Major William Colby, later to become head of the CIA, was a member of a Jedburgh team codenamed Bruce. His two Free French team-mates are shown.

JACQUES FAVEL: CODENAME GALWAY

LOUIS GIRY: CODENAME PIASTRE

WILLIAM COLBY: CODENAME BERKSHIRE

Cocking rod

Firing lever

Armband

Elastic strap

Foresight

Silencer

Rear sight

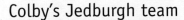

Silenced Hi-Standard Model B .22-caliber pistol

The Hi-Standard pistol was commercially available before World War II. This silenced version, however, was made for the Research and Development Branch of the OSS. The pistol was accurate and quiet, and did not produce a muzzle flash.

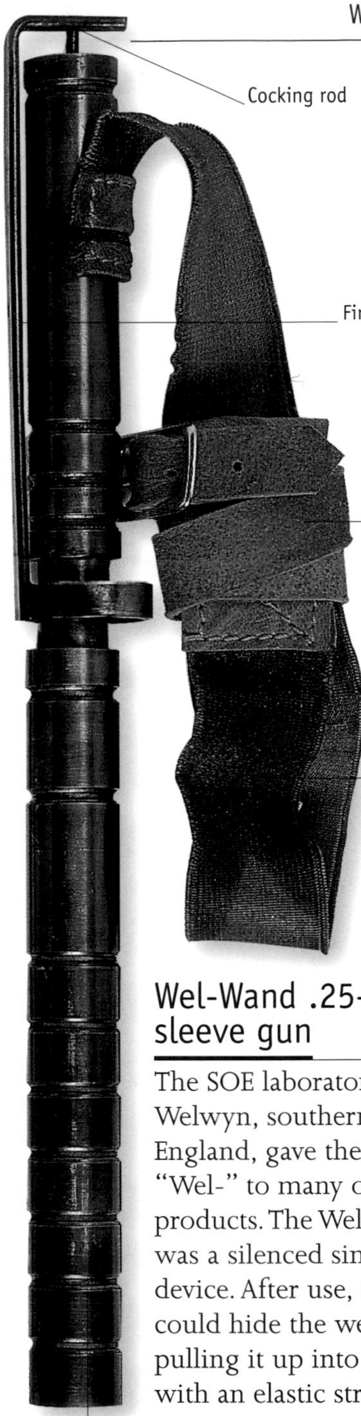

Trigger

Ten-round ammunition clip

Wel-Wand .25-caliber sleeve gun

The SOE laboratory in Welwyn, southern England, gave the prefix "Wel-" to many of its products. The Wel-Wand was a silenced single-shot device. After use, the user could hide the weapon by pulling it up into his sleeve with an elastic strap.

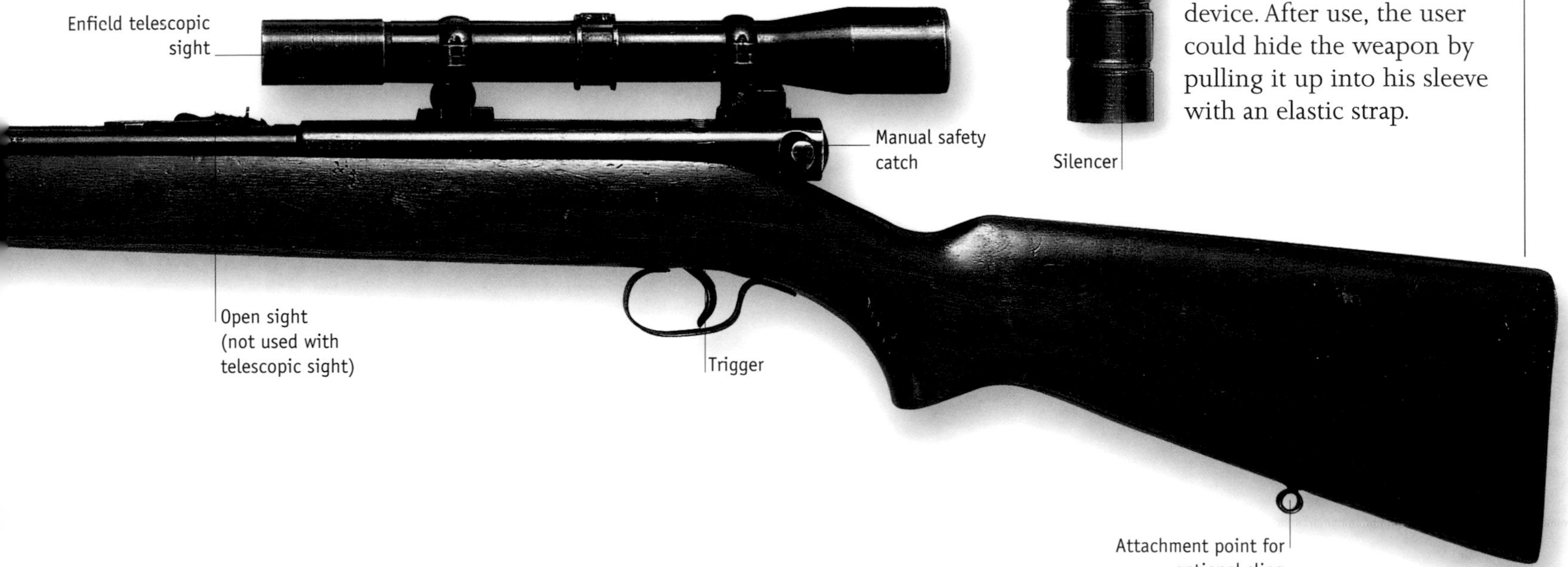

Silencer

Enfield telescopic sight

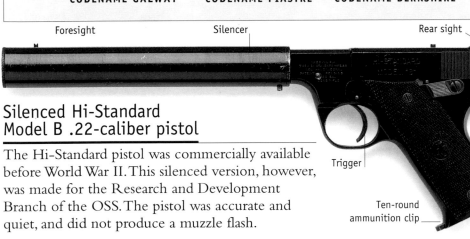

Manual safety catch

Open sight (not used with telescopic sight)

Trigger

Attachment point for optional sling

Crossbows and darts

MANY INTELLIGENCE AGENCIES have tried to develop weapons capable of firing silently and without emitting a muzzle flash. During World War II, some designs were based on earlier weapons: medieval crossbows and slingshots were the inspiration for the Big Joe 5 crossbow, while a close-range weapon called the bigot was a pistol adapted to fire a dart. But, after tests proved that these weapons were less effective than the newly improved silenced guns, they were not adopted. Weapons invented since World War II include a steel crossbow developed for British special forces.

Adapted Colt .45
semiautomatic pistol

BIGOT

Dart-firing pistol

Invented in the United States in 1944, the bigot was a pistol adapted to fire a dart. This was launched from a structure known as a spigot, which protruded from the gun's muzzle. The dart's flight was powered by the blast from a blank cartridge located inside the forward end of the fin tube. The weapon fired without making a visible flash.

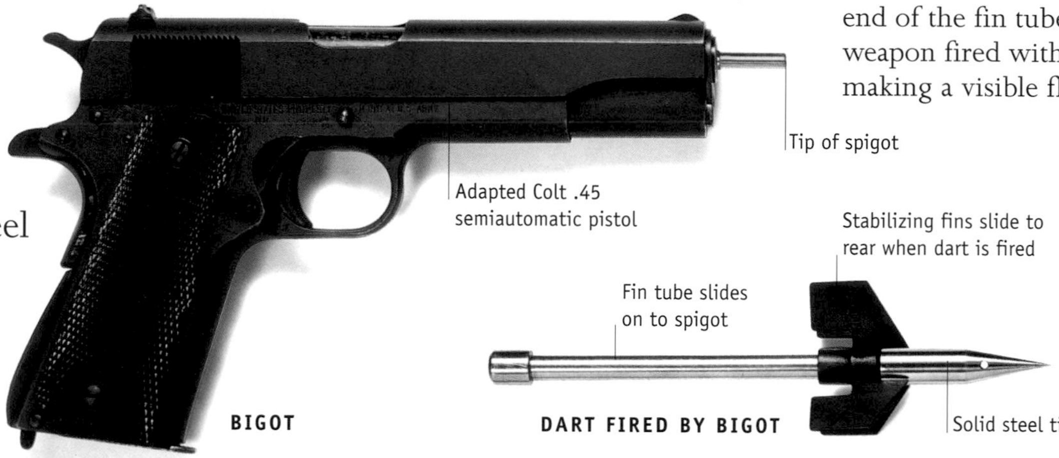

Tip of spigot

Stabilizing fins slide to rear when dart is fired

Fin tube slides on to spigot

DART FIRED BY BIGOT

Solid steel tip

Steel crossbow

This lightweight British weapon from the 1970s has a powerful metal bow. It shoots either a normal steel bolt or a knife blade. Originally meant for use in assassinations or combat missions, in practice the crossbow has mainly been used for killing guard dogs.

BOW

Reinforced section

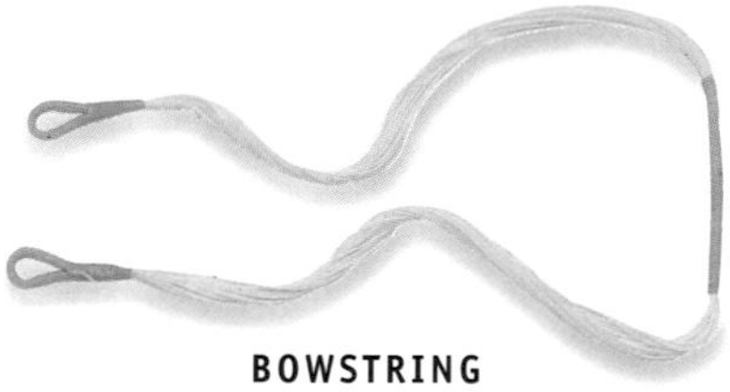

BOWSTRING

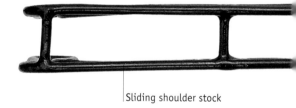

Sliding shoulder stock

Metal tip

Plastic flight

BOLT

KNIFE BLADE

Allen key for disassembly

Bowstring sear

Receiver

Lever for securing shoulder stock

Bow locking attachment

Fore-grip

Trigger

Sliding shoulder stock

SIDE VIEW

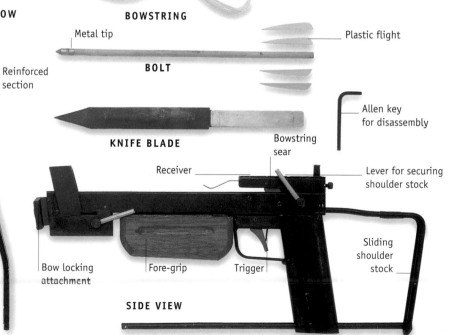

Testing the Big Joe 5 crossbow
Trials showed that the crossbow had a maximum range of 200 yd (183 m), but in practical terms it was less useful than the new silenced firearms.

Big Joe 5 crossbow

This American design was tested during World War II by the SOE
(see p. 30) and the OSS (see p. 32), but was not used in action. The
crossbow was powered by rubber loops, which were tensioned by a
windlass before firing. The front frame and shoulder stock could be
folded for easier transportation and concealment. Ammunition was
either a normal bolt with a steel head that could inflict deep wounds,
or a flare bolt that could be used to illuminate targets.

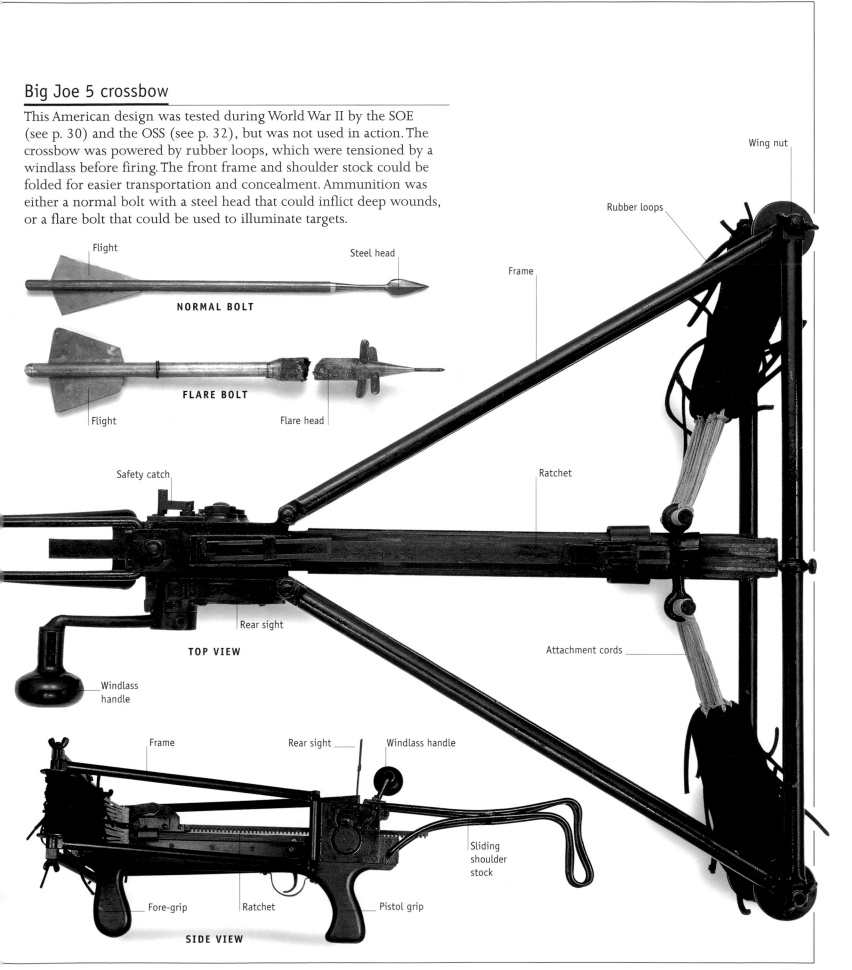

Flight

Steel head

NORMAL BOLT

FLARE BOLT

Flight

Flare head

Wing nut

Rubber loops

Frame

Safety catch

Ratchet

Rear sight

TOP VIEW

Attachment cords

Windlass
handle

Frame

Rear sight

Windlass handle

Sliding
shoulder
stock

Fore-grip

Ratchet

Pistol grip

SIDE VIEW

Close-combat weapons I

CLOSE COMBAT is something for which all special operations personnel must be trained and equipped. Specialized close-combat weapons – such as blades, knives, coshes, and garrottes – enable them to overcome an opponent in a swift, silent attack, or to defend themselves in an emergency and hopefully escape alive. The weapons tend to be used as a last resort, perhaps when a silenced firearm is unavailable. Those who are likely to face the dangers of close combat make their own preparations and often buy weapons privately, although some are issued officially.

Garrotte

The most common use of a garrotte is to strangle sentries. The wire is looped over the victim's head, around the neck, and pulled tight from behind until the target is dead. Other garrottes have serrated wires that double as escape saws.

Thrust weapon

The brass pommel of this weapon rested in the palm of the hand to add force to a thrusting movement. The lanyard was twisted around the hand to prevent the blade from being lost in action. British marine special forces used this weapon in World War II. Small items (suicide tablets, for instance) could be carried in the pommel.

Hidden garrotte

Some British special forces in World War II used a condom to conceal a garrotte. It also prevented rust by sealing out moisture. Because condoms were commonly carried, the garrotte might be overlooked if the person carrying one was searched by the enemy.

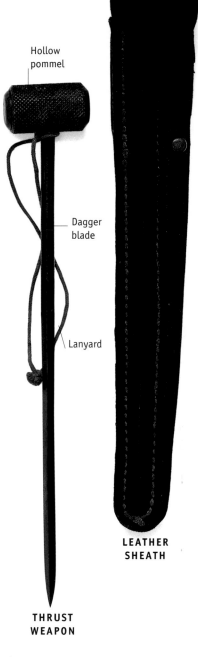

Hollow pommel

Dagger blade

Lanyard

LEATHER SHEATH

THRUST WEAPON

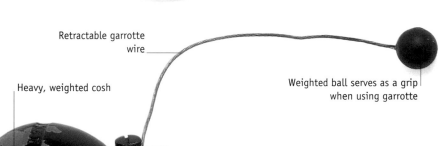

Brass handle

Wire

Garrotte rolled up inside condom for concealment

Retractable garrotte wire

Weighted ball serves as a grip when using garrotte

Heavy, weighted cosh

Peskett close-combat weapon

Named after its inventor, John Peskett, this multi-purpose weapon was designed for World War II special operations. It is a combination of a cosh, garrotte, and dagger, complete with wrist strap.

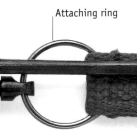

Attaching ring

Button to release dagger and lock it in place

Brass knuckles

Brass knuckles serve as a metal brace to give extra force to a punch. Brass knuckles are bought privately by some intelligence personnel as protection from street crime in some of the rough areas where they operate. During World War II, brass knuckles were occasionally issued officially to members of covert action units.

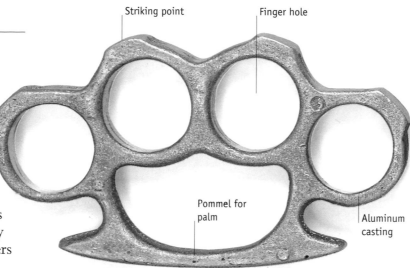

Striking point

Finger hole

Pommel for palm

Aluminum casting

Push dagger

The three-finger grip of this British weapon from World War II allowed the operator to exert tremendous force at close range.

Finger hole

Leather strip for attachment to clothing

Round blade to penetrate clothing and body tissues

PUSH DAGGER

LEATHER SCABBARD

Coshes

Coshes are often used to stun or injure, but a hard blow to the temple or the back of the head can be fatal. The upper cosh was used by the East German Stasi (see p. 91) as a method of crowd control during demonstrations. The lower one was carried by CIA officers operating in Europe during the 1960s as a means of self-defense.

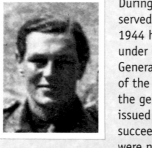

SPY PROFILE | **William Stanley-Moss**

During World War II, Captain Stanley-Moss served in British special operations. In 1944 he was in a team sent to Crete (then under German occupation) to capture General Kreipe, the German commander of the island. The team planned to kidnap the general by ambushing his car, and was issued with coshes for this purpose. They succeeded, although in the event coshes were not used. The general was smuggled to Egypt by submarine.

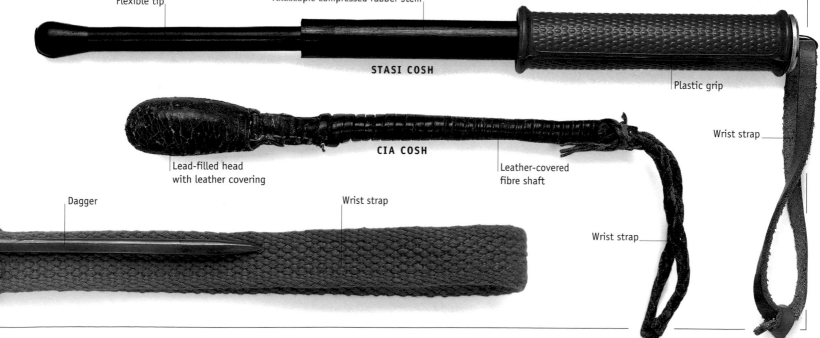

Flexible tip

Telescopic compressed rubber stem

STASI COSH

Plastic grip

Wrist strap

CIA COSH

Lead-filled head with leather covering

Leather-covered fibre shaft

Dagger

Wrist strap

Wrist strap

Close-combat weapons II

Thumb knives and scabbards

Thumb knives (these are from World War II) are tiny knives that can be hidden in clothing or a uniform. In use, they are gripped with the thumb and forefinger.

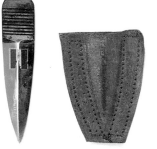

KNIFE WITH FRENCH TRICOLOR

KNIFE WITH CANADIAN MAPLE LEAF

X-troop

10 Commando was a British army unit made up of foreign nationals during World War II. Its No. 3 troop, also known as X-troop, was made up of anti-Nazi Germans, many Jewish. X-troop personnel performed a variety of roles in front-line service. As German speakers, they were specially helpful in intelligence work. But they risked execution as traitors if captured. Many carried escape aids such as the knife below.

X-TROOP DETACHMENT

X-TROOP ESCAPE KNIFE

Clandestine blade kit

During World War II, the SOE (see p. 30) sent this blade kit to the OSS (see p. 32) for evaluation, but it was not accepted there for official issue. However, many OSS personnel acquired the blades privately, while attending SOE training schools in Britain.

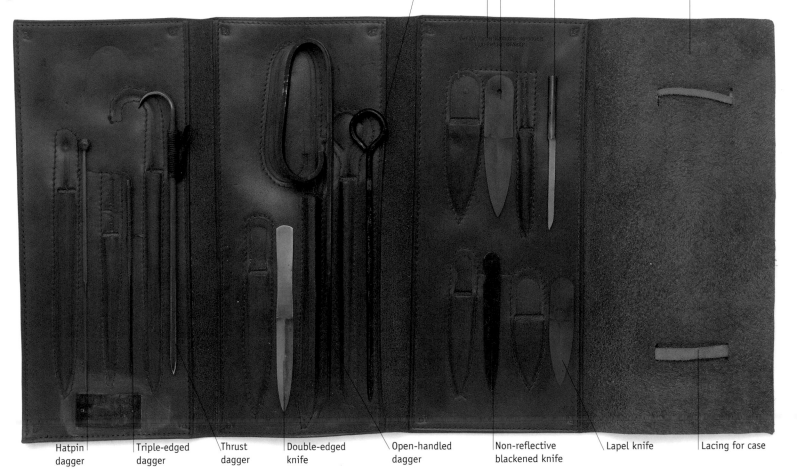

OSS marking

Thumb knife

Ring dagger

Triple-edged dart

Folding leather case

Hatpin dagger

Triple-edged dagger

Thrust dagger

Double-edged knife

Open-handled dagger

Non-reflective blackened knife

Lapel knife

Lacing for case

Instructor's blade kit

SOE instructors used an assortment of blades for training new personnel during World War II. Packed in wax-sealed containers and wrapped in chamois leather, the kit could also be buried for recovery and use during an operation. This example, buried in the 1940s, was recovered during the 1980s in perfect condition. The blade pack includes thumb and bodkin knives, and a tire-slasher for sabotaging vehicles.

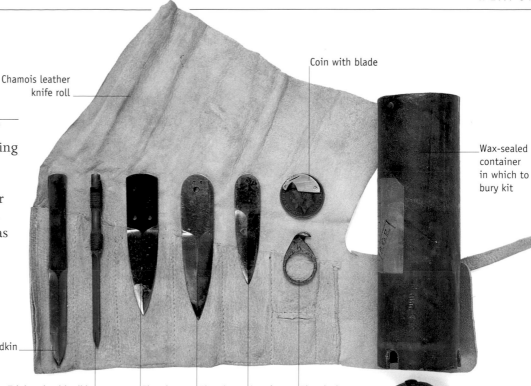

Chamois leather knife roll

Coin with blade

Wax-sealed container in which to bury kit

Double-edged bodkin

Triple-edged bodkin

Thumb knife

Thumb knife

Lapel blade

Tire slasher

Lid of container

Knuckleduster knife

During World War II, a knife was designed for British commandos operating in North Africa and the Middle East. The knife's brass grip could be used to knock out sentries.

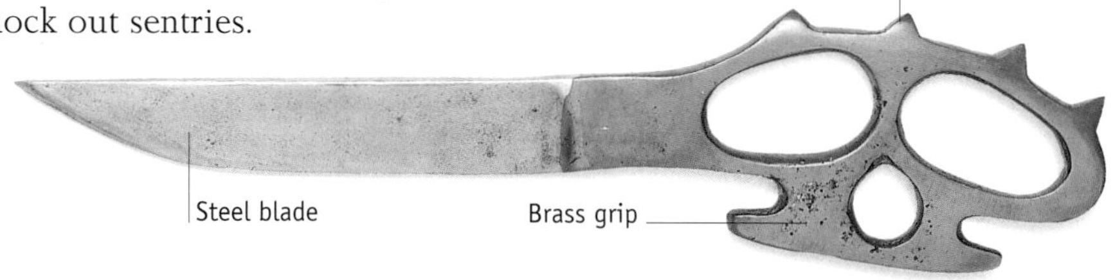

Brass knuckles point

Steel blade

Brass grip

Fairbairn–Sykes fighting knife

This weapon was designed in 1940 by two British officers, Captain W. E. Fairbairn and Captain E. A. Sykes. They had gained experience in close combat while serving with the Shanghai Police. Their knife was designed so that a trained user could strike at the vulnerable points of an opponent's body and attack the vital organs, killing the target quickly. The first knives were made in 1941 and were quickly accepted. They were issued to British commando units and used on raids in Norway in 1941. Fairbairn was later loaned as an instructor to the OSS, for which he created a special version of the knife. Successive versions continued to be produced into the 1990s.

Instructor and inventor
W. E. Fairbairn (1885–1960) in the uniform of a lieutenant colonel, a rank he attained in August 1944.

LEATHER SCABBARD

FAIRBAIRN–SYKES FIGHTING KNIFE

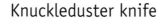

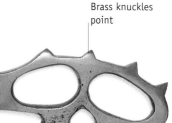

Concealed weapons I

IN CLANDESTINE WARFARE, situations arise in which hidden weapons, perhaps of an unconventional or unexpected kind, may tilt the balance between success and failure. Because concealment generally means limited size, such weapons are likely to be very basic, without refinements such as silencers or magazines of extra bullets. Weapons of this type can also be used for assassinations, as they allow the killer to get close to the victim without arousing alarm. These weapons are issued only to people who have serious need of them and are not carried by those engaged in normal intelligence work. Anyone found in possession of them would be suspected of covert activity.

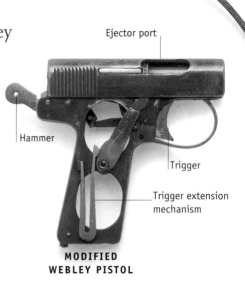

Trigger remote control

Ejector port

Hammer

Trigger

Trigger extension mechanism

MODIFIED WEBLEY PISTOL

Belt pistol

This belt and pistol were developed for use by British special operations personnel during World War II. A modified .25-caliber Webley pistol was worn on the belt on the user's right side, facing forward, hidden under the clothing. The trigger was activated by a length of cable that ran to the user's hand.

Cable end attached to trigger extension mechanism

Attachment plate for pistol

BELT WITH PISTOL PLATE

Trigger cable

Single-shot cigar pistol

A .22-caliber firing device was disguised as a cigar for use by SOE personnel (see p. 30). It was fired by pulling on the string. Its effective range was just 3 ft (1 m).

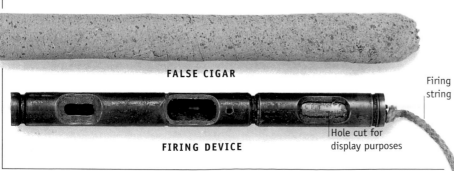

FALSE CIGAR

FIRING DEVICE

Firing string

Hole cut for display purposes

Single-shot cigarette pistol

This .22-caliber device disguised as a cigarette was developed at the SOE's Welwyn laboratory. The device was fired when the user pulled on a string with his teeth. Because of its short barrel it had a range of only about 3 ft (1 m) and was very loud.

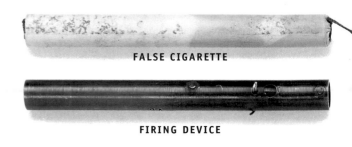

FALSE CIGARETTE

FIRING DEVICE

Single-shot pen gun

Known as the En-Pen, this 22-caliber device was made at the Royal Small Arms Factory at Enfield, north of London, for the SOE. The gun was fired by pulling back the pocket clip. This kit, issued to SOE instructors, included a cartridge ejector rod and a tool for cleaning out wax left in the chamber after firing blanks.

Pocket clip

Hole cut for display purposes

Rod used to push out spent cartridges

Blanks were used for practice firing

Leather holder

CROSS-SECTIONED VIEW OF GUN

CARTRIDGE EJECTOR ROD

SET OF BLANK CARTRIDGES

CLEANING TOOL

Single-shot gas and poison pens

The KGB assassination pen fired a small charge that shattered an ampoule of hydrocyanic acid. This was then projected from the pen as a lethal gas. The pellet pen (also KGB) was used to inject a small pellet impregnated with ricin poison into a victim. The tear gas pen was developed for the SOE during World War II. It had a range of up to 6 ft (2 m).

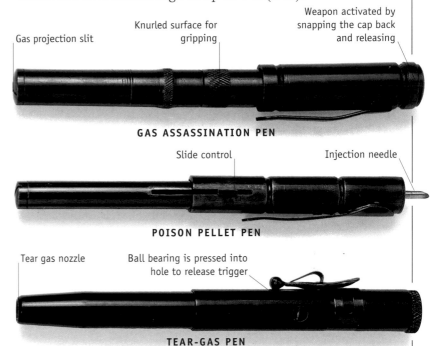

Gas projection slit

Knurled surface for gripping

Weapon activated by snapping the cap back and releasing

GAS ASSASSINATION PEN

Slide control

Injection needle

POISON PELLET PEN

Tear gas nozzle

Ball bearing is pressed into hole to release trigger

TEAR-GAS PEN

Stanley Lovell

During World War II, the OSS (see p. 32) began the practice of using industrial resources and the universities to develop new clandestine technology, an innovative approach that came to be widely adopted during the later Cold War years.

Stanley Lovell (1890–1976) was recruited from an academic background. He was personally selected by the OSS chief William Donovan to be OSS director of research and development. Under Lovell's direction, the OSS developed a number of devices for use in clandestine warfare. Among these were the Hi-Standard pistol (see p. 171), the Beano grenade (see p. 118), and the Matchbox camera (see p. 85). Other ideas included an explosive disguised as flour, which could even be baked without exploding, and a plan (never implemented) to attack Japanese cities by releasing bats to which incendiary bombs had been attached.

Wrist pistol

This small .25-caliber firing device was designed to be worn on the wrist of SOE personnel, so that it was readily available without having to be held in the hand. The device was fired by a string attached to the inside of a shirt or jacket. Any sudden forward movement of the arm would be enough to fire the device.

Barrel points in same direction as the outstretched fingers

Strap for tightening band on wrist

Wrist band

Concealed weapons II

Major Christopher Clayton Hutton

CLAYTON HUTTON WITH M19 DEVICES

During World War II, Christopher Clayton Hutton (b.1894) worked in MI9, a British organization set up by the armed forces to help British prisoners of war escape, and to assist special forces behind enemy lines. He created numerous weapons, concealments, and escape and evasion aids. One of his inventions was a clandestine airstrip beacon that was only faintly luminous so that it could be seen by an approaching pilot, but would be hard to spot at ground level.

Major Clayton Hutton designed an air-powered firing device for the French resistance in Paris. The device was disguised as a pen and fired a gramophone needle. Although this weapon was unlikely to be lethal, the resistance would be able to spread a rumor among the Germans that the needles were poisoned. French units expressed interest in the weapon, but MI9 was unable to supply the quantity required.

Barrel unscrews for loading

Needle-firing pen
This pneumatic weapon was devised by Clayton Hutton for use by French resistance fighters during World War II.

Pocket clip   Trigger

Cap pulled back to prime weapon

Single-shot firing device (stinger)

The Stinger was developed for the CIA during the post-World War II years. A reloadable .22-caliber device, the Stinger was issued with a spare barrel and seven rounds of ammunition in a camouflaged lead foil tube.

Lead foil tube

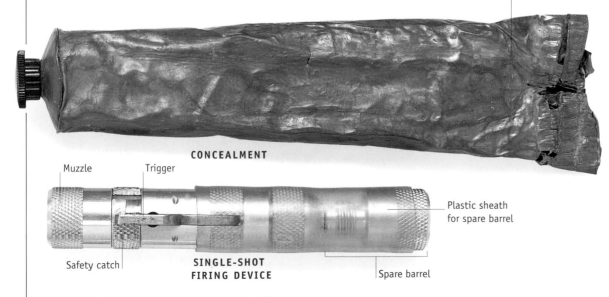

CONCEALMENT

Muzzle   Trigger

Plastic sheath for spare barrel

Safety catch

SINGLE-SHOT FIRING DEVICE

Spare barrel

Single-shot rectal pistol

This KGB 4.5mm firing device is packaged in a rubber sheath to facilitate concealment in the rectum. This is a common way of hiding items from cursory searches. The device was fired by holding the knurled ring, and twisting the barrel a quarter turn.

Muzzle

Barrel

SAFETY COVER   **FIRING DEVICE**

Single-shot pocket flashlight pistol

This 4.5mm device, disguised as a pocket flashlight, was used by the KGB in the 1950s and 1960s. Its mechanism was the same as in the pistol above. This example was seized at a British airport from the pilot of a Soviet civil aircraft.

Safety catch

Flashlight casing

Pipe pistol

Common items carried on the person were capable of being transformed into lethal firing devices. This World War II device was designed for use by SOE personnel (see p. 30). It was fired by removing the mouthpiece and twisting the bowl while grasping the barrel.

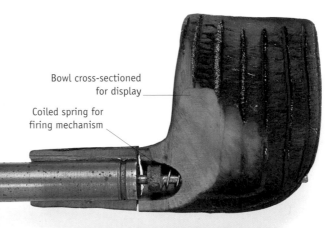

Bowl cross-sectioned for display

Coiled spring for firing mechanism

Device concealed inside mouthpiece of pipe

Safety wire removed before firing

Muzzle

Mechanical pencil pistol

Casing contains spring-loaded hammer

Button pulled back and released to fire

Tip unscrewed to load cartridge

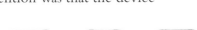

Unusual in that it functioned without a barrel, this 6.35mm weapon fired its bullet straight from the cartridge, which was loaded into the top section of the pencil. The device was sold commercially in Europe at the time of World War II.

Cartridge

Pencil concealment for thrusting weapon

MI9 designed a variety of small thrusting weapons that could be concealed inside pencils and pens. The intention was that the device would pass unnoticed through an initial search and could then be used in an escape attempt.

Hole cut for display purposes

Cruciform blade

Twine-wrapped grip

Leather glove

Plunger

Barrel

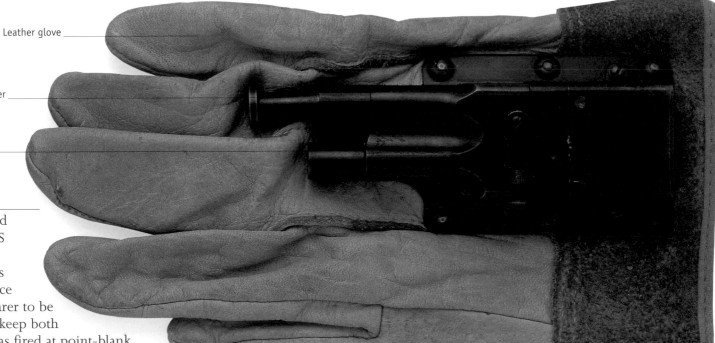

Glove pistol

Devised in World War II by the US Office of Naval Intelligence, this .38-caliber device allowed the wearer to be armed and still keep both hands free. It was fired at point-blank range by pressing the plunger into an opponent's body while striking a blow.

Assassination devices I

INTELLIGENCE AGENCIES are sometimes ordered to assassinate individuals who are considered by their governments to be a threat to national interests. In most cases, such killings have to be discreet, quiet, and untraceable to the assassins. Sometimes they are performed in such a way as to give the impression that the victim died of natural causes. Some killings, however, can serve as warnings, and might be done more blatantly. The need for discretion has led to the development of many types of assassination device, some of which are shown here. Secret services of the Soviet bloc countries used to specialize in assassinations. They devised a variety of methods, and even established a special workshop to experiment with poisons.

Single-shot assassination device

Developed during World War II by the technical department of the Abwehr (see p. 34), this device could be used for assassinations or for suicides. It fired a single 4.5mm bullet a short distance, and worked by pulling back and then releasing the rear section of the device. It is shown here at its actual size.

Knurled base | Brass casing | Barrel

Poison pellet cane

The KGB developed this cane in the 1950s. It is operated by pressing the tip against a body. The pressure rotates the tip to extend a large needle. When the needle is extended, a poison pellet is fired through it and into the victim, with fatal effect.

Handle

Powder charge and poison pellet

Spring

Rotating cam

Tip through which large needle protrudes

TIP OF POISON PELLET CANE

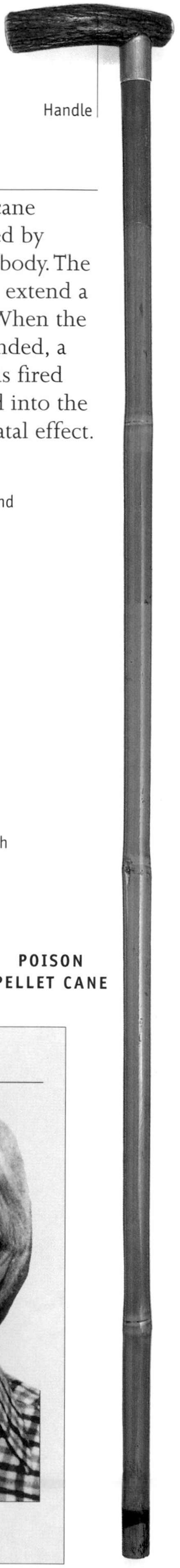

POISON PELLET CANE

The Bulgarian umbrella

In 1978 Georgi Markov, a Bulgarian dissident living in London, was killed on the orders of the Bulgarian leadership. The Bulgarians had asked the KGB to give technical assistance in devising an assassination method, and the KGB offered three choices: poisoned food; poisonous jelly to be smeared on Markov's skin; or a poison pellet.

A pellet filled with the lethal poison ricin was chosen. This was injected into Markov's thigh by means of a device disguised as an umbrella, which was jabbed at Markov as he stood on Waterloo Bridge, in London (see p. 187). He died soon afterward. At first his death was a mystery, as no one understood how it had happened. Eventually, however, murder began to be suspected, and Markov's corpse was exhumed. The pellet was found in the course of an autopsy, and the cause of his death understood.

BULGARIAN SECRET SERVICE CREST

GEORGI MARKOV

Cigarette pack with gas-firing device

A Soviet cigarette pack was adapted to conceal this poison-gas device, which is removed for firing. The single-shot weapon fires a cartridge containing a glass vial of acid. When fired, the vial is crushed and the acid vaporizes in the victim's face. A mesh screen stops glass splinters from reaching the victim's face and thus revealing the cause of death.

Mesh screen

Cartridge

Cocking and firing lever

GAS-FIRING DEVICE

CIGARETTE PACK

The foiled assassination

In 1954 Soviet assassin Nicolai Khokhlov (b.1922) was sent to Frankfurt, West Germany, to kill anti-Soviet agitator Georgi Okolovich. Before departing on his mission, Khokhlov married and converted to his wife's Christian beliefs. Because of these new beliefs, Khokhlov felt unable to carry out the assassination. When he arrived in Frankfurt, he warned Okolovich of the plot to kill him. Khokhlov defected with information about Soviet assassination devices, including the poison-pellet cigarette pack that was meant to kill Okolovich (see p. 186).

An assassin meets his intended victim
Soviet assassin Nicolai Khokhlov (right), defected rather than attempt to kill his intended victim, Georgi Okolovich, whom he warned of the assassination plot.

Silenced assassination gun

This Soviet weapon is designed to be carried in and fired from a rolled-up newspaper. It is a single-shot device, fired by squeezing the external lever on the rear section of the weapon. It is silenced by an internal suppressor, and further muffled by being pressed up against the victim as it is fired. A later adaptation of this gun, which fires gas, is shown on p. 184.

Mesh inside tube to muffle sound

Hole cut for display purposes

End connected to firing chamber

INTERNAL SUPPRESSOR

Thread screws into rear section of weapon

Hole cut for display purposes

Cocking rod

Outer tube serves as a handle

Recessed surface receives suppressor

FIRING CHAMBER

Firing lever

REAR SECTION OF WEAPON

Assassination devices II

Poison gas assassination cane

A gas assassination device has been hidden in this cane for the blind. The trigger is concealed by the white tape, which was peeled back for use. When the device was fired, it emitted gas from an opening in the handle, which was held close to the victim's face.

Firing port for poisonous gas

Tape to simulate a cane used by the blind

Trigger mechanism

CANE

HANDLE OF CANE

Poison gas assassination gun

This Soviet weapon had the capability to kill almost instantly if fired directly into the victim's face. It is a gas-firing version of the gun shown on p. 183 and, like that gun, was hidden in a rolled-up newspaper. The firing lever activated a firing pin, which detonated a percussion cap, rupturing an ampoule of acid. The acid vaporized into poisonous gas and was propelled out of a small hole. The gas gun is just 7 in (18 cm) long.

Antidotes for poison gas

KGB personnel who used gas assassination weapons were equipped with antidotes, which they took as a precaution against accidental inhalation of the lethal gas. The tablet of sodium thiosulphate was swallowed 30 minutes before an attack, and the ampoule of amyl nitrate was broken and inhaled immediately after the assassination had taken place.

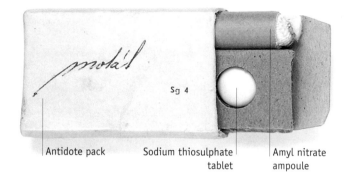

Antidote pack

Sodium thiosulphate tablet

Amyl nitrate ampoule

Bogdan Stashinsky

In 1957, KGB officer Bogdan Stashinsky (b.1931) killed the Ukrainian dissident leader Lev Rebet in Munich, using a gas assassination gun concealed in a newspaper. Rebet's death was ascribed to a heart attack. In 1959, Stashinsky assassinated the Ukrainian dissident Stefan Bandera, using an improved gas gun. The cause of death was correctly identified this time. Stashinsky defected to West Germany in 1961. He was convicted of the murders but received a short sentence.

Cocking rod

Firing lever

Outer tube serves as a handle

Attaching screw

Rubber ring to absorb recoil

Plots to assassinate Fidel Castro

Between 1960 and 1965, the CIA was involved in eight White House-authorized plots to assassinate Fidel Castro (b.1926), leader of communist Cuba. (Communist Cuba was considered a particular threat to the United States due to its close proximity.) Equipment and such materials as poisons were provided by the CIA Technical Services Division. Some plots went no further than the planning stage; others progressed further, but none resulted in a serious assassination attempt. One plot twice reached a point at which poison pills were sent to Cuba and agents were despatched to carry out the task. In another plot, weapons were furnished to a Cuban dissident. There was even a plan to impregnate one of Castro's cigars with deadly botulism bacilli. Non-lethal attacks were planned, aimed at destroying Castro's credibility with the Cubans. Such projects included putting thallium salts in his boots to make his beard fall out, and spraying him with hallucinatory drugs while he made a broadcast to the Cuban nation.

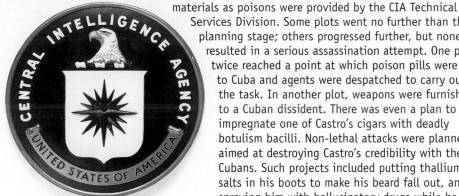

CREST OF THE CIA

FIDEL CASTRO

Gas-firing cartridge assassination wallet

A poison-gas firing device is concealed in this KGB wallet, which also has compartments for gas antidotes to protect the assassin. When the trigger was fired, the primer charge crushed a glass ampoule of poisonous acid that turned into a vapor and killed the victim. A screen over the cartridge prevented shards of glass from the ampoule embedding in the victim and so revealing the cause of death.

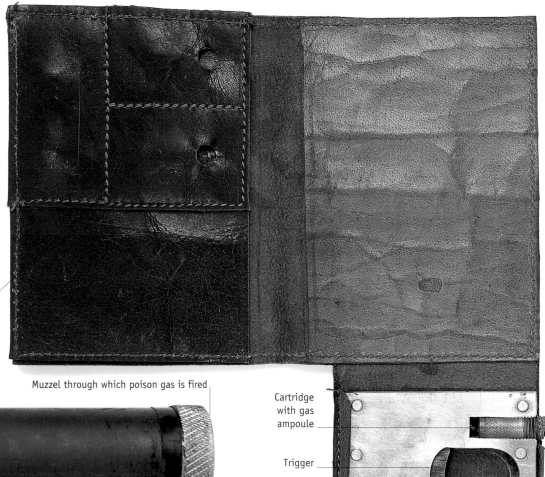

Compartment for antidotes

Muzzel through which poison gas is fired

Cartridge with gas ampoule

Trigger

Metal casing

Assassination devices III

SSG-82 sniper rifle

The East German Ministry for Security (MfS) recognized the need for a precision sniper rifle capable of delivering a lethal round with pinpoint accuracy for use by airport antiterror units and other security forces. The rifle is a bolt-action, manual repeater with a five-round detachable box magazine. The barrel is hammer-forged and is equipped with a Zeiss 4X fixed-power telescopic sight. The length of the wooden stock can be adjusted with rubber inserts.

Erich Mielke
Colonel General Erich Mielke headed the East German Ministry for State Security from 1957 to 1989. He is shown here demonstrating how the SSG-82 is held and aimed.

Telescopic sight

Barrel

Trigger

Adjustment dial for telescopic sight

Shoulder stock

Cigarette-case pistol

In 1954, the KGB's Operational–Technical Department issued a cigarette-case pistol to Nikolai Khokhlov, an internal police officer. The pistol, which fired poison-filled bullets through a fake-cigarette insert, was intended for the assassination of the anti-Soviet émigré Georgii Okolovich. The assassination plan failed because Khokhlov defected to the West (see p. 183).

Fake cigarettes

Barrel

Cocking lever

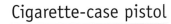

Fake cigarette that conceals cocking lever

INSERT WITH FAKE CIGARETTES

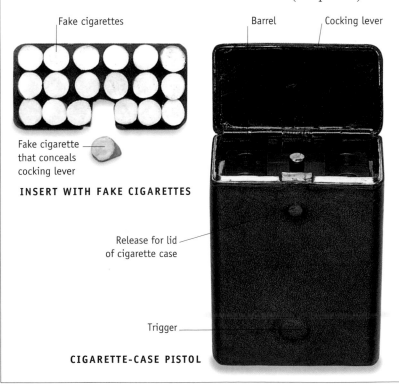

Release for lid of cigarette case

Trigger

CIGARETTE-CASE PISTOL

Assassination ring

In the 1940s and '50s, Special Laboratory No. 12 of the KGB's Operational–Technical Department employed chemists, doctors, and technologists to make a variety of poisons and assassination devices. The turquoise stone of this assassination ring unscrewed to reveal a sharp point covered with poison.

Turquoise stone

Sharp, poison-covered point

TURQUOISE STONE

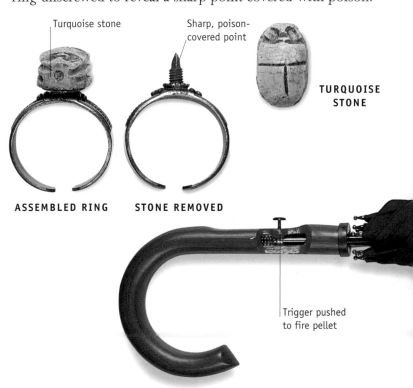

ASSEMBLED RING

STONE REMOVED

Trigger pushed to fire pellet

Cigarette-lighter pistol

This European-style lighter appears functional and unmodified and could be carried without suspicion in a pocket or purse. However, it converts into an electrically fired pistol with a disposable barrel, which slots into the top of the lighter. The action of pulling back and rotating the rear of the lighter to form the handle automatically raises the rear sight into position. When the trigger is pressed, an internal electric magneto sends an impulse that fires the pistol.

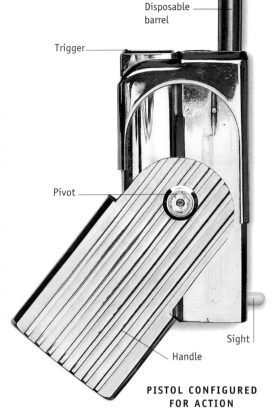

Disposable barrel

Trigger

Pivot

Sight

Handle

PISTOL CONFIGURED FOR ACTION

.22-Caliber firing device

Slighter longer than a cigarette, this US firing device is easy to conceal in a purse or pocket. It is cocked by pulling on the knurled ring at the rear and fired by depressing the raised firing lever.

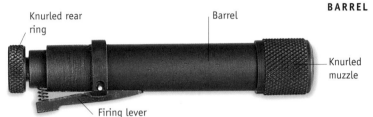

Knurled rear ring

Barrel

Knurled muzzle

Firing lever

Barrel

BARREL　**PISTOL CAMOUFLAGED AS LIGHTER**

Assassination umbrella

On September 7, 1978, dissident Georgi Markov (see p. 182), an outspoken critic of the Zhivkov regime in Bulgaria, was assassinated in London. His attacker used an umbrella that had been converted into a pneumatic weapon. When the tip was jabbed into Markov's thigh, it fired a pellet the size of a pinhead that entered Markov's skin. The pellet was filled with the biotoxin ricin, a deadly derivative of the castor-oil seed. The umbrella was purchased in

Washington, D.C., by the KGB but modified in Moscow at Laboratory No. 12 of the Central Scientific Investigation Institute for Special Technology (TsNIIST). Throughout the Cold War, the KGB orchestrated assassinations globally as a way of stifling dissidents who had spoken out against hard-line Communist regimes. The assassin of Georgi Markov has never been arrested and the case is still under investigation.

Cutaway section

Umbrella tip

Rolled umbrella

Pellet filled with ricin poison

Tip of injector

Cutaway section of tip

Cylinder with compressed gas to fire pellet

REPLICA OF ASSASSINATION UMBRELLA

ENLARGED MODEL OF UMBRELLA TIP

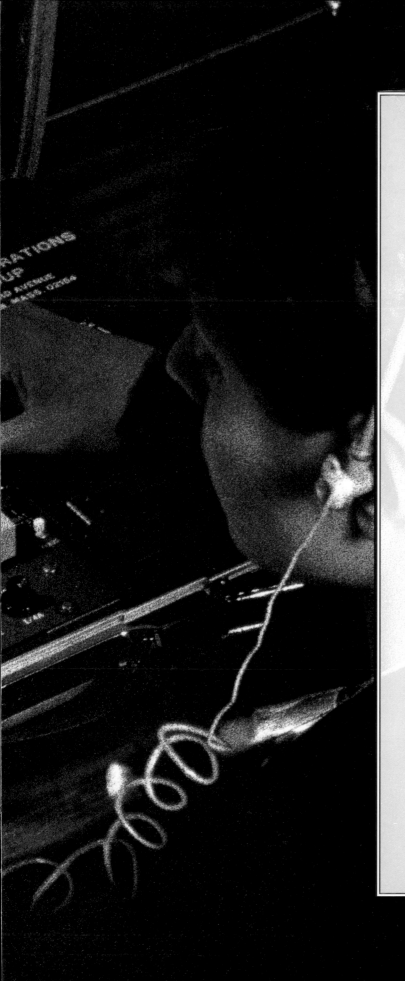

HOW TO BE A SPY

Many people want to be spies, attracted by the glamour they see in films or read about in novels, but very few actually achieve their ambition. Some intelligence agencies, such as the CIA, do advertise for new recruits, but most agencies approach potential members individually. Once an agency has recruited someone suitable, he or she has to be trained. This can take years, as the potential spy must painstakingly learn all the tradecraft – the techniques for living, working, and communicating surreptitiously. If the spy is going to live under cover in a foreign country for a long period of time, then meticulous attention must be paid to ensure that the spy's cover story is perfect. The life of a spy is not one of constant action, but rather one of quiet, often boring work. If a spy or his or her controller makes the smallest mistake, the spy can suddenly be in great danger. The life of a spy can be precarious. This section covers all the aspects of how a spy works, from recruitment and training, and developing a cover, to the spy's fate.

Training and recruitment I

SPIES ARE RECRUITED by different means according to the skills or abilities required. Personnel needed by the technical support branch of an intelligence service, for example, can often be recruited simply by advertising for people with the required expertise. If scientific knowledge is required, in computing or nuclear physics, for instance, it may be possible to recruit directly from universities. Linguists can also be acquired in this way. Thousands of specialists are employed by the big intelligence agencies, though few of the recruits will play active roles in intelligence-gathering overseas.

Physical training
Intelligence officers, particularly those expected to engage in clandestine warfare like these wartime SOE agents, undergo rigorous physical training.

Intelligence-gathering is the preserve of career intelligence officers, known as case officers, and agents recruited by them. When working abroad, case officers are usually attached to the staff of embassies. They operate there under the guise of diplomatic personnel, often making stringent efforts to disguise their role in intelligence work. Their primary task is the recruitment and control of agents, through whom intelligence can be gathered. When seeking potential recruits, case officers usually target the personnel of foreign intelligence services and foreign embassy employees.

Intelligence officers are of obvious value if they can be recruited as moles, but anyone who has access to information can prove useful. Chauffeurs, secretaries, or maintenance staff can all provide information that may lead to the recruitment of more agents. For instance, they are likely to know which of their colleagues have personal problems, such as financial difficulties or alcoholism, and which may be having extramarital affairs. Such gossip can help intelligence officers identify the people who are vulnerable, and who might therefore be successfully recruited.

Friendly spies

Case officers who are responsible for recruiting agents need to have friendly, likeable personalities. They must be affable and socially adaptable, and appear open to other people's points of view. Soviet case officers with these qualities were known to spend much time in clubs and bars around Washington, DC,

Scaled-down Fairbairn-Sykes knives
Three-quarter-sized versions of this famous fighting knife (see p. 177) had the advantage of concealability. The ball tip was added for safety in training.

SPY PROFILE — Aldrich Ames

Finding himself in debt, CIA officer Ames (b.1941) offered his services to the KGB in 1985. He became the Counterintelligence Branch Chief in the Soviet Division of the Directorate of Operations and betrayed every secret that came his way, leading to the deaths of at least 10 CIA agents. For the information that Ames gave them, the KGB paid a total of $2.7 million. Ames was arrested in 1994 and was convicted and sentenced to life imprisonment.

hoping to fall into the company of US government staff, military personnel, or business people. The case officer will typically form a friendship with a likely recruit. This friendship is often based on a supposedly shared interest; for example women, drinking, gambling, or even an innocent hobby such as fishing or stamp collecting. As the friendship develops, the case officer will subtly probe for any character weaknesses that can be used to control the new friend. At this point, the potential recruit is referred to as a developing agent. The first information sought from them may seem totally innocuous. But slowly, new recruits

George Blake

Communist Party member George Blake (b.1922) was a British citizen recruited by MI6 (see p. 201) because of his linguistic skills. Sent to Korea as Head of Station during the Korean War (1950–53), he was taken prisoner by the North Koreans. On his return to England in 1953, he started to pass secrets to the KGB, badly affecting British intelligence. In 1961 Blake was arrested and jailed for 42 years. After six years, he escaped to the Soviet Union.

will be drawn closer into a web of deceit and espionage. Some will be persuaded to agree to clandestine activities in return for cash, and later made to sign a receipt for money received. Once they have gone this far, there is little chance that they will turn back. They will have become recruited agents. The threat of having their new activities revealed, coupled with the lure of money, will be enough to ensure their continued loyalty to their handler.

Handlers, who may not be the same case officers who recruited the agent, will attempt to reinforce this loyalty by building strong bonds of friendship and trust with their agents. Even after his arrest, CIA traitor Aldrich Ames was able to talk of the great affection he still held for his former handlers.

Training padlock
This special padlock was used for training recruits how to open combination locks.

Types of agent

Apart from those recruited specifically to procure intelligence, several other types of agent exist. Contact agents and access agents are used to identify and facilitate access to potential recruits. Agents of influence are used to affect public opinion or events. Support agents assist other agents by acting as couriers or maintaining safe houses, for example.

Double agents are those who work against their original intelligence services while under the control of another service. They may be driven by motives of money, ideology, compromise, or ego, or they may be trying to save their lives or to regain their freedom after capture by their original enemy.

Moles are intelligence personnel who are in the employment of one service while being controlled by another.

Sleeper agents are those who are sent into foreign countries to live apparently normal lives until activated, perhaps in time of national emergency or pending war, when their mission is likely to be one of sabotage or assassination.

"Illegals" (see p. 194) are spies who adopt elaborate false identities to work in foreign countries. They are difficult for the enemy to detect, but run the risk of heavy punishment as they operate without any diplomatic immunity. Apart from gathering information, their role may sometimes also be to spot potential new recruits or run other agents.

Instruction in tradecraft
Tradecraft is the word for the range of technical skills used in espionage. Here, SOE recruits (see p. 30) learn about methods of opening locks.

Training and recruitment II

Once recruited, new employees of an intelligence service may follow any one of a number of different paths. Major intelligence agencies, such as the CIA and the KGB (now partially replaced by the SVR), need large numbers of technical and analytical experts to support their operations. Personnel who have been recruited to take these roles will receive a general introduction to the various elements of intelligence work

Communications training
The use of Morse code for radio communication can be one of the most intensive and time-consuming elements of intelligence training.

TRAINING KEY

EARPIECE

Morse training key
This practice key and earpiece were used to train CIA recruits in the use of Morse code during the 1960s.

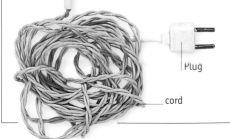

Plug

cord

before being sent on for training in their individual specialties. They may continue to work within these specialized areas throughout their careers. A recruit who is destined for a career as an intelligence officer or case officer will go through a far more intensive and wide-ranging course of training. Many of the elements that have characterized Western intelligence training since 1945 have their origins in the early, wartime training programs that were devised for the British SOE (see p. 30) and the American OSS (see p. 32).

Wartime recruitment and training

Originally, the SOE discovered many of its trainees through word-of-mouth recommendations and similar informal contacts. Individuals who had excellent foreign language skills, who were also willing to volunteer for unspecified service, were in demand. Besides this, the SOE received some of its recruits via the War Office Department MI1x, which also provided recruits for MI5 (see

p. 196) and MI6. These agencies carried out their own direct recruiting, sometimes in competition with the SOE. The SOE preferred to recruit people from a middle-class background, who had no affiliations to extreme political groups. Less respectable individuals, such as forgers and burglars, were hired for their specialized skills.

The OSS also began by informal recruitment of personnel. By late 1943, however, its growing manpower needs led to a more systematic approach. The OSS joined with the SOE to set up a system of psychological assessment for sifting recruits; this system was combined with training programs designed in such a way that unsuitable trainees could be filtered out at various stages. In both organizations trainees would undergo a period of basic training. Subjects included fieldcraft (survival skills), communications, sabotage, and the various forms of combat. After that, more advanced courses followed to prepare agents for specialized tasks or work in specific countries.

John Vassall

Admiralty clerk John Vassall (b.1924) was working at the British Embassy in Moscow when he was recruited by the KGB, who used evidence of his homosexuality as blackmail. He was trained to use a Minox camera and started work for the KGB. He continued to spy on his return to London in 1956. After passing many naval secrets to Moscow, Vassall was arrested in 1962 and convicted of spying. He served 10 years of an 18-year sentence.

Hugh Hambleton

Hugh Hambleton (b.1922) was recruited in 1947 by the MGB (later KGB), lured by their intellectual flattery and his craving for adventure. From 1956 to 1961 he worked for NATO and supplied secrets to Moscow. He returned to Canada, became a professor, and continued to pass secrets. The RCMP security service (see p. 166) discovered his espionage equipment in 1979. He was later sentenced to 10 years in prison in Britain.

Silencer   Trigger   Grip safety   Cocking handle

Combined magazine and pistol grip

Welrod pistol
Designed during World War II at the SOE laboratories in Welwyn Garden City, near London, this silenced weapon remained in service in the postwar years.

Firearms training
Intelligence services may train their officers to use a variety of firearms, choosing weapons that will best meet the anticipated operational needs.

CIA training

The system of training instituted by the OSS had a strong influence over the methods adopted by the CIA. During the 1950s, trainee CIA officers received basic training at a camp codenamed Isolation. This former naval base in Virginia was also known to recruits as Camp Swampy,

due to the marshy land in which the camp was situated. The basic elements of clandestine operations were still taught using the OSS manual.

Trainees were also given a thorough grounding in the special vocabulary of the world of espionage. They were taught the differences between types of agents, and learned the skills required to recruit them. Their role as case officers was expressed as providing the "link between the intelligence bureaucracy that wants the secret information and the agents that have access to the information." Technical experts lectured the students on espionage tradecraft, such as clandestine photography, secret writing, surveillance, and dead drops.

In the later stages of their training, the trainees would be taken to the nearby city of Norfolk, to practice their newly acquired skills.

Soviet training

Soviet recruits to the KGB and GRU (see p. 38) were taught much the same basic skills. The KGB's main training center was School 101 (later renamed the Red Banner Institute) near Moscow. The GRU trained its personnel at the Military Diplomatic Academy.

KGB training was based on a textbook entitled *The Foundation of Soviet Intelligence Work*, which covered the tradecraft and case-officer skills required of an intelligence officer. KGB and GRU recruits were not taught to gather intelligence but to persuade others to do this for them by betraying their countries. The work of recruiting and running agents was studied from actual cases, with the aid of experienced instructors with firsthand knowledge. The final stage of training was to learn a foreign language, and this was selected to best meet the current operational requirements of the service.

Operational training
SOE recruits learned the importance of terrain in planning an operation. Here, an instructor shows a group how to use a topographical model.

Covers and legends

IN ESPIONAGE, A COVER is a form of deception designed to conceal a spy's true identity. For simple operations, a cover need not be elaborate – perhaps just a false name. A legend is a sophisticated cover that amounts to an entire artificial background and life history. Legends are created for spies living secretly in a foreign country for as long as a few years without the benefit of diplomatic immunity – in KGB terms, an "illegal" (see p. 201). The equivalent CIA term is NOC (nonofficial cover). A legend has to stand up to scrutiny by counterintelligence. The time and care spent creating a cover or legend are determined by three factors: the importance of the mission, the length of time the identity has to be maintained, and the degree of scrutiny it must endure.

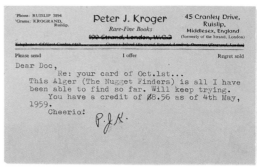

LEGEND-BUILDING POSTCARD WITH "HOUSE OF SPIES" ADDRESS (see p. 50)

Cover or legend?

A short-term false identity, for which little preparation is needed, is called a cover. For example, a member of MI6 visiting an electronics trade show in a British town need only sign in under a false name, carry cards relating to a nonexistent business, and set up a telephone line answered in that company's name.

But an illegal needs greater preparation. Elie Cohen (see p. 126) took a year establishing his legend in Argentina before he began his mission, spying for Israel in Syria.

False identities

Spy agencies maintain stockpiles of paper samples from around the world to be able to duplicate most identification

SOVIET FORGERY OF A BLANK (UNCOMPLETED) DRIVER'S LICENSE FORM

documents exactly. Such work must be flawless: the identity of a German spy posing as a Soviet citizen during World War II was discovered because stainless steel staples – not available in the Soviet Union – were used on his documents. The absence of rust marks on his papers was enough to expose him.

The credibility of a false identity can be helped by the careful use of "pocket litter," such as ticket stubs or receipts, to lend support to the cover story. It is vital that a spy carries nothing that would reveal his or her true identity.

Sometimes spies are able to obtain the documents that allow them to assume the identity of a person who has died. The research involved in basing a legend on the identity of a dead person must be

done thoroughly. For example, care must be taken in checking that the spy conforms to the physical details of the deceased person. A small error can be disastrous, as in the case of the KGB illegal Konon Molody (see p. 51).

Avoiding discovery

Even if a legend has been constructed perfectly, a spy must behave in the right manner. For an operative working at home or in a friendly country this will not be too demanding, since the legend will not be closely scrutinized. However, a spy using a legend in a hostile country must make every effort to "live" that legend constantly and be very careful not to say anything, even in a casual conversation, that might cast doubt on it. Actions must be in keeping with the character. In World War I, a German officer trying to infiltrate Canada was discovered because he was dressed in shabby clothes but was traveling in the first-class compartment of the train.

SOVIET FORGERY OF A UNITED STATES PRESS CARD

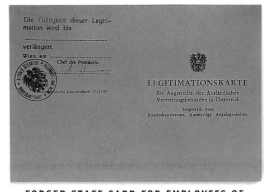

FORGED STAFF CARD FOR EMPLOYEES OF FOREIGN MISSIONS IN AUSTRIA

Forest Frederick Edward Yeo-Thomas

British World War II secret agent Edward Yeo-Thomas (1901–64) was a former Royal Air Force (RAF) officer who volunteered for service with the SOE (see p. 30). He undertook three missions to France, where he worked with the resistance. In 1944, he was captured and tortured by the Gestapo, but he managed to survive captivity until the end of the war. For his bravery Yeo-Thomas was later awarded the George Cross, one of the highest British honors. The items shown below include his SOE file card and RAF identity disks, and an SOE disk knife. The other items relate to legends that were created for his first two missions in France. The identity card in the name of Thierry (born in Arras, northern France) was used on his first mission. The papers in the name of Tirelli (born in Algiers) relate to his second mission in France and include an identity card, ration card, driver's license, and a French Air Force demobilization certificate.

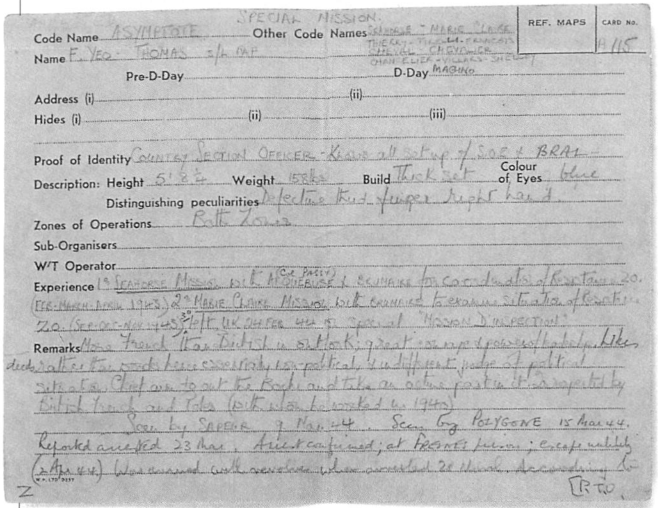

Paper is aged to simulate a certificate that is two years old

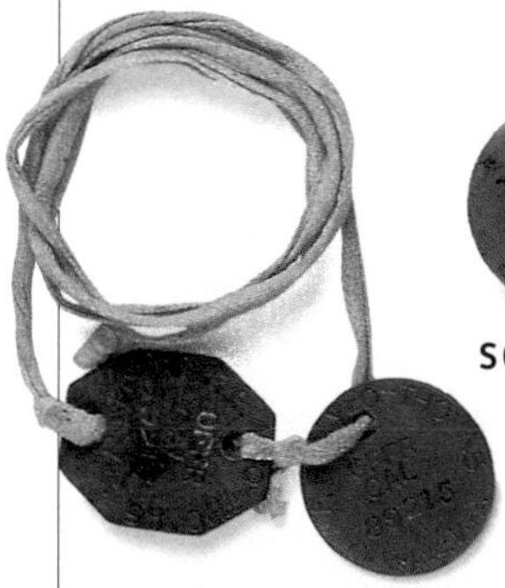

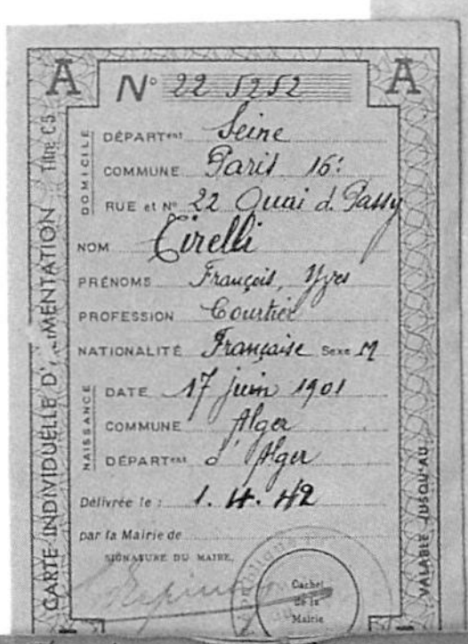

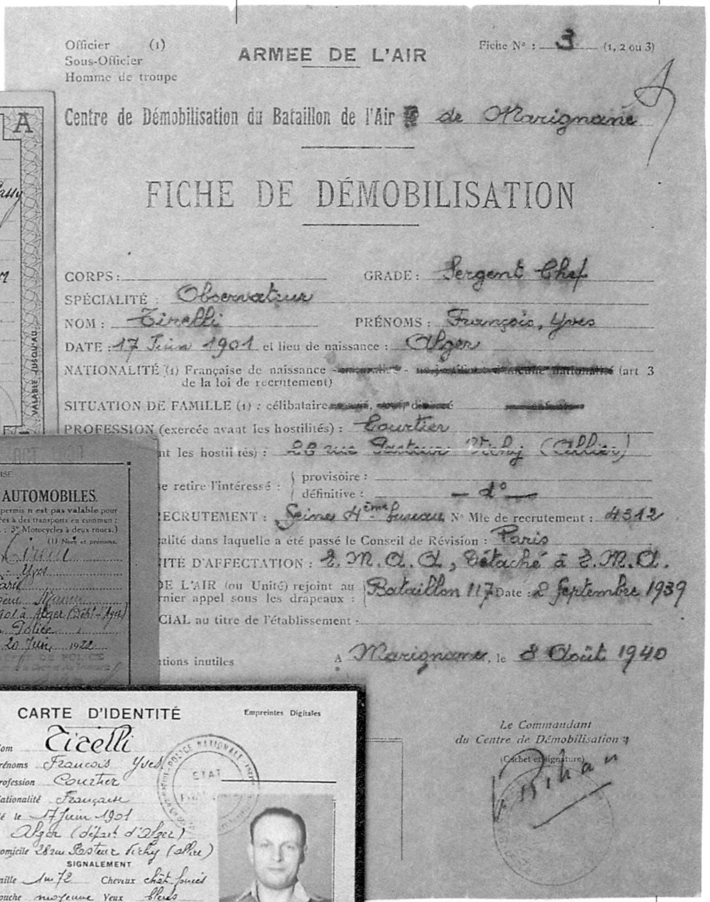

SOE FILE CARD

FRENCH RATION CARD

SOE DISK KNIFE

RAF IDENTITY DISKS

Photograph of Yeo-Thomas

Signature adopted for assumed identity

FRENCH IDENTITY CARD

FRENCH DRIVER'S LICENSE

Signature adopted for assumed identity

UPDATED FRENCH IDENTITY CARD

FRENCH AIR FORCE DEMOBILIZATION CERTIFICATE

Spy networks

A SPY NETWORK IS A GROUP of agents working under the supervision of a controller. Each person in the network reports to a single superior but may control more than one person. Consequently, networks have a pyramidal structure, with many agents at the bottom and only a few controllers at the top. An example of a controller might be a CIA case officer, working under diplomatic cover, or a Soviet "chief illegal" (a senior "illegal" officer, see p. 201) under an assumed identity.

Controllers need to know as much as possible about their agents to be able to handle them effectively. For the sake of security, agents are told as little as possible about their controllers and nothing about fellow agents. This principle, called compartmentalization, ensures that an arrested agent cannot betray those above him or those in other branches of the network. Without compartmentalization, the entire network may be put at risk.

Sometimes, for reasons of operational expediency, controllers of spy networks have chosen not to apply the principle of compartmentalization. This was the case in the Cambridge network in Britain (see opposite) and in some of the American networks of World War II.

RUDOLF IVANOVICH ABEL

Abel's cuff links
Microdots could be concealed in a cavity within these cuff links, which were found in the possession of Rudolf Abel.

Hollow nail
The Abel spy network used this specially constructed nail as a dead drop in which microfilm could be hidden.

MI5 – the British security service

Despite the letters MI in the names of MI5 and MI6 (see p. 201), neither body is now a component of military intelligence. MI5 is responsible for counterintelligence and counterespionage and monitors activities of subversive and terrorist groups and foreign nationals in Britain. During World War II, MI5 had great success in detecting German spies. In 1991, Stella Rimington became head of M15, the first woman to head an intelligence agency in a major country.

the FBI to locate Abel himself. Abel was arrested but was later traded in a spy swap for Francis Gary Powers (see p. 52).

Abel's network had contacts with Ethel and Julius Rosenberg, agents working for the Soviet Union who were convicted of treason and executed in 1953. Damage to the rest of the network after their arrest was limited by compartmentalization.

The Abel spy ring
The spy ring operated by the Soviet illegal Colonel Rudolf Ivanovich Abel (1903–71) was put at risk by lack of compartmentalization. Working from his apartment in New York, Abel kept in contact with Soviet agents who were involved in trying to steal American atomic secrets. In 1954 another illegal, Reino Hayhanen, became Abel's assistant. He proved unreliable, and Abel had him recalled to Moscow. While in transit, Hayhanen defected. He gave details of Abel's cipher to the FBI and, having been to Abel's apartment, was able to help

JULIUS ROSENBERG

ETHEL ROSENBERG

GUY BURGESS

ANTHONY BLUNT

DONALD MACLEAN

HAROLD (KIM) PHILBY

The Cambridge spies

In Britain during the 1930s, the KGB recruited a number of agents. Among these were five men who had all been pro-communist students at Cambridge University. They were later controlled by NKVD (later KGB) officer Yuri Modin.

In 1951, two of these agents, Foreign Office officials Donald Maclean and Guy Burgess, defected to the Soviet Union, as they were under suspicion. Their friend Kim Philby was forced to resign from a high-ranking post with MI6 as a result of these defections. He worked in journalism until, in 1963, he also defected. Philby, once regarded as a possible future chief of MI6, had betrayed many operations to the KGB.

The fourth man in the network was Sir Anthony Blunt, who was an officer in MI5 from 1940 to 1945. He later functioned as a spy while serving as Surveyor of the Queen's Pictures. His guilt had been known to MI5 before it was publicly revealed in 1979.

The last of the five to be publicly named was John Cairncross. He had a career that included positions in MI6, a wartime signals intelligence agency known as GC & CS (later GCHQ), and other government ministries.

Mossad spy network

Mossad networks operate under the cover of Israel's embassies in other countries. Illegals are controlled directly from Israel, working without diplomatic cover or support from embassy staff. In each country there is a Head of Station who works under diplomatic protection inside the embassy, and when necessary can direct even the ambassador to support Mossad activities. The *sayanim* register is a list of volunteers in the Jewish community available to help when required – this helps keep Mossad manning levels low. Each station imports technical specialists when they are needed, rather than keep them as full-time members of the station.

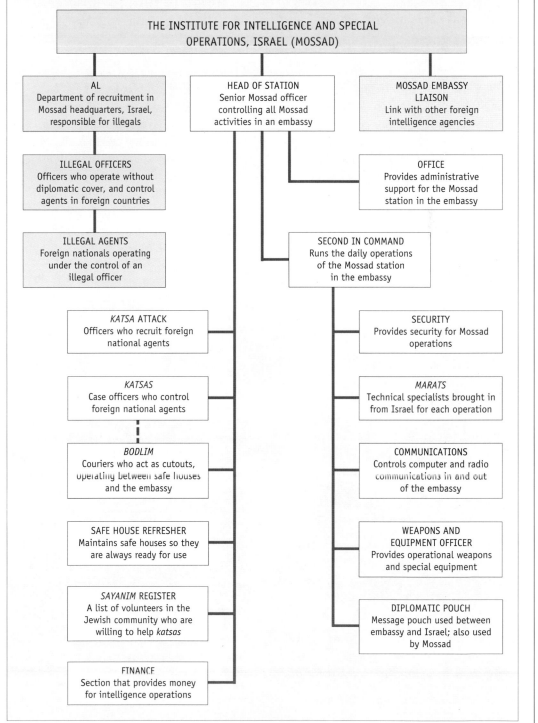

THE INSTITUTE FOR INTELLIGENCE AND SPECIAL OPERATIONS, ISRAEL (MOSSAD)

AL
Department of recruitment in Mossad headquarters, Israel, responsible for illegals

HEAD OF STATION
Senior Mossad officer controlling all Mossad activities in an embassy

MOSSAD EMBASSY LIAISON
Link with other foreign intelligence agencies

ILLEGAL OFFICERS
Officers who operate without diplomatic cover, and control agents in foreign countries

OFFICE
Provides administrative support for the Mossad station in the embassy

ILLEGAL AGENTS
Foreign nationals operating under the control of an illegal officer

SECOND IN COMMAND
Runs the daily operations of the Mossad station in the embassy

KATSA ATTACK
Officers who recruit foreign national agents

SECURITY
Provides security for Mossad operations

KATSAS
Case officers who control foreign national agents

MARATS
Technical specialists brought in from Israel for each operation

BODLIM
Couriers who act as cutouts, operating between safe houses and the embassy

COMMUNICATIONS
Controls computer and radio communications in and out of the embassy

SAFE HOUSE REFRESHER
Maintains safe houses so they are always ready for use

WEAPONS AND EQUIPMENT OFFICER
Provides operational weapons and special equipment

SAYANIM REGISTER
A list of volunteers in the Jewish community who are willing to help *katsas*

DIPLOMATIC POUCH
Message pouch used between embassy and Israel; also used by Mossad

FINANCE
Section that provides money for intelligence operations

Fate of a spy

Poisoned pin
American spy pilot Francis Gary Powers carried this poison-tipped pin, concealed in a silver dollar.

SPIES OPERATE UNDER constant threat of detection and capture, which may result in them facing anything from a period in custody to the death penalty. "Legal" officers – those under cover of diplomatic immunity – are sometimes well known to enemy counterintelligence and are often treated leniently: a few hours of detention may be followed by release into the custody of representatives from the embassy of their own country.

Those personnel who operate without diplomatic protection, and are known as illegals (see p. 201), face far greater risks. Illegals are at the mercy of the judicial system of the country in which they are arrested. The agency controlling them may try to offer protection, but may have difficulty because knowledge of the illegals' identity is compartmentalized: the illegal agents are known only to those directly needed to support and control their activities.

Betrayal

Despite taking precautions, spies are always vulnerable to betrayal by moles (see p. 12). Moles work from within intelligence agencies and are often able to identify spies to the enemy service that is controlling them. The KGB mole Aldrich Ames (see p. 194) operated within the CIA and was

able to betray at least 10 agents operating in the Soviet Union for the CIA. Most of these were killed. Ames also betrayed Oleg Gordievsky, a KGB officer who worked as a mole for the British intelligence service MI6. The latter helped Gordievsky defect to Britain and avoid capture and possible death. Other important moles have included those of the Cambridge spy ring (see p. 197) who operated for years, betraying many agents.

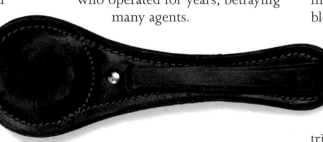

Interrogation cosh
This weapon was used in KGB interrogations. The flat end contains a lead weight which is covered in leather to avoid inflicting fatal blows while still causing great pain to the victim.

Cyanide vial and rectal concealment
This tube, which could be concealed in the rectum, was made for Germany's World War II security service, the SD. It held a glass vial of cyanide.

Punishments

The sentence for espionage varies from country to country and is affected by many circumstances. The former Soviet bloc countries generally executed those convicted of spying. Oleg Penkovsky, a GRU (Soviet military intelligence) officer who worked as a mole both for the CIA and for MI6, was executed after a well-publicized show trial, to make an example of him as a warning to other potential traitors.

Illegals, too, may face execution if they are operating in particularly hostile circumstances. For example, the Arab

The man in the trunk

Mordecai Louk, an Israeli, was a double agent working for both Mossad and Egyptian intelligence. In 1964, when Louk was living in Rome, the Egyptians suspected him and decided to bring him in for questioning. Louk was seized, drugged, and put in a specially designed trunk to be flown secretly back to Cairo. Inside the trunk, Louk was strapped in a leather seat, his feet were clamped to the floor of the trunk, and his hands and head were held in special fixtures. At Rome's Fiumicino airport, however, a delay allowed the effect of the drugs to wear off. Customs officers heard Louk's voice and released him. Later, Louk returned to Israel. Ironically, he was convicted and jailed on account of his contacts with the Egyptians.

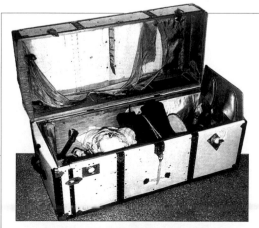

HUMAN TRANSPORTATION TRUNK

MORDECAI LOUK

states almost always execute captured Israeli illegals. Such a grim prospect has led members of the Israeli intelligence organization, Mossad, to refer to the Arab states as "The Land of the Dead."

In post-World War II America and Western Europe, convicted traitors have generally received prison sentences. An important exception occurred in the case of Ethel and Julius Rosenberg (see p. 196), who were executed in 1953 for passing American atomic bomb secrets to the Soviets during World War II. The couple were the first American citizens to be executed for treason since the end of the Civil War.

Illegal agents operating in the relative safety of the industrialized countries, where political violence is less prevalent – such as Western Europe or North America – may receive prison terms but may not have to complete them. They may be exchanged for prisoners held by other countries, in spy swaps.

Interrogation and torture

Counterintelligence services interrogate and occasionally torture captured spies to extract vital information from them. Some spies choose to commit suicide rather than risk being forced to give information that may compromise their mission and those involved in it. World War II SOE operatives (see p. 30) were often issued with "L" pills, capable of

Glienicke Bridge, Berlin
The Glienicke Bridge across the River Spree between East and West Berlin. The bridge became well known as the site of several important exchanges of convicted spies.

causing almost instant death; the U-2 spy pilot Francis Gary Powers (see p. 52) carried a poison-tipped suicide pin.

Turning a spy

In certain cases, captured spies may be offered their lives or freedom in return for becoming double agents (see p. 13). Many German spies detected by British intelligence during World War II took this option. The Germans, too, tried to turn spies. One of their main successes was in the case of an SOE agent whom they captured in Holland. He agreed to help the Germans by asking the SOE to send more men to Holland. Hoping to warn the SOE of his fate, the captured agent did not use the SOE security code when radioing his controllers. SOE headquarters failed to recognize this omission as a warning, however, and sent more than 50 operatives to Holland. All were immediately captured by the Gestapo.

One World War II spy, codenamed Cicero, met an ironic fate (see p. 34). He worked as a butler to the British ambassador to Turkey, and also as a spy for Germany. However, it was only after the war that he discovered that the Germans had paid him in forged English banknotes. Cicero's fate was to end his days in poverty.

Greville Wynne

While in Moscow in 1961, British businessman Greville Wynne (1919–90) became a courier working between Soviet military intelligence officer Colonel Oleg Penkovsky and British intelligence. Wynne would visit Eastern Europe on business and collect material from Penkovsky to take back to England. In 1962 the KGB arrested Penkovsky and Wynne. Penkovsky was executed; Wynne was released in a swap for Konon Molody (see p. 50).

The last cigarette
This Russian spy was captured by Austrian forces in the Balkans in World War I. This picture was taken moments before his execution.

Glossary

Words in SMALL CAPITALS refer to other entries in this glossary.

Abwehr
German military intelligence, established before World War II. It was the primary organization for foreign intelligence-gathering until its merger with the SD in 1944.

Agent
A person, often a foreign national, who works for, but is not officially employed by, an intelligence service.

Assassination device
A special weapon selected for use in carrying out assassinations. These devices are usually concealable and some are designed to leave no traces at the site of the assassination.

Audio surveillance
A technique for surreptitious eavesdropping, often using electronic devices.

BfV
(Bundesamt für Verfassungsschutz) German counterintelligence agency, founded in West Germany in 1950.

BND
(Bundesnachrichtendienst) German foreign intelligence-gathering organization, established in 1956 in West Germany.

Case officer
An intelligence officer who controls or is responsible for an agent. See HANDLER.

Cheka
(Russian abbreviation for Extraordinary Commission for the Struggle against Counter-revolution, Espionage, Speculation, and Sabotage) Russian secret police organization founded in 1917 to serve the Bolshevik Party; replaced in 1922 by the GPU, later the OGPU.

CIA
(Central Intelligence Agency) Founded in 1947; the American agency responsible for the combined tasks of worldwide intelligence-gathering and COUNTERINTELLIGENCE abroad.

Cipher
A form of CODE in which numbers or letters are substituted systematically for those in a plain text message, so as to prevent unintended recipients from understanding the message.

Code
(1) A system designed to obscure the meaning of a message of any kind by substituting words, numbers, or symbols (from a code book or by any other previous arrangement) for plain text. Not every code is a CIPHER; in some codes, a symbol can represent an idea or even convey a whole message.
(2) A nonclandestine letter substitution system such as MORSE CODE.

Concealment device
An object that has been altered for the secret storage and transportation of messages, ciphers, electronic bugs, or other TRADECRAFT items.

Counterespionage
COUNTERINTELLIGENCE operations that involve the clandestine penetration of a hostile intelligence service.

Counterintelligence
Broader category than COUNTERESPIONAGE, including action against foreign intelligence, and protecting information, personnel, equipment, and installations from espionage, sabotage, and terrorism.

Countersurveillance
Techniques used to detect hostile surveillance, and also to frustrate it.

Counterterrorism
COUNTERINTELLIGENCE operations aimed at foiling the plans and actions of terrorists.

Courier
A person who carries secret material for an intelligence service, either wittingly or unwittingly. A courier may also be a CUTOUT.

Cryptanalysis
Also known as code-breaking, this is the study of CIPHERS and other kinds of CODES in order to reveal the original message, without having access to official keys or encryption systems.

Cryptography
The use of codes and ciphers to render communications that have been originally written in plain text unintelligible and secure except to the intended recipients.

Cutout
A person acting as an intermediary between members of intelligence services or spy networks, improving network security by preventing contact between members.

Dead drop
A secure location, usually with a concealed container, used for secret communication and exchange of material between a spy and his controller. Dead drops remove the need for potentially dangerous personal meetings.

Defector
A person who, by choice, physically leaves the control of a country or intelligence service to serve the interests of another country. Such people often provide information of high value to the host intelligence service.

DGSE
(Direction Générale de la Securité Extérieure) French external intelligence service. Founded in 1981, the DGSE is similar in function to the CIA and Britain's MI6.

Digital espionage
The use of digital technology, especially involving computers and satellites, for espionage activities.

Double agent
An agent of one intelligence service who is recruited and controlled by another intelligence service to work secretly against their original service. A double agent should not be confused with a MOLE.

ECM
(Electronic countermeasures) The use of devices that render the electronic equipment of an enemy ineffective. ECM is applied extensively in warfare, and also in COUNTERINTELLIGENCE.

Enigma
An electromechanical, rotor-based CIPHER machine invented by German engineer Walter Scherbius in 1923. Versions of the Enigma were used for enciphering and deciphering messages by the German military and civil organizations during World War II.

FBI
(Federal Bureau of Investigation) Founded in 1924, the bureau is responsible for COUNTERINTELLIGENCE, internal security, and some other law enforcement duties within the United States.

Flaps and seals
TRADECRAFT term for opening, examining, and resealing envelopes and packages without raising the suspicions of the recipient. The procedure originally involved clandestine manipulation of envelope flaps and wax seals, from which its name is derived.

FSB
(Russian abbreviation for Federal Security Service) Internal security service in Russia, successor to KGB Second Chief Directorate.

GCHQ
(Government Communications Headquarters) The British signals intelligence center, similar to the NSA in the United States.

Gestapo
(Abbreviation for Geheime Staatspolizei) World War II German secret state police. Founded in April 1933, it was controlled by the Nazi Party and had responsibility for internal security throughout Germany.

GPU
See CHEKA.

GRU
(Russian abbreviation for Chief Intelligence Directorate) Founded in 1918 as the Soviet military intelligence service. The GRU survived the fall of the Soviet Union in 1991 and has continued serving the state of Russia.

Handler
A person, usually an intelligence officer (also usually a CASE OFFICER) who is responsible for, or controls, an agent.

HUMINT
(Abbreviation for human intelligence) Refers to information directly collected by human sources, such as AGENTS, as opposed to that collected via technology such as satellites.

HVA
(Hauptverwaltung Aufklärung) East German Foreign Intelligence Service, founded in 1952.

"Illegal"
A intelligence officer belonging to an agency of the former Soviet Union (KGB or GRU), an allied country, or to present-day Russia (SVR or GRU), operating in a hostile country without diplomatic protection but with the benefit of a legend (see p. 194). An illegal usually has no direct contact with his or her embassy, being controlled directly from Moscow.

Industrial espionage
The clandestine acquisition of information about business; may be carried out by a competitor, or by an intelligence agency.

Intelligence
This term can be applied to the profession of espionage, the information collected by espionage, or the final analyzed product.

KGB
(Russian abbreviation for Committee for State Security) Founded in 1954 as the intelligence and security organization of the Soviet Union, and the successor during the Cold War of the CHEKA. In 1991, the KGB First Chief Directorate (for foreign intelligence-gathering) was dissolved but later re-formed as the SVR. The Second Chief Directorate (for internal security) was renamed the FSB.

"Legal"
An intelligence officer protected by diplomatic immunity and belonging to an agency of the former Soviet Union or one of its allies; since 1991, the equivalent in the case of Russia.

Listening post
A site at which signals received by means of electronic audio surveillance are monitored.

MI5
(Originally an abbreviation for Military Intelligence, section 5) MI5 has no military connection and is now officially called the Security Service. Founded in 1909, it is the British internal security organization. Like the FBI in the United States, MI5 is responsible for domestic COUNTERINTELLIGENCE.

MI6
(Originally an abbreviation for Military Intelligence, section 6) MI6 no longer has any military connection and is now officially known as the Secret Intelligence Service (SIS). Founded in 1909, it is Britain's foreign intelligence service. The role of MI6 is similar to that of the CIA in the United States and MOSSAD in Israel.

MICE
(Money, Ideology, Compromise, and Ego) These are considered to be the four prime motivating factors that may be of use in recruiting a potential agent.

Microdot
An optical reduction of a photographic negative to a size that is illegible without magnification. In practice, a microdot is considered to be 1 mm or smaller in size.

Minox
A subminiature camera, using 9.5mm film, that has a wide range of uses in clandestine photography. The Minox was first produced in Riga, Latvia, in 1938. After World War II, a new Minox company was founded in West Germany. This company was, in 2002, still making cameras based on the original design.

Mole
An employee or officer of an intelligence service who agrees to work for another intelligence service. Some would-be DEFECTORS who approach an intelligence service they wish to work for are persuaded to remain in their posts and function as moles.

Morse code
Developed by an American, Samuel Morse, in 1838 for the electromagnetic telegraph, this code substitutes a series of dots and dashes for letters and numbers. The code is still in use and is internationally recognized.

Mossad
(Hebrew abbreviation for the Institute for Intelligence and Special Operations) Mossad was founded in 1951 and is Israel's external intelligence-gathering organization. It is similar in function to the CIA and Britain's MI6.

NKVD
(Russian abbreviation for the People's Commissariat for Internal Affairs) The internal security and (despite the name) worldwide intelligence organization of the Soviet Union that succeeded the OGPU from 1934 to 1946.

NOC
(Nonofficial cover) An intelligence officer who belongs to an American agency and operates without diplomatic immunity.

NSA
(National Security Agency) The American agency, formed in 1952, responsible for information security, foreign signals intelligence, and CRYPTOGRAPHY.

OGPU
(Russian abbreviation for the Unified State Political Directorate) Founded in 1923 as the organization responsible for internal security and intelligence for the newly formed Soviet Union. It succeeded CHEKA and the GPU, and was replaced by the NKVD.

Okhrana
The secret police that operated in Russia under the Czars between 1881 and 1917.

One-time pad
A set of paper or silk sheets, each bearing a series of random numbers or letters that is used only once for encipherment and decipherment of a message. The CIPHER is usually printed in groups of five letters. If each CIPHER is used only once, it is considered unbreakable. Pads for individual sheets are sometimes converted into MICRODOTS.

Operative
An officer or AGENT operating under the control of an intelligence service.

OSS
(Office of Strategic Services) Operational between 1942 and 1945, this American organization was the forerunner of the CIA.

OTS
(Office of Technical Service) The makers of gadgets and special devices for the CIA. Also the designation of the former makers of special equipment for the MfS (STASI) of East Germany.

OTU
Operational–Technical Department of the KGB and SVR, responsible for producing espionage equipment for Soviet and Russian spies.

Polyalphabetic substitution
The use of two or more CIPHER alphabets in a prearranged pattern to provide multiple substitutes for a particular letter in a message.

Receiver
Electronic equipment used to receive signals from electronic surveillance devices.

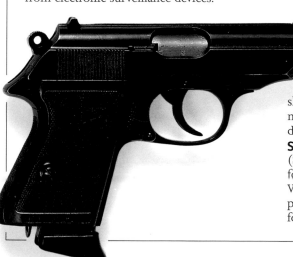

Reconnaissance
A mission undertaken to secure information, usually in advance of a secret operation.

Red Orchestra (Rote Kapelle)
The German name given to the successful Soviet military spy network that operated in Europe before and during World War II.

Resistance group
An indigenous underground organization that makes use of guerrilla warfare techniques and conducts sabotage and intelligence operations against an occupying power. Clandestine services of a country at war may work with resistance groups in enemy-occupied territory.

Safe house
A house or apartment that is thought to be unknown to foreign intelligence or COUNTERINTELLIGENCE and is considered temporarily safe for clandestine meetings.

SD
(Sicherheitsdienst, or Security Service) The SD was founded in 1934 as the political intelligence and COUNTERINTELLIGENCE service of the Nazi Party. In 1944 the SD was merged with the ABWEHR and became the dominant force in wartime Germany for intelligence-gathering and counterintelligence.

Secret writing
TRADECRAFT terminology for the use of secret inks (wet system) or special carbon papers impregnated with chemicals (dry system) for clandestine communication. Both systems use reagents to reveal the message.

SIGINT
(Abbreviation for signals intelligence) Refers both to intelligence gathered by eavesdropping on enemy electronic transmissions and to the process of gathering such intelligence.

Silenced weapon
A weapon modified by a noise suppressor attached to the end of the barrel. Such weapons are not completely silent, but it may be difficult to identify the source of the noise.

Sleeper
An AGENT or officer who lives in a foreign country for years as an ordinary citizen. When a hostile situation develops, the sleeper is activated on preassigned missions of sabotage, assassination, or intelligence collection.

SMERSH
(Abbreviation for Smert shpionam, a Russian slogan meaning "death to spies") Soviet military COUNTERINTELLIGENCE organization during World War II.

SOE
(Special Operations Executive) A British special forces organization founded in 1940 during World War II to conduct sabotage operations and provide equipment, training, and leadership for resistance groups in Nazi-occupied Europe.

Spy satellite
An orbiting satellite that uses sensors to record photographic or electronic intelligence.

Stasi
(Abbreviation for Staatssicherheitsdienst) Founded in 1950, dissolved in 1989; East German state security, with a component (HVA) conducting foreign intelligence operations.

StB
(Statni tajna Bezpecnost or State Secret Security) Founded in 1948; the Czech intelligence and security service.

Steganography
The science of hiding messages, for example in MICRODOTS or as SECRET WRITING. Digital steganography involves hiding messages or images in digital media, such as computer files.

Support agent
An AGENT who services another agent or a network. This might involve replenishing SAFE HOUSE supplies or acting as a CUTOUT.

SVR
(Russian abbreviation for Russian Foreign Intelligence Service) Succeeded the KGB's First Chief Directorate in the 1990s.

Telephone tapping
Using specialized electronic devices to listen to and record telephone conversations. Inductive taps are those that do not require physical connection to the telephone circuit.

Tokko
The Special High Police Bureau of the Tokyo Metropolitan Police Department. During World War II, Tokko carried out domestic COUNTERINTELLIGENCE.

Tradecraft
The procedures, techniques, and devices used in clandestine intelligence operations.

Visual surveillance
The observation of a person, place, or thing, using visual means.

Index

Page numbers in **bold** type denote the main reference to a spread title. Page numbers in *italic* type indicate an illustration or its caption.

Acknowledgments

The author would like to thank the following for their assistance in preparing this book:
Al, Christopher Andrew, Annette, Inge Atwood and the late Col. Jim Atwood, Nick Benigsen, Ralf Beyer, Willi Bickel, Sid Boorstein, Janusz Borowski, Carl Boyd, Chase Brandon, David Brown and the John Brown family, Beth Bruins, Robin C., Rusty Capps, Dave Carey, CIA Museum, CIA Public Affairs Office, Tom Clinton, Jerry Coates, Peter Deriaban, Jr., Rich Di Sabatino, John Edwards, Dr. Charles Ewing, Dennis Flinn, Steve Gold, Oleg Gordievsky, Mick Gould, Sam Halpern, Chet Hanson, Michael Hasco, The Hon. Richard Helms, Herb Hetu, Toni Hiley, Col. William Howard, Lyle Hunger, Jack E. Ingram, James G. Joyce, Brian K., Maj. Gen. Oleg Kalugin, David Kharab, Steve Klindworth – Supercircuits, John Koehler, Jim Lecroy, Richard Lovell, Peter McCollum, David G. Major, Peter Mason, Prue Mason, Scott Meinket, Dawn Melton, Tony and Jonna Mendez, Ambassador and Mrs. Hugh Montgomery, Dr. Paul D. Moore, Seth Moore, Morris Moses, Dan Mulvenna, Dave Murphy, Jack Naylor, NSA – Office of Public Affairs, Victor Ostrovsky, Dr. Oto, Jon Paul, Hayden B. Peake, Walter Pforzheimer, Rufina Philby, Jim Phillips, Carolyn Reams, Liane Reinecke, Gerald "Jerry" Richards, Gordon Rocca, Douglas St. Denny, Lloyd Salvetti, Jerrold L. Schecter, Rick Schroeder, R. Harris Smith, Glenmore Trenear-Harvey, Bob Troisi, Dr Helmut Trotnow, Oleg Tsarev, Detlev Vreisleben, Bob Wallace, Ron Weingarten, Nigel West, Glenn Whidden, Reade Williams, Gen. Markus Wolf, Capt. Greg Woody.

Dorling Kindersley would like to thank the following for their assistance:
Nicola Powling for jacket design and Jane Oliver-Jedrzejak for jacket copywriting; David Cooke, Jill Hamilton, Mary Lindsay, Lesley Malkin, Mukul Patel, and Cathy Rubinstein for editorial assistance; Raúl López Cabello and Almudena Díaz for dtp design assistance; Neville Graham, Nicola Hampel, Nathalie Hennequin, Philip Ormerod, Helen Taylor, Hans Verkroest, Chris Walker, and Mark Wilde for design assistance; Ray Allen, John Bullen, Diana Condell, Paul Cornish, and Mike Hibberd at the Imperial War Museum; Susan M. Rodgers at the Special Forces Club; Theresa Bargallo, Nick Goodall, Neville Graham, Louise Tucker, Nicholas Turpin, and Mark Wilde for modeling.

Index Julie Rimington.

Illustrators Mick Gillah, the Maltings Partnership.

Special photography Andy Crawford, Steve Gorton, and Gary Ombler.
Additional photography Bruce Chisholm, Geoff Dann, Philip Gatward, Tim Ridley, and Clive Streeter.

PICTURE CREDITS
Dorling Kindersley would like to thank the following for their kind permission to reproduce the photographs:
a = above; b = bottom; c = center; l = left;
r = right; t = top; crb = center right below

Archive Photos 38tr; 40tc; 119bl; 157tl; 197tl
Archiv für Kunst und Geschichte 18cr/**Palazzo Venezia, Rome** 20cl; 21br
Associated Press 9br; 12br, 14bl; 58tr; 66bl; 67t; 120bl; 167cr; 192bc; 198bl; 199bl/**Dennis Cook** 67b
Courtesy of Elizabeth Bancroft 58bl
Bildarchiv Preussischer Kulturbesitz 34cl
Bilderdienst Süddeutscher Verlag 146bl
Professor Carl Boyd 36tr
David Brown 137tc
Bundesarchiv, Koblenz, Germany 38cl
Cambridge University Library 37tr
Camera Press 8br; 11tc; 41br; 51bc; 52bl; 191tc
Courtesy of the Central Intelligence Agency, Washington, DC 47tl; 59tl; 113cr
William Colby 33bl; 183cl-c-cr
Corpus Christi College, Cambridge 20bcr
Couvrette/Ottawa 1994 74bl
Crypto-AG 145cr
Ian Dear 176ca
Peter Deriaban, Jr. 185bc
Deutsche Presse-Agentur GmbH 34bl; 199tr
The Devan Adair Company 13bc; 168cr
Richard Dunlop 33tr
Mary Evans 23bl
Courtesy of the Federal Bureau of Investigation, Washington, DC 1c; 54cl; 54bc; 55t; 55cl; 55c; 55b; 74br; 88tr; 160c; 160bl; 160bc; 196cl
Brian Fraser-Smith 116bcl
Willis George 132c
Hatfield House 21tl & ca
Jason Hawkes Aerial Library 68bl
Hulton 22tr & bc; 26bl; 27br; 37br; 45t; 169tr; 192ca; 197tc
Imperial War Museum/G.M Hallowes, Esq. 12tl; 30bl; 31bl; 35cl; 40b; 117tc; 117cl; 136bl; 136bc; 190tr; 191b; 192cl; 193cla; 193bc
Courtesy of Jack Ingram, Curator, National Cryptologic Museum/NSA, FT. Meade, Maryland 29bl; 36bl; 36br; 41bl; 42cr; 104tr & cr

Katz Pictures/Levy/Gamma Liaison 66br/**Najlah Feanny/SABA** 66bc
David King Collection 165tl
Library of Congress (BH82-4864A) 22bl; (LC-US262-11182) 25tr
Lockheed Martin Skunk Works/Denny Lombard 42tl; 52–53t
Los Angeles County Sheriff's Department 59bl
Peter Mason 180bl
Courtesy of Jim Minnery 178br; 194c; 194bl; 194br
Morris G. Moses 89br
Museum of the Confederacy, Richmond, Virginia 18bl/**Katherine Wetzel** 23tl; 23cr
National Archives 41tr
National Security Agency, Public Affairs 47tr
Courtesy of Victor Ostrovsky 180cr
Jim Phillips 140bl
Popperfoto 8bl; 29tl; 44cl; 50cl; 50bl; 51tl; 51c; 51tr; 51bl; 180bc; 190bc; 197cl
Anthony Potter 126tc
Press Association 166br
Range 9cl; 11crb; 15tc; 41tc; 46bl; 47br; 59tc; 114br; 127cl; 198br
Rex Features/Sipa Press 56b
Royal Marines Museum 122cr
Scala/Palazzo Vecchio, Firenze 20cr
Jerrold L. Schecter & Peter S. Deriaban 98cr
Science Photo Library/David Parker 68tr
Courtesy of the Security Service and the College of Arms 196cr
Carl Strahle 32bl
Topham 11br; 37bl; 39cr; 53cr/**Paul Elliott** 83cl; 98tc; 103br; 109br; 112bc; 114bl; 164bc & br
Oleg Tsarev 197c
US Airforce Office of Special Investigations, Public Affairs 148tc
WorldMap International Limited/Ian Wilkinson 15bl; 59br
Philip Zimmermann 69b

All other images are from the collection of **H. Keith Melton (www.spyimages.net).**

Every effort has been made to trace the copyright holders. Dorling Kindersley apologizes for any unintentional omissions and would be pleased, if any such case should arise, to add an appropriate acknowledgment in future editions.